NEWMAN UNIVERSITY

Transactions of the Royal Historical Society

SIXTH SERIES

CAMBRIDGE
UNIVERSITY PRESS

Published by the Press Syndicate of the University of Cambridge
The Edinburgh Building, Cambridge CB2 2RU, United Kingdom
40 West 20th Street, New York, NY 10011–4211, USA
477 Williamstown Road, Port Melbourne, VIC 3207 Australia
Ruiz de Alarcón 13, 28014 Madrid, Spain

A catalogue record for this book is available from the British Library

First published 2005

ISBN 0 521 849969 hardback

SUBSCRIPTIONS. The serial publications of the Royal Historical Society, *Royal Historical Society Transactions* (ISSN 0080–4401) and Camden Fifth Series (ISSN 0960–1163) volumes may be purchased together on annual subscription. The 2005 subscription price (which includes print and electronic access) is £77 (US$124 in the USA, Canada and Mexico) and includes Camden Fifth Series, volumes 26 and 27 (published in July and December) and Transactions Sixth Series, volume 15 (published in December). Japanese prices are available from Kinokuniya Company Ltd, PO Box 55, Chitose, Tokyo 156, Japan. EU subscribers (outside the UK) who are not registered for VAT should add VAT at their country's rate. VAT registered subscribers should provide their VAT registration number.

Subscription orders, which must be accompanied by payment, may be sent to a bookseller, subscription agent or direct to the publisher: Cambridge University Press, The Edinburgh Building, Shaftesbury Road, Cambridge CB2 2RU, UK; or in the USA, Canada and Mexico; Cambridge University Press, Journals Fulfillment Department, 100 Brook Hill Drive, West Nyack, New York 10994–2133, USA. Prices include delivery by air.

SINGLE VOLUMES AND BACK VOLUMES. A list of Royal Historical Society volumes available from Cambridge University Press may be obtained from the Humanities Marketing Department at the address above.

Printed and bound in the United Kingdom at the University Press, Cambridge

CONTENTS

Transactions of the RHS 15 (2005), pp. 1–27 © 2005 Royal Historical Society
doi:10.1017/S0080440105000368 Printed in the United Kingdom

TRANSACTIONS OF THE

ROYAL HISTORICAL SOCIETY

PRESIDENTIAL ADDRESS

By Janet L. Nelson

ENGLAND AND THE CONTINENT IN THE NINTH CENTURY: IV, BODIES AND MINDS

READ 26 NOVEMBER 2004

ABSTRACT. In the long ninth century, in both England and on the Continent, Christianity penetrated more deeply than before into social practice, as rulers and churchmen urged greater self-discipline on their people. This essay examines some of the ways in which the symbolism of bodily weakness, and reparability, was used to inscribe new ideas on minds, and new ideas impinged on the ways bodies were treated. Particularly close attention is paid to the evidence of poetry and prayer which both affected and reflected lives lived at court and elsewhere. This takes us to the heart of projects for political and religious correction, and reveals an unexpected amount of human agency.

Friends and colleagues, I must begin by giving special thanks to those of you who have stayed with these lectures from beginning to end, and then I must welcome all of you here for my fourth and last set of reflections on England and the Continent in the long ninth century. In the previous three lectures, I tried to capture some distinctive aspects of an age and its historiography. This evening I hope to convince you that in the ninth century western European minds focused on bodies in new ways; and that this was no coincidence, for Christianisation now acquired a new reach, not just horizontally in making contacts with pagans, that is, potential new Christians – and about that I shall not be speaking, important though it is – but also vertically within societies that called themselves Christian.[1] To ask, as Charlemagne invited his counsellors to do, 'are we

[1] For horizontal extension and its limits, see H. Reimitz, 'Conversion and Control: The Establishment of Liturgical Frontiers in Carolingian Pannonia', in *The Transformation of*

really Christian?' was to scrutinise bodies and minds with a new care and discipline.[2] Some ninth-century people, not all of them preacher-men, found much in contemporary conduct that needed correction. They wanted to live lives as monks or nuns, clergy or layfolk that, as far as they were concerned (and that surely has to be *our* concern), were compatible with Christian ideals and standards. One important kind of identity came to be defined in Christian terms. The English word 'Christendom' is a ninth-century coinage, in the Old English translation of Orosius's *History against the Pagans*, made during the reign of Alfred and perhaps at his court.[3]

The ninth century was the age par excellence of translations in another sense: transfers of holy bodies from martyrs' tombs, especially in Rome, to gold-covered, jewel-encrusted shrines north of the Alps.[4] It was an age when fears of Viking attacks caused new transfers of holy bodies to places of safety, followed, more often than not, by triumphant restorations to their old sites or to new homes, when the raiders had moved on, or settled down.[5] It was an age when more texts than ever before tell of pilgrimages to St Peter's body, when a letter or a treaty-text, put into the shrine over that body, was believed to have become charged with holy power;[6] when in thousands of new-minted miracle stories (in a curiously inverted ratio to Lives of new saints), frail or damaged living bodies, in contact with the

---

Frontiers from Late Antiquity to the Carolingians, ed. W. Pohl, I. Wood and H. Reimitz (Leiden, 2001), 189–207; J. T. Palmer, 'Rimbert's *Vita Anskarii* and Scandinavian Mission in the Ninth Century', *Journal of Ecclesiastical History*, 55 (2004), 235–56. For vertical extension, see J. M. H. Smith, 'Religion and Lay Society', in *New Cambridge Medieval History*, ed. R. McKitterick, III (Cambridge, 1995), 654–78; M. de Jong, 'Charlemagne's Church', in *Charlemagne. Empire and Society*, ed. J. Story (Manchester, 2005), 103–35.

[2] Monumenta Germaniae Historica, Capitularia regum Francorum [hereafter MGH Capit.], ed. A. Boretius and V. Krause (2 vols., Hannover, 1883–97), I, no. 71 (811), c. 9, p. 161, 'utrum vere Christiani sumus'; cf. no. 33 (802), c. 3, p. 92: 'ut unusquisque et persona propria se in sancto Dei servitio . . . conservare studeat secundum intellectum et vires suas, quia ipse domnus imperator non omnibus singulariter necessariam potest exhibere curam et disciplinam'.

[3] *The Old English Orosius*, ed. J. M. Bately, Early English Text Society, Extra Series 6 (London, 1980), 156. For indirect reflections on the association of this work with Alfred's court, see M. Lapidge, 'Asser's Reading', and S. Irvine, 'The Anglo-Saxon Chronicle and the Idea of Rome in Alfredian Literature', both in *Alfred the Great*, ed. T. Reuter (Aldershot, 2003), 27–48 at 41, and 63–78, at 72–3.

[4] J. M. H. Smith, 'Old Saints, New Cults: Roman Saints in Carolingian Francia', in *Early Medieval Rome and the Christian West. Essays in Honour of Donald Bullough*, ed. J. M. H. Smith (Leiden, 2000), 317–40.

[5] See P. Riché, 'Translations de reliques à l'époque carolingienne', *Le Moyen Age*, 82 (1976), 201–18, M. Heinzelmann, *Translationsberichte und andere Quellen des Reliquienkultes*, Typologie des sources du moyen âge occidental 33 (Turnhout, 1979), and F. Lifshitz, 'The Migration of Neustrian Relics in the Viking Age', *Early Medieval Europe*, 4 (1995) 175–92.

[6] J. L. Nelson, 'Charlemagne – The Man', in *Charlemagne*, ed. Story, 22–37, at 30–1.

bodies of the holy dead, became whole.[7] It was an age when devotion was directed towards the wounded, resplendent body of the crucified God.[8] It was an age when clergy considered how the difference between men's and women's bodies should affect differential access to holy bodies, and came up with different answers; when clergy questioned whether even women should be allowed beyond the chancel rail in churches; when clamouring women might be allowed entry to a saint's shrine exceptionally, yet denied it in the everyday.[9] It was an age when the minds of laymen were required seriously, and for the first time, to subject their bodies to penitential discipline, and through fasting and sexual abstinence at required times to discipline their own bodies, regarding them with the anxious solicitude that had previously characterised the professionally celibate. At least, I think that is the most plausible inference from dozens of ninth-century manuscripts of penitentials, dozens of episcopal instructions to priest-confessors, and of serious questions to experts about actual cases.[10] Max Weber thought western Christian culture's most distinctive trait was rational restlessness.[11] In the ninth century, alongside that, and in part responsible for it too, was an insistent preoccupation, widely shared and widely represented in written and visual sources, with frail, vile bodies that had the potential to be purged, restored and glorified. Was the aptest punishment for oath-breakers the loss of the right hand with which the oath had been sworn on the bodies of saints?[12] Was the aptest, because so

[7] M. Rouche, 'Miracles, maladies et psychologie de la foi à l'époque carolingienne en Francie', in *Hagiographie, cultures et sociétés, IVe – XIIe siècles* (Paris, 1981), 319–37, reads miracle-stories rather as pathologists' case-notes, but has the merit of taking these texts seriously. See further A. Bauch, *Ein bayerische Mirakelbuch aus der Karolingerzeit: die Monheimer Walpurgis-Wunder der Priesters Wolfhard* (Regensburg 1979), and Einhard, *Translatio et miracula SS Marcellini et Petri*, trans. P. E. Dutton, *Charlemagne's Courtier. The Complete Einhard* (Peterborough, ON, 1998), 69–130, with comments at xxiv–xxx.

[8] C. Chazelle, *The Crucified God in the Carolingian Era. Theology and Art of Christ's Passion* (Cambridge, 2000).

[9] Nelson, 'Les femmes et l'évangelisation', *Revue du Nord*, 68 (1986), 471–85; Smith, 'Women at the Tomb: Access to Relic Shrines in the Early Middle Ages', in *The World of Gregory of Tours*, ed. K. Mitchell and I. Wood (Leiden, 2002), 161–80.

[10] P. Payer, 'The Humanism of the Penitentials and the Continuity of the Penitential Tradition', *Medieval Studies*, 46 (1984), 340–54; R. Meens, 'The Frequency and Nature of Early Medieval Penance', in *Handling Sin: Confession in the Middle Ages*, ed. P. Biller and A. Minnis (Woodbridge, 1998), 35–61; S. Hamilton, *The Practice of Penance, 900–1050* (Woodbridge, 2001), esp. 4–24; de Jong, 'Charlemagne's Church', 123, 128–9.

[11] M. Weber, quoted in M. Mann, *The Sources of Social Power* (2 vols., Cambridge, 1986), I, 388.

[12] MGH Capit. I, no. 20 (779), c. 10, p. 49: 'De eo qui periurium fecerit, nullam redemptionem, nisi manum perdat'; no. 33 (802), c. 36, p. 98: 'Si quis . . . in periurio probatus fuerit, manum dextera se perdere sciat.' For Anglo-Saxon application of this penalty to counterfeiters, see P. Wormald, *The Making of English Law* (Oxford, 1999), 306, 444.

literally defacing, punishment for those involved in oath-swearing against the king that they slit each others' noses?[13] Should priests celebrate mass with bare legs?[14] How should fasting be calibrated to take account of age and infirmity?[15] Did Christ when on earth see God with bodily eyes or only spiritually?[16] If a man committed buggery with an animal, what should happen to him, and what should happen to the animal?[17]

At the beginning of the long ninth century, where bodies were concerned, England, in (Christian) Europe yet not entirely of it, could look like a marginal case. Some Anglo-Saxon attitudes were curious.[18] Some men behaved badly. It was to investigate and correct such bad behaviour that a mission (and the word mission seems right in more senses than one) went from Rome to Mercia, then Northumbria, in 786, led by two papal legates and advised by two Anglo-Saxon clerics. They took evidence and then issued decrees, ten for clergy, ten for laity. The second list included the following decision:

> God formed man beautiful in body and appearance (*pulcher in decore et specie*), but pagans, at the Devil's prompting, have superimposed [on bodies] most hideous marks (*cicatrices teterrimae*) . . . Anyone who sustains this injury of tattooing (*haec tincturae iniuria*) for God's sake, shall have great reward. But whoever does it out of the superstition of pagans, it will no more profit him for salvation than bodily circumcision benefits Jews without the faith of the heart.

The decree then turned into a little sermon:

> You wear clothes in the manner of the pagans whom your forefathers with their weapons, by God's help, drove out of the world . . . And you cut your horses with a filthy custom, you slit their nostrils and you clip their ears and make them deaf, and you dock their

[13] MGH Capit. I, no. 44 (805), c. 10, p. 124; cf. no. 20 (779), c. 12, pp. 49–50.

[14] Synodal report of the papal legates George of Ostia and Theophylact of Todi, edited as Alcuin Ep. 3, by E. Dümmler, MGH Epistolae [hereafter Epp.] IV (Berlin, 1895), c. X, p. 23. See C. Cubitt, *Anglo-Saxon Church Councils c. 650 – c. 850* (Leicester, 1995), 153–90.

[15] MGH Capit. I, no. 124 (807), p. 245; cf. no. 21 (793 – I prefer the dating of P. D. King, *Charlemagne. Translated Sources* (Lambrigg, 1986), 27–8, to that of Dümmler), p. 52. Cf. S. Hindle, 'Dearth, Fasting and Alms: The Campaign for General Hospitality in Later Elizabethan England', *Past and Present*, 172 (2001), 44–86.

[16] Candidus, Ep. ad amicum, Epistolae variae, no. 39, MGH Epp. IV, p. 558.

[17] Hrabanus Maurus Ep. 41 (ad Regimboldi sacerdotis quaestiones responsa), ed. E. Dümmler, MGH Epp. Karolini Aevi III (Berlin, 1899), 480 (with reference to Leviticus 20: 15–16).

[18] '"What curious attitudes he goes into" [said Alice] . . . (For the Messenger kept skipping up and down and wriggling like an eel . . . .) "Not at all", said the King,"He's an Anglo-Saxon messenger and those are Anglo-Saxon attitudes."' L. Carroll, *Alice Through the Looking-Glass* (London 1871), ed. M. Gardner, *The Annotated Alice*, rev. edn (London 1970), 279: in re-presenting the Mad Hatter and the March Hare (from *Alice in Wonderland*) as two Anglo-Saxon messengers, Hatta and Haigha, Carroll was 'spoofing the Anglo-Saxon scholarship fashionable in his day'.

tails – and because you could have them unharmed, but refuse to do that, you make them hateful to all.[19]

Something of the natural, divinely created value set on human bodies seems here to be extended to equine bodies, while ancestral masculine virtue is set up against the degenerate practices of present-day men. One of the two Anglo-Saxon clerics who evidently drafted these decrees was Alcuin, formerly master of the cathedral school of York, in 786 recently recruited into the service of Charlemagne.[20] The pagan-style clothes and haircuts of lay Northumbrians were objects of ongoing concern to Alcuin, who wanted to underscore the dividing-line between Christian and pagan *habitus*. Of no less concern was the bodily comportment of clergy and the dividing-line between them and laymen. When Alcuin, now retired to St Martin's, Tours, and a busier scholarly life than ever, heard that Archbishop Æthelheard of Canterbury would be visiting Charlemagne's court en route for Rome, he wrote to tell him about the appalling reputation English clergy had on the Continent.

> Their way of life has long been corrupt and grown vile, and almost equals the worthlessness (*vanitas*) of laymen, so that the tonsure now seems the only thing that distinguishes them, and in all other respects their conduct seems largely the same, whether in the vanity of their clothes, their arrogance, their excessive feasting, and other things that your holy sagacity knows perfectly well already[21] ... If you come to the lord king [Charlemagne], tell your retinue, especially the clerics among them, to behave themselves with due decorum (*honorifice*) in their religious observance, in their clothing, and as befits their ecclesiastical rank ... Tell them not to wear gold [ornaments] or silk robes in the lord king's sight, but go out in humble attire (*humilis habitus*) as is the custom for servants of God. Everywhere you travel, behave peacefully and with conduct becoming (*conversatio honesta*), for the [approved] practice and custom of this people is known to you. And I have sent you a saddle that I use when I go on horseback, prepared in the way pastors of churches are accustomed to have their saddles in this part of the world; and a horse capable of carrying the saddle and you on it.[22]

[19] Alcuin Ep. 3 (Synodal report), c. XIX, pp. 26–7. The report goes on to complain about the eating of horses, 'which not [even] any of the eastern Christian do' ('quod nullus Christianorum in orientalibus facit'). See J. Story, *Carolingian Connexions: Anglo-Saxon England and Carolingian Francia, c. 750–870* (Aldershot, 2003), ch. 3, esp. 85–7. P. Wormald, 'In Search of King Offa's "Law Code"', in *People and Places in Northern Europe 500–1600. Studies Presented to Peter H. Sawyer*, ed. I. Wood and N. Lund (Woodbridge, 1991), 25–45, at 33, suggested very plausibly that the pagans (*gentes*) here are Picts. The objects of criticism here would be Northumbrians, then.

[20] D. Bullough, *Alcuin: Achievement and Reputation* (Leiden, 2004).

[21] Cf. MGH Epp. 19 (793), 43 (795), 286 (post-793), 53–6, 87–9, 444–5 – all to Northumbrian clergy. Boniface earlier, and Pope John VIII later, voiced similar criticisms: see J. L. Nelson, 'A King across the Sea: Alfred in Continental Perspective', *Transactions of the Royal Historical Society*, 5th ser. 36 (1986), 45–68, at 62.

[22] MGH Ep. 230 (datable to 801), 374–5. The reference is apparently to clergy riding side-saddle: another notable indicaton of a distinct masculinity anticipating eleventh-century reform ideas.

Again codes of deportment link horses and men; and the practices complained of divide Anglo-Saxons from 'this people', that is, the Franks. Fellow-courtiers laughed at Alcuin because he ate porridge and drank beer, but in essentials, as everyone knew, Alcuin's *habitus* was exemplary: Christian and Frankish.

On 25 April 799, 'armed men gathered satanically, full of evil thoughts', to attack Pope Leo III as he advanced on horseback, surrounded by an unarmed crowd, along the processional route of the spring ceremony 'that everyone calls the Major Litany'. This ancient fertility festival was still practised, then, at Rome, with the pope in a central role – a nice example of the syncretism V. J. Flint diagnosed in the early medieval rise of magic.[23]

> The unarmed crowd fled, the armed men, like Jews despising God and man and the pope's office and like wild beasts throwing the pope to the ground, mercilessly cut off his clothes, and tried to pluck out his eyes and blind him. They cut off his tongue and left him, so they thought, both blind and dumb in the middle of the road.[24]

The attack on Leo III caused shock waves throughout Christendom. In Francia, Alcuin lamented an extreme example of wickedness (*extrema impietatis exempla*): Leo's attackers, blind in their hearts, had blinded their own head. This was wickedness even more extreme than the fate of the governor of the empire of second Rome (i.e. Byzantium), slain not by foreigners but by his own men and fellow-citizens (*non ab alienis sed a propriis et concivibus*).[25] In Rome, some alleged that Leo had been guilty of adulteries, hence deserved to be deposed; there was also horror because the chief attacker was a papal official, named and shamed by the author of Leo's Life as 'the wicked and unspeakable Paschal' who as Leo was riding out from the Lateran palace on 25 April had 'come forward to meet him *not wearing a chasuble* [my stress], with the hypocritical excuse, "I have had to come without a chasuble because I am ill."' The excuse was lame as well as false. But the papal biographer was making a significant point. Clerical bodies should be clad in appropriate liturgical vestments on great ceremonial occasions. Instead Paschal betrayed his internal disorder by an external sign that things were amiss, that is, by looking like a layman (clearly this was not just an Anglo-Saxon attitude) – and he would go on to act like a particularly vicious one in wielding his knife on the pope's body.

[23] V. J. Flint, *The Rise of Magic in Early Medieval Europe* (Oxford, 1991).

[24] *Liber Pontificalis*, Vita Leonis III, cc. 11–12, ed. L. Duchesne, rev. C. Vogel, *Le Liber Pontificalis* (3 vols., Paris, 1955–7), I, 4–5.

[25] Alcuin, Ep. 174, p. 288. The *gubernator imperii* was Constantine VI. See also *Annales regni Francorum*, ed. F. Kurze, MGH Scriptores rerum Germanicarum in usum scholarum (Hannover, 1895), s.a. 798, pp. 104–5; Theophanes, *Chronographia*, ed. C. de Boor, Corpus Fontium Historiae Byzantinae (Leipzig, 1883–5), Anno mundi 6289 (AD 796–7), 472 , trans. C. Mango and R. Scott, *The Chronicle of Theophanes Confessor* (Oxford, 1997), 649.

By early May, word on the Roman street was that the mutilated Leo had been cured by God, had been rescued and was on his way north to visit Charlemagne.[26] There were those, in Rome as well as in Francia, who doubted divine intervention here. Others in the west, and they prevailed in the long run, accepted Leo's recovery as an authentic miracle.[27] The most emphatic exponent of this view was the Frankish author of a lengthy poem written very soon after the event, perhaps in 799 itself: the Paderborn Epic, so called because Paderborn in Saxony was the place where Charlemagne, busy with war and mission, staged the ritual reception of Leo after his flight from Rome.[28] Of the poem's 536 lines, no fewer than 200 are concerned (intermittently) with the pope's mutilation and healing. First, lines 326–34 tell how Charlemagne, while taking a nap during a hunt, had a dream of Leo

> standing there, pouring forth sorrowful sobs,
> His eye-sockets were empty, his face was stained with blood,
> l. 330 His tongue was cut out, and he showed many horrible
> Wounds. Cold horror overwhelmed the care-loaded limbs of the Augustus. . . .
> [334] he marveled at what the sad dream might mean . . .

Then as Charlemagne returned to Saxony

> [344] Suddenly a sadder report spread and reached them,
> l. 345 That the apostolic light had succumbed to savage wounds

[26] Vita Leonis III, c. 13, p. 5.

[27] Story, *Carolingian Connexions*, 123–4, compares the record of the miracle in Northumbrian annals, in Frankish annals, and in the *Liber Pontificalis*, suggesting 'Frankish' and 'Roman' versions. But there were more than two: compare the 'original' and 'revised' versions of the *Annales regni Francorum*, s.a. 799, pp. 106–7, where one author sounds as if he believed Leo had been blinded and deprived of his tongue (the modern editor depicts this as the account given by 'the earliest messengers'), while the other inserts into his version the suggestive phrase 'ut aliquibus visum est' ('as it appeared to some people'). Vita Leonis III, c. 12, p. 4, says that the mutilations were 'attempted' in the street, then (p. 5) that they were carried out a second time at a neighbouring monastery, then (c. 13, p. 5) that the attackers' 'attempt' was 'destroyed' by God. Theophanes, *Chronographia*, 472, trans. 649, says that Leo's attackers forbore to carry out the blinding because they were humane (*philanthropoi*).

[28] The poem, the surviving third book of an otherwise lost work, was edited by E. Dümmler in MGH Poetae Latini Karolini Aevi (Berlin, 1881), I, 366–84. P. Godman, *Poetry of the Carolingian Renaissance* (1985), 22–4, discussed the poem helpfully but briefly, and, 196–207, translated lines 1–176, which do not include the material about Leo. (The translation below is my own.) A. T. Hack, 'Das Zeremoniell des Papstempfangs 799 in Paderborn', in *Kunst und Kultur der Karolingerzeit. Karl der Große und Papst Leo III in Paderborn*, ed. C. Stiegemann and M. Wemhoff (Mainz, 1999), 19–33, at 22–4, dates the poem between 799 and 814. F. Stella, 'Autore e attribuzioni del *Karolus Magnus et Leo Papa*', in *Am Vorabend der Kaiserkrönung. Das Epos 'Karolus Magnus et Leo Papa' und der Papstbesuch in Paderborn 799*, ed. P. Godman, J. Jarnut and P. Johanek (Berlin, 2002), 19–33, reviews the arguments. The discussion at the Paderborn Conference following Stella's paper included reaffirmation of the possibility of a date in 799.

By a cruel death; for the fierce and terrible Serpent

. . .

Persuaded everyone, blinding their minds, to rage
l. 350 Against an innocent man, and servants to slaughter a mighty master.
The dreadful foulness, once dropped, stuck to minds and senses . . .

. . . .

[358] The demented mob and the stupid people, and the raving young men,
With clubs and swords . . .
l. 360 Attacked the highest pastor in a violent onrush,
Blind, raging, suddenly driven by an urge to destruction.
They tortured the priest's sacred limbs with scourges;

. . .

They wrenched from his forehead his two eyes
l. 365 And from his lacerated body they cut out his swift tongue.

. . .

But a bountiful hand offered medicines for the Father's torn-out eyes
And repaired his face with new light.*
l. 370 A pallid countenance gazed astonished at the faces of foreigners,
And the truncated tongue gave a brief explanation.
With a few companions the great priest fled from that place.
He secretly made for the town of Spoleto, to seek help . . .

. . .

[376] He heard that there had arrived in Italy faithful *missi*
Of the Franks, and that the usual 'safety' of the Romans was something
They refused to endure, since their own mighty lord, who was guiltless,
The Romans had crucified with torments. Learning that the *missi* were there,
l. 380 He soon ordered these men to come before him, and he
Began to address them thus, his tongue that had been mutilated moving beneath his palate With its short range, enunciating a calm little speech . . . *

. . .

[396] A cohort of Franks mixed with Latins
Surrounded him, giving grateful thanks to the Lord
Who had given back new eyes to the highest pontiff
And re-fixed in his mouth the tongue he had despaired of.*

. . .

l.405 Then they joyfully began their journey and set off with rapid
Steps.

. . .

Numberless crowds came up everywhere to watch as they passed,

. . .

[412] And when they saw in that old head new eyes for seeing
They were amazed, and they were astonished at the tongue for speaking
Now received anew, and his swift speech with voice recreated.*

. . . .

The pope's messenger meanwhile approached the royal hall,
And reported that the highest pontiff was coming,
l. 435 Leo, who had been expelled from the Roman see
By his own citizens; and he described how many

Wounds he had borne, telling how light had been extinguished from his face,
Then told how his tongue had clearly been cut from his throat,
And how, now, with God as doctor, he had been healed of all these
l. 440 Sufferings.* The entire army were astounded in their minds
At hearing all this; and Charles, recollecting the dream he had had earlier,
And recognizing by the signs of what had gone before that he had seen the footsteps,
Had no doubt of what was to come, since he had seen some time before in his dream
This very same pontiff pouring forth sad sobs.

...

[504] The king, father of Europe, and Leo the highest pastor in the world,
l. 505 Having met, together enjoyed discussing various subjects.
Charles asked various questions about what had happened, and listened to the story
Of the pope's tribulations: he was stunned by the impious deeds of the wicked people.
He marveled at the two eyes so recently
Extinguished, and the face now repaired with light,
l. 510 And he was amazed that the tongue, mutilated by the pincers, could now speak.*

...

[512] with equal steps they make for the high throne-places.
In front of the gates of the sacred temple stand priests
Chanting songs of praise antiphonally,
l. 515 And repeatedly giving thanks and praises to the Creator
Who restored new eyes to the highest pontiff
And re-implanted a tongue in his mouth when he had despaired of that.*

I make that five separate mentions of the savage mutilation, and no fewer than seven of the miraculous healing (marked with an *).

The emphasis put in this text on the miracle of Leo's recovery, attested by multiple audiences, is very direct evidence for the importance attached to the restoration of Leo's personal credibility by Charlemagne, his counsellors (one of whom surely wrote this poem) and the Franks, here represented by the Frankish army. By August 799, Alcuin had consigned to the fire a letter reporting the scandalous allegations about Leo's adulteries.[29] In the letters written during these months, Alcuin evoked the apocalyptic connotations of dangerous times (*tempora periculosa sunt*).[30] Roasting in the flames of an August heatwave (*canicularibus decoctus flammis*) Alcuin learned that Leo had arrived in Francia, and wished desperately that he might be allowed to go to meet him 'to soothe the flames of his mind'.[31] But you did not go to Charlemagne without a summons, and no summons came. Repeatedly protesting (perhaps too much?) the enfeebled state of his own poor little body, Alcuin had to resign himself to being, as Donald Bullough put it, out of the loop.[32] But during these

[29] Alcuin Ep. 184, p. 309.

[30] W. Brandes, 'Tempora periculosa sunt', in *Der Frankfurter Konzil von 794*, ed. R. Berndt (2 vols., Mainz, 1997), I, 44–88.

[31] Alcuin Ep. 179 (to Arn), pp. 296–7.

[32] D. Bullough, unpublished paper delivered at the Paderborn Conference in October 1999. Cf. the English version of the late Donald Bullough's 'Die Kaiseridee zwischen Antike

sweltering weeks, the reality of the miracle performed by God on Leo became the Franks' official line. It was the line that led directly to Rome and Charlemagne's coronation as emperor on Christmas Day 800. On the crucial meaning of the integrity of Leo's body, Franks and Romans could unite.

Before leaving the hothouse atmosphere of that fin-de-siècle, I want to note two further points about the ways bodies were treated and mistreated. The first concerns mutilation as a legal punishment. Charlemagne and the Franks decreed the loss of an eye as the penalty for brigandage for a first offence, for a second, nose-slitting, for a third, death. Charlemagne had captured rebels blinded in 786, but as far as I know, this is a unique instance of his imposing that penalty for treason.[33] Then there is mutilation as exclusion from royal succession. In 806, in his plan for the future division of his empire between his sons, Charlemagne decreed 'as regards our grandsons', that 'our sons should not in any circumstances cause any of them accused before him to be put to death or corporally mutilated or blinded or tonsured against his will without lawful trial and inquiry'.[34] Perhaps Charlemagne had done something of the kind to his own nephews and felt guilty.[35] To calibrate blinding as distinct from capital punishment was difficult. Louis the Pious had his nephew Bernard blinded, and the lad died three days later of his injuries. Louis's son Charles the Bald had his own son blinded, and he survived for several years. Charles the Fat had his cousin Hugh blinded and put into a monastery.[36] These punishments were horrible, yet justified, in contemporary law, by the charge of treason. Given the amount of Carolingian intra-familial tension and conflict, this is not a large haul. In roughly the same period, a dozen Anglo-Saxon kings died violently – in the Old English of the *Anglo-Saxon Chronicle* the verb is *ofslogen* – through internecine strife rather than in battle against external enemies. Twice as many died of natural causes: they 'fared forth'. In Wessex, with a single exception, no king-slaying is recorded, and there seems to have been a royal preference for family-management rather than of –

und Mittelalter', in *Kunst und Kultur*, ed. Stiegemann and Wemhoff, 36–46, now edited by David Ganz in *Early Medieval Europe*, 12 (2004), 377–87: the final paragraph emphasises that influences other than Alcuin's must explain the imperial coronation of Charlemagne.

[33] *Annales Nazariani* s.a. 785, ed. G. Pertz, MGH Scriptores I, 42.

[34] *Divisio regni*, MGH Capit. I, no. 45, c. 18, pp. 129–30.

[35] W. Schlesinger, 'Kaisertum und Reichsteilung. Zur Divisio regnorum von 806', in his *Beiträge zur deutschen Verfassungsgeschichte des Mittelalters* (2 vols., Göttingen, 1963), I, 193–232, at 196.

[36] G. Bührer-Thierry, '"Just Anger" or "Vengeful Anger"? The Punishment of Blinding in the Early Medieval West', in *Anger's Past. The Social Uses of an Emotion in the Middle Ages*, ed. B. Rosenwein (Ithaca, NY, 1998), 75–91, offers an exemplary reading of the evidence. (Hugh, son of Lothar II, was Charles the Fat's first cousin once-removed.)

sloging it out. Patrick Wormald may have been right to connect this with Wessex's eventual ascendance.[37] It is perhaps methodologically unwise to generalise about pre-Conquest England's 'savage political *mores*' from Bede to Edward the Confessor.[38] But to distinguish cultures more or less given to mutilation is methodologically very wise, because it invites consideration of how far cultural difference can be linked with economic difference. Categorising cultures is the rub. Was the ninth-century world really one of gift-exchange rather than monetary values? Was it a world in which there were so few strongholds from which territory could be controlled that there was no sensible alternative to, in John Gillingham's neatly conclusive phrase, 'putting [enemies] out of action'?[39] Gift was clearly important both north and south of the Humber, and in both Saxony and Italy. So too was coin-use, though with intensities that varied greatly between regions.[40] Monasteries, the strongholds of God, served quite effectively to keep enemies out of political action. Both in England and on the Continent cultural traits included attitudes to bodies which were not just governed by economics.

In thinking about bodies, we also think about minds. For historians, at least, the two simply cannot be kept apart. What we know about bodies, we know because of what authors thought fit to tell. Whether or not clergy in Charlemagne's palace were really as decorous as Alcuin said, if we want to expose curiously cohabiting attitudes at court, recognisably high ideals embedded alongside tolerance of what by that age's own standards was louche not to say loose conduct, we should stay with poetry: the ninth century's private genre par excellence but also a very public genre, the vehicle of political as well as personal rivalry, and of moral critique.[41] Poetry exposes the paradox, and helps resolve it. No politically correct attitudes at Charlemagne's court restrained the wit of court poets. Alcuin joked gently about the chief notary Erchambald, to whom he gave the nickname Zacchaeus, after the publican in St Luke's Gospel (19: 3–4) who had had to climb a tree in order to see Christ: 'little Zacchaeus climbs a high wooden writing desk to watch the crowd of scribes running around'.[42] Theodulf joked more acerbically about little Erchambald along with little Einhard and little Osulf, one of Alcuin's students, nicknamed Corydon

[37] P. Wormald, 'The Ninth Century', in *The Anglo-Saxons*, ed. J. Campbell (London, 1981), 140.

[38] J. Gillingham, *The English in the Twelfth Century* (Woodbridge, 2001), 55–6.

[39] *Ibid.*, 54.

[40] M. McCormick, 'New Light on the "Dark Ages": How the Slave Trade Fuelled the Carolingian Economy', *Past and Present*, 177 (2002), 17–54, does not persuade me that slaving was as important as he claims.

[41] Key works here are Godman, *Poetry*, and D. Schaller, *Studien zur lateinischen Dichtung des Frühmittelalters* (Stuttgart, 1995).

[42] Alcuin, *Carmen* XXVI, 246.

after Vergil's lovely shepherd: 'if those three were joined together, they would make three legs of a table'.[43] Theodulf mocked three Byzantine envoys who were eunuchs: 'these three bodies can't make up even one man'.[44] The mockery became deadly serious in another of Theodulf's poems.[45] Here he mocked Osulf again, in a pastiche of Vergil's Second Eclogue, into which he inserted the transpyrenean slang word for a muslim catamite:

> O Mochanaz, my pipe is coming to the end of the song; what are these which my persistent love urgently scourges? O Mochanaz, Mochanaz [if you know the Second Eclogue you will catch the echo of 'O Corydon, Corydon'], what are these fields that you are so happy in, what are these fetters that bind you, tell me, I ask you, O you who move so fast?

The poem itself is addressed to Charlemagne's eldest son Charles, of whose entourage Osulf/Mochanaz was a member. The rest of the poem praises Charles to the skies – and Charles's father, grandfather and great-grandfather are invoked to beat Mochanaz with sharp scourges. But since Mochanaz/Corydon/Osulf is one of Alcuin's former students, one he specially loved, the poem is a coded attack on Alcuin for failing to guide his beloved boy in the strait way. Some time ago, the late John Boswell argued from Alcuin's own poems that Alcuin himself was gay. Maybe he was; and maybe Charlemagne's court harboured the tolerance that Boswell yearned to find.[46] But not everyone was tolerant, or tolerated. Though Theodulf and Alcuin had coexisted at court for a few years, from the mid-790s (and remember Alcuin left court in 796), rivalry between them turned nasty. Alcuin is the butt of this rather unpleasant poem. Is it also an attack on the Young Charles, who remained unmarried? I do not think so. The rest of the poem eulogises him, and its target, anyway, is not gays in general but Alcuin and his coterie in particular.

Angilbert was another cleric-about-court, and another old student of Alcuin, who nicknamed him Homer. In a letter-poem about Charlemagne's court, Angilbert described the royal family one by one, including the king's second daughter Bertha, 'a maiden worthy of the Muses' songs'.[47] In the Paderborn Epic (which some experts think

[43] Theodulf, *Carmen* XXV, 487.

[44] *Ibid.*, 493.

[45] *Ibid.*, 526–7, Ad Carolum regem. I am much indebted to Franz Fuchs, who has allowed me to read and cite the paper on Theodulf's poems in which he unveiled new manuscript evidence for the original version of *Carmen* XXXV. This paper was given at a conference at St-Gallen in 2004, and my warm thanks go to David Ganz who heard it, told me about it and put me in touch with Professor Fuchs.

[46] J. Boswell, *Christianity, Homosexuality and Social Tolerance* (Chicago, IL, 1980), 188–91.

[47] Angilbert, *Carmen* II, ed. Dümmler, MGH Poetae I, l. 50, p. 361, and cf. ll. 72, 75–7, p. 362, sending his poem to 'David', that is, Charlemagne himself, and urging the poem 'decies dic mille salutes/atque pedum digitis da basia dulcia sacris'. Cf also Theodulf, *Carmen* XXV,

Angilbert/Homer may have written), Bertha is described in the family procession at Aachen in 799 as particularly like Charlemagne: 'she shines forth radiant . . . / With voice, manly spirit, bearing and gleaming face, she has a mouth, a bearing, eyes and a heart that all resemble her father's.'[48] Angilbert in 790 had become abbot of the monastery of St-Riquier; in the 790s he was Bertha's lover and they had two sons who seem to have been brought up at their grandfather's court. Bertha's sister Rotrude was a nun at the convent of Chelles (Alcuin's nickname for her was Dove) and she too had a lover and a son who was apparently brought up at court (in his forties he became abbot of St-Denis).[49] This surely was what Einhard had in mind when he wrote in his *Life of Charlemagne*:

> Instead of giving his daughters in marriage to his own men or to foreigners, Charlemagne kept them with him in his household until the very day of his death, maintaining that he could not live without their company. The consequence was that he had some unfortunate experiences but he shut his eyes to all that happened and pretended that no suspicion of immoral conduct ever reached him.

Einhard, also in this section on 'Charlemagne's domestic and interior life', lists the king's successive wives and four of his concubines and then refers to 'another one whose name I cannot remember'. Einhard mentions fifteen children and there is evidence for two more.[50] Now imagine the palace, the private apartments, the women, the nurseries, the entertainments. Alcuin warned yet another of his former students resident at the palace: 'May the crowned doves who flit through the apartments not come to your windows . . . Take no interest in dancing bears but in psalm-singing clergy.'[51]

It was difficult to square a model of parallel but separate clerical and lay orders with the realities of life at the palace. Yet Charlemagne was determined not just to discipline everyone's bodies and minds, but to get them to discipline themselves. He did so, especially in the years after 800, by creating a Christian court culture in which men and to some extent women too learned new kinds of deportment and new aspirations.

---

l. 19, p. 484: 'pectora, crura, pedes, est non laudabile cui nil' ('chest, legs, feet, there's no part of him that is not worth praising').

[48] *Karolus Magnus et Leo Papa*, 371, ll. 220–3.

[49] For Angilbert and Bertha, and Rotrude, see J. L. Nelson, 'La cour impériale de Charlemagne', in *La royauté et les élites dans l'Europe carolingienne*, ed. R. Le Jan (Lille, 1998), 177–91, repr. in J. L. Nelson, *Rulers and Ruling Families in Early Medieval Europe* (Aldershot, 1999), ch. XIV.

[50] Einhard, *Vita Karoli Magni*, c. 18, ed. O. Holder-Egger, MGH Scriptores rerum Germanicarum [hereafter SRG] (Hannover, 1911), 22–3; see also J. L. Nelson, 'La famille de Charlemagne', *Byzantion*, 61 (1991), 194–212, repr. in Nelson, *Rulers and Ruling Families*, ch. XII.

[51] Alcuin, Ep. 244, p. 392, quoting Isaiah 60: 8, which referred to doves but not 'crowned doves'.

The grandchildren were little students too. This did not exclude secular pastimes but subsumed them. The poetry is our entrée to a world in which paradox dissolves; and what might seem to us contradictory modes and models were more or less comfortably reconciled. Court conversations that happen to have been recorded were about the meaning of Gospel miracles, and about theological problems.[52] Thanks to Alcuin's teaching, Boethius's *Consolation of Philosophy* was so well known to the circle at Aachen that, as the late Margaret Gibson said in a paper to this Society, 'Alcuin could count on fairly oblique references being recognised.'[53] Theodulf in 799/800 addressed to the court a long poem on *Justice* replete with references to Virgil, Ovid and Boethius as well as Augustine: Laurence Nees observed here 'sources and terms that would have been widely known and already part of the court's universe of discourse'.[54] This poem was clearly aimed at judges – that is, above all at lay notables. It was an intervention in a debate about how the regime would deliver its social and political programme. It was a well-thought-out attack on bribery: at once *pièce d'occasion* and policy document, it was, if 'not a training manual for Carolingian *missi dominici*',[55] then legible as a code of practice for the officers of a new state in the new ninth century.

To get a closer look at these laymen, their minds and their attitudes to bodies, it is worth looking at another poem, the *Waltharius*, which some scholars, at least, think early Carolingian.[56] The eponymous hero, Walter,

[52] See J. L. Nelson, 'Was Charlemagne's Court a Courtly Society?', in *Court Culture in the Early Middle Ages*, ed. C. Cubitt (Turnhout, 2003), 39–57.

[53] 'Boethius in the Carolingian Schools', *Transactions of the Royal Historical Society*, 5th ser. 32 (1982), 43–56, at 53.

[54] Theodulf, *Carmen* XXVIII, 493–517; L. Nees, *A Tainted Mantle. Hercules and the Classical Tradition at the Carolingian Court* (Philadelphia, PA, 1991), 123. The first half of Nees's book, a probing analysis of Theodulf's poem on *Justice* in literary and historical contexts, offers uniquely valuable insights into the thought and practice of the Carolingian elite at the fin-de-siècle and for long afterwards. See also the thoughtful comments of Godman, *Poetry*, 13–16.

[55] Nees, *A Tainted Mantle*, 91.

[56] I have used the edition of K. Strecker, *Nachträge zu den Poetae Aevi Karolini*, I (Weimar, 1951), repr. in the MGH Poetae Latini Medii Aevi VI/1 (Munich, 1978). Also invaluable are the edition, translation and commentary of D. Kratz, *Waltharius and Ruodlieb* (New York, 1984), and the verse translation and notes of B. Murdoch, *Walthari*, Scottish Papers in Germanic Studies vol. 9 (Glasgow, 1989). My translation is indebted to theirs. I have found especially helpful (though sometimes dissented from) P. Dronke, 'Waltharius-Gaiferos', in P. and U. Dronke, *Barbara et antiquissimi carmina*, Publicaciones del seminario de literatura medieval y humanistica (Barcelona, 1977), 27–79, esp. 66–79, 'The Date and Provenance of Waltharius'; R. Schieffer, 'Zur neuen Thesen über den *Waltharius*', *Deutsches Archiv*, 36 (1980), 193–201; D. M. Kratz, *Mocking Epic: Waltharius, Alexandreis and the Problem of Christian Heroism*, Studia Humanitatis (Madrid, 1980); D. Schaller, 'Ist der *Waltharius* frühkarolingisch?', *Mittellateinische Jahrbuch*, 18 (1983), 63–83; K.-F. Werner, '*Hludovicus Augustus*. Gouverner l'empire chrétien – Idées et réalités', in *Charlemagne's Heir. New Perspectives on the Reign of Louis the Pious*, ed. P. Godman and R. Collins (Oxford, 1990), 3–123, at 101–23; and a paper read in October

is an Aquitanian hostage at the court of Attila the Hun. There he meets two other hostages, Hagano a Frank, and a girl, Hiltgund, a Burgundian. She and Walter had been betrothed by their parents when they were still children, before their captivity. Hagen eventually escapes and joins the court of King Gunther of the Rhineland Franks, then Walter and Hiltgund do likewise. I will quote two passages. The first is from the scene in the palace of Attila where Walter proposes flight to Hiltgund:

> Walter came upon Hiltgund sitting alone
> After he'd embraced and kissed her sweetly he said:
> 'Bring me a drink quickly, I'm gasping with weariness!'
> Swiftly she filled a precious goblet with undiluted wine
> And handed it to the man, who made the sign of the cross and took it,
> And clasped the maiden's hand in his own . . .
> 'Together we have endured exile for a long time now
> well aware of what our parents decided
> Between themselves about our future.
> For how long are we to keep silent about this?'
> Hiltgund, thinking her betrothed had spoken thus
> In irony, was silent for a moment, then said:
> 'Why do you feign with your lips what you abhor in your innermost feelings?
> Why do you urge in speech what in your heart you deny?
> Would it be some kind of great shame to take such a bride?'
> The wise man countered this and said:
> 'May what you say be far from the truth! Look at things in the right way.
> You know I've said nothing with a deceiving mind.
> Believe there is nothing hidden or false in my speech!
> No-one is here except for us two:
> If I were sure that you were offering me your willing mind
> And would keep faith in everything with careful vows,
> I'd want to lay bare to you all the mysteries of my heart.'
> Finally Hiltgund sank before the man's knees and said:
> 'Wherever you call me, my lord, I will follow you devotedly.'
> ll. 229–47

Though it follows Virgil's *Aeneid* closely, in fact is full of echoes of Book IV, the story of Dido and Aeneas, the emphasis here is on thoughts and motivations. Hiltgund's suspicion of irony is a back-handed tribute to interiority.[57] Walter counters the charge of having a 'deceiving mind' by appeal to a 'willing mind' and the truthful exposure it invites. Walter, unlike Aeneas, is not about to abandon the woman who loves him, but to flee with her. The irony of Hiltgund's mistrust is one we appreciate – or

2004 at the Harvard Conference on New Interpretations of the Early Middle Ages by Jan Ziolkowski, 'Of Arms and the (Ger)man: Literacy and Material Culture in the Weapons and Warfare in *Waltharius*', to appear in *New Directions in Early Medieival History*, III, ed. M. McCormick and J. R. Davis (Cambridge, MA, forthcoming), and his comments in discussion afterwards.

[57] Nees, *A Tainted Mantle*, 61–2, 95–6, stresses the significance of irony, and its openness to misinterpretation. See also Kratz, *Mocking Epic*.

will appreciate – because that mistrust is itself misplaced: Walter, unlike Aeneas, is true. Walter, unlike Aeneas, will follow not imperial duty but his own heart, whose directives coincide with their parents' wishes. His invocation of divine approval is implied in his signing of the goblet before he takes the wine from Hiltgund's hand in a powerful sign of relationship that combines Christian and non-Christian symbolism. The passage perfectly represents the blending of ancient forms, classical and 'barbarian', and their adaptation to a self-reflective Christian ethic as preached at the Carolingian court. That is also, I think, one of the main reasons that many critics have refused to date the poem to the age of Charlemagne: as if love between man and woman was simply out of place in a Carolingian context, as if the age of epic had to be quite distinct from the age of romance![58]

The second scene is from the end of the poem: Walter and Hiltgund have escaped, and reached the Rhineland, where Gunther, along with (though despite the advice of) his follower Hagen and a retinue of twelve, arrives to capture them and take the treasure they have brought with them. Walter prepares, with God's grace, to fight; then slays all Gunther's followers except for Hagen. In the end only Hagen, Gunther and Walter are left alive, all three severely wounded. Now read on:

> The battle was over.
> His wound, and exhaustion, warned each man
> To lay down his weapons.
>
> . . . After the end had come, each man was marked by honourable signs:
> King Gunther's leg lay there, and the right arm
> Of Walter, and the still-quivering eye of Hagen.
> Thus, thus, did they divide the Avar arm-rings!
> Two of them sat down, and the third could only lie down,
> Trying to staunch with foliage the wave of blood that flowed.
> Then Alphere's son [i.e. Walter] called the frightened girl with a shout
> And she came and bound up all their wounds.
> When all this had been done, her betrothed told her,
> 'Now pour some wine, and offer it to Hagen first!
> He is a good warrior, if he keeps laws to faith.'
> . . .
> Then Hagen the hawthorny one,[59] and the Aquitanian,
> Unconquered in their minds, although exhausted in the whole of their bodies,
> After the various warcries and the tremendous blows,

[58] W. P. Ker, *Epic and Romance* (London, 1896), had an enduring influence, especially over Oxford men: thus R. W. Southern, *The Making of the Middle Ages* (London, 1953), 276, acknowledges the source of the title of his final chapter, 'From Epic to Romance', and asserts that Ker's book 'retains all its freshness and value'. Granted! But a less welcome effect was to make sharply distinguished narrative genres the basis of a cultural divide between the earlier Middle Ages and the twelfth century which has since persisted in English historical thinking and curricula. It is high time medieval historians read Kratz as well as Ker.

[59] This is a pun, across languages, on the Germanic word for 'hawthorn'.

As they drank played in joking conflict (*scurrili certamine*).
The Frank said: From now on, when you hunt stags, my friend,
You can make yourself a pair of gloves from their skin as often as you like
But I advise you to stuff the right glove with soft wool,
So that you can deceive with your counterfeit hand those who are not in the know!
But hey! what are you going to say when you breach the custom of your people
And you are seen girding your sword on your right side?
And what about your wife, when desire for her comes over you,
Are you going to put your left arm round her, Oh! In a cackhanded embrace?
Why am I going on like this? Look, you will have to do everything from now on
With your left hand.
ll. 1401–33

Since this poem has long been in the hands of literary scholars, many of them nowadays in North America, you will not be surprised to hear that one of them has recently opined that the epic's last 500 lines look 'more or less like the Rhineland Chainsaw Massacre', citing Carol Clover, famous American medievalist and also author of *Men, Women and Chainsaws*, on 'low-budget horror films that complicate the gendered semiotics of the cinematic gaze'.[60] There are serious points here. There is indeed irony in the poem's ending, and an affirmation of heroism, but a qualified one. The intended audience (*fratres*) surely included monks and warriors, but why not some women as well? The literary colleagues certainly offer fresh insights. Can a bog-standard historian get closer to the where and when of this poem's origin?

The idea that the *Waltharius* is a version of a much older oral poetic tradition is confirmed by the existence of two small fragments of an Old English analogue, the poem *Waldere*.[61] One of the fragments has Hildegyth urging on Waldere to fight Guthhere in single combat. The other has Waldere and Guthhere exchanging taunts about weapons, and Waldere expressing trust in God's judgement 'in every righteous cause'. Neither bears any close relation to any passage in the *Waltharius*. Cross-Channel contacts do not have to be assumed, therefore. But it seems to me plausible to hypothesise that both *Waltharius* and *Waldere* assumed written form in courtly milieux. Indicative traits in one or both include: the important role of the Avars, alias the Huns, both in the poem and in Frankish annals of the early 790s, and thereafter in court concern with the Avars' conversion; the interest in the various peoples, Franks and

[60] D. Townsend, 'Ironic Intertextuality and the Reader's Resistance to Heroic Masculinity in the *Waltharius*', in *Becoming Male in the Middle Ages*, ed. J. J. Cohen and B. Wheeler (New York and London, 2000), 67–86, at 69, 71.

[61] The fragments, in a West Saxon form and hand of *c.* 1000, were discovered in 1860 in the binding of a book now in the Royal Library of Copenhagen. See the edition by J. Hill, *Old English Minor Heroic Poems* (Durham, 1983), and translation by S. Bradley, *Anglo-Saxon Poetry* (London, 1995), 510–12. Ker, *Epic and Romance*, 79–83, offers an interesting comparison of *Waldere* with Beowulf and other epics.

Aquitanians and Burgundians, identities highly topical in an imperial, that is, multi-gentile, realm; the author's display of special knowledge of weapons and armour and horses that chimes with references in early ninth-century capitularies;[62] the warriors' names, and their titles – usually *comes* (count), *satellites* and *socii* (followers) and the very occasional *vassus*, terms familiar in early ninth-century narrative and annalistic sources; the presence among Gunther's retinue of an exile from Anglo-Saxon England;[63] the fact that the author can assume an audience so familiar with *Aeneid* Book IV and Ovid's *Metamorphoses* that allusions, including the explicit recourse to *hyronia*, irony, will be picked up;[64] an audience with a refined sensibility and at the same time a taste for laddish jokes; an audience responsive to Christian gesture and also to stark and frankly realistic depictions of what happens to male bodies in hand-to-hand combat; attitudes to bodies and minds, conveyed through a mix of biblical, liturgical and classical references, that look paradoxical unless you situate them in a living context where these very paradoxes are there to be encountered: an audience familiar (like the Frank, Hagen) with the contending demands of manly duty to avenge kin and manly loyalty to a former comrade; an audience interested in complicated representations of noble masculinity, and (quantitatively small but qualitatively significant) of femininity; an audience including monks, warriors and women. Such multiple elements and cultures did actually coexist and interact at the courts of Charlemagne and his successors, and, *mutatis mutandis*, of Alfred and his.[65]

By 823, Charlemagne himself was a memory. But that memory was the stuff of dreams and political propaganda. In the imperial monastery on the Reichenau in Swabia, a monk named Wetti had a vision of the next world in which, guided by a spirit, he was taken to a certain place:

> Considering also a man in the fields which they had surveyed,
> Ausonia's sometime ruler and master of the mighty
> Roman people, standing rooted to the spot,
> Opposite him was a savage beast tearing at his genitals,
> Lucky were the rest of his limbs on his body not covered in blood.

[62] This point I owe particularly to Jan Ziolkowski (see above, n. 56).

[63] Ekifrid taunts Walter: 'Are you a flesh and blood man, damn you, or a spirit man of the woods?' To which Walter replies 'Your Irish turn of phrase shows you come from a people whom Nature's made excel all others in joking!', 'Celtica lingua probat te ex illa gente creatum/cui natura dedit reliquas ludendo praeire!', ll. 765–6. See the comments of B. Murdoch in his edition of the poem (cited above, n. 56), 98–9.

[64] Godman, *Poetry*, 86–7.

[65] Werner, '*Hludovicus Augustus*', argued for Ermold's authorship of the *Waltharius* and an intended audience at the court of Pippin I of Aquitaine in the 830s. A courtly origin (Mercian or West Saxon) has been suggested for Beowulf, and though I am not aware of any such suggestion in the case of the *Waldere*, it may be time to propose one. For Alfred's court, see below, p. 26.

Under this impression, staggered and terrified Wetti cried out:
'Sheer luck among men made of him, while he bore this life in his body,
Instigator of justice and in the modern age.
Mighty was the witness he bore to the cause of the Lord,
Protection and defence were duly given by him to God's people,
Eminence of a special kind he achieved, as it seemed, in this world,
Righteousness he desired, moving swiftly through his realms with sweet favour.
Awful is the savage plight in which he is held here.
Terrible, too, is the heavy punishment and grim affliction he endures.
O I beg you, explain!' Then his otherworldly guide explained: 'In these agonies he
Remains, because he befouled his good deeds with filthy lust,
And thinking that his unlawful acts would be blotted out by the mass of his
Good deeds, he wished to finish his life in his accustomed
Filthiness. Yet he will attain the best life
And rejoicing he will move into the honour ordained for him by God.'[66]

The first letters of these lines form an acrostic, sure sign of a poem meant to be read as well as heard. The man suffering carefully targeted torment in the next world was *Carolus imperator*. This vision of Charlemagne in a place of purgation can be read as part of campaign to vilify the dead emperor and so accentuate the virtues of his son, Louis the Pious.[67] On his father's death, Louis had 'expelled from the palace that whole female mob, which was very large', no doubt to place his own men in positions of power at court, but also to fix his own identity and reputation as a clean-liver, by contrast with his late 'befouled' father, the man who had a series of mistresses and turned a blind eye to the fornication of the daughters he loved so much. Louis, to be sure, had sown his own wild oats, fathering twins before he was fifteen; but so far as is known, he was a faithful husband thereafter, and married off his daughters as expected. Louis's sins were of another kind: the 'putting out of action' of close kin by monastic confinement, the blinding of his nephew. Pressures for a reconciliation built up and a preliminary rapprochement took place in 821, followed by a full-scale ritual occasion at the assembly of Attigny in 822, when 'Louis undertook a voluntary penance, imitating the great emperor Theodosius', and his leading men, ecclesiastical and lay, followed suit.[68] Penance involved mental confession and bodily abasement through fasting and prostration, followed by the restoration of the penitent to full communion with the faithful. At Attigny, the emperor's credibility

[66] Walahfrid Strabo, *Visio Wettini*, ed. and trans. Godman, *Poetry*, no. 27, p. 214 (I have made some slight changes but appreciate Godman's skill in keeping the acrostic in translation).

[67] See P. E. Dutton, *The Politics of Dreaming in the Carolingian Empire* (Lincoln, NE, and London, 1994), pp. 60, 55–7, and D. Ganz, 'Charlemagne in Hell', *Florilegium*, 17 (2000), pp. 175–94.

[68] Astronomer, *Vita Hludowici* c. 35, ed. E. Tremp, MGH SRG, 406–7; see M. de Jong, 'Power and Humility in Carolingian Society: The Public Penance of Louis the Pious', *Early Medieval Europe*, 1 (1992), 29–52.

was rapidly re-established. But in fact this penitential mode had already been pioneered by Charlemagne, not least in the Aachen years.[69]

At the same assembly, but unrecorded in any strictly contemporary source, another notable event took place. Hincmar of Rheims, an eye-witness, recalled it in 860 in the context of his hefty negative response to King Lothar II's request for a divorce from his queen:[70]

> We have thought it necessary to recall an event to memory, since it is written that 'You should not transgress the boundaries set by your Fathers', whose examples are for us true doctrine to be imitated. The event is as follows: some of our people [Hincmar's fellow-monks of the monastery of St-Denis] in the time of our lord the pious emperor Louis of happy memory, were present at the palace of Attigny when there was a universal synod of the whole empire, at which legates of the Roman see were also present, and a general assembly. A certain woman of not ignoble birth, Northild by name, made a complaint publicly to the emperor about certain dishonourable acts (*quaedam inhonesta*) between herself and her husband, who was named Agembert. The emperor sent her to the synod, so that episcopal authority should decree what was to be done. But the generality of the bishops remitted her to the judgement of laymen and married men, so that they might judge between her and her husband, because those laymen were cognisant of such affairs and possessed of extremely expert knowledge in the laws of the world, and therefore that woman should subject herself to the legal judgements of those men, and she should hold to what they might decide concerning her charge without any [right of] appeal ... This discretionary decision (*discretio*) of the bishops pleased the lay nobles, because judgement concerning their wives had not been taken away from them, nor had prejudice been done to civilian laws by the episcopal order. So [the lay nobility] declared the law in response to the woman's legal complaint, and by a lawful judgement they put an end to her plea.[71]

The judgement was that she must return to her husband, with no separation allowed. What were these dishonourable acts which had caused Northild to seek a separation? A plausible reconstruction is that Agembert had expected Northild to comply with his desire for forms of intercourse prohibited by canon law, i.e., everything but the missionary position, and/or perhaps intercourse repugnant to lay custom. Northild, to escape further sin and humiliation, was prepared to expose the secrets of the marriage bed to public view; and she believed that the emperor, as protector of the powerless (*pauperes*), including women, would declare in favour of a legal separation. According to some texts of secular law, such a separation was licit when both parties agreed, or when one or the other party had committed a particularly heinous sexual offence such as incest. Hincmar cited the Northild case, after all, not only to make a point about private bodies and the body politic, but to show that marriage was

[69] See above, n. 10; also J. L. Nelson, 'Did Charlemagne Have a Private Life?', forthcoming in a Festschrift.

[70] For the case, and Hincmar's work, see above all S. Airlie, 'Private Bodies and the Body Politic in the Divorce Case of Lothar II', *Past and Present*, 161 (1998), 3–38.

[71] Hincmar, *De divortio Hlotharii et Tetbergae*, Responsio V, ed L. Böhringer, MGH Concilia IV, Supplementum 1 (Hannover, 1992), 141–2.

part of secular and natural law, and he quite clearly approved of laymen's handling of it. The bishops in 822 shoved responsibility sideways, having been nudged in that direction, perhaps, by the emperor. For what Louis wanted in 822 was the restoration of consensus. Where judgement over wives and defence of secular laws were concerned, patriarchs united. I have begun to suspect that the whole case was stage-managed by Louis, with the not ignoble Northild as fall-doll, and reaffirmed patriarchy the prize.

Another case in 846 looks similarly well plotted, in this case by Louis's son Charles the Bald. In 846, Charles the Bald's situation looked worse than his father's had been in 822; recent military defeat;[72] grim weather; wolves in armies of 300 at a time on the roads of Aquitaine devouring the inhabitants;[73] an assembly in June at which entente between bishops and lay notables had cracked open when the laymen threw out proposals designed to remove lay encroachments on church property.[74] Then a man was brought before the assembly for judgement – he had been in custody since Lent, when he had been caught in the act of sexual intercourse with a mare. The assembled Franks condemned him to be burnt alive. After that a measure of consensus was doubtless restored. What the war on terror or gay marriages can be in the early twenty-first century – rallying-cries for strapped politicians – bestiality could be for ninth-century Franks.

Enough of *inhonesta*, and victims whose fate after all these centuries still distresses me! I turn with some relief to another Frankish noblewoman, Dhuoda, whom I briefly want to introduce as a bearer and exponent of views on body and mind that she had learned at the courts of Louis the Pious and, perhaps, Charlemagne, and passed on, in a work of maternal instruction, to her just-adult son William as he joined a new Carolingian court.[75] According to Michael Wallace-Hadrill, the programme of spiritual exercises she offered William 'might have strained a monk'.[76] That is a statement that seriously underestimates the capacity for prayer of

[72] J. L. Nelson, *Charles the Bald* (London, 1992), 147.

[73] Annales Bertiniani s.a. 846, ed. F. Grat, J. Vielliard and S. Clémencet (Paris, 1964), 51–2, trans. Nelson, *The Annals of St-Bertin* (Manchester, 1991), 62–3.

[74] *Ibid.* Hincmar's view of this episode is preserved in Hague MS 1: MGH Capit. II, no. 257, p. 261.

[75] Dhuoda, *Liber Manualis*, ed. and trans. M. Thiébaux, *Dhuoda. Handbook for her Warrior Son* (Cambridge, 1998), cited hereafter as *LM*. See further J. L. Nelson, 'Dhuoda', in *Lay Intellectuals in the Carolingian World*, ed. P. Wormald (Cambridge, forthcoming). I should like to acknowledge the recent important work of two young scholars, Rachel Stone and Cullum Chandler.

[76] J. M. Wallace-Hadrill, *The Frankish Church* (Oxford, 1983), 286; cf. J. L. Nelson, 'Monks, Secular Men and Masculinity c. 900', in *Masculinity in Medieval Europe*, ed. D. M. Hadley (London, 1999), 121–42, at 128.

the Carolingian lay elite and of Carolingian rulers themselves.[77] Dhuoda took her cue from Alcuin's handbook for a layman, *Virtues and Vices*, but she affirmed with a force and consistency essayed, or risked, by no other Carolingian moralist, that a life of Christian mindfulness was compatible with the life, and the lifestyle, of a layman, and a layman at a Carolingian court.[78]

One passage illuminates Dhuoda's method and intent especially well. VII, 1 stands out as a key point in the book's structure.[79] It is headed, uniquely, *Admonitio singularis utilissima*. In her prologue, she said she would deal with *utrumque negotium*, that is, 'being useful in the world (*saeculum*) and pleasing God'.[80] In VII, 1, Dhuoda picked up this dual theme. She had served her son up to now as his *ordinatrix*, the one who put him in line (an apt military metaphor), organised him, as regards *temporalia*, so that he could advance confidently and calmly while he lived 'on active service', and was concerned with worldly office; but now, and from now on, she would admonish him on how to advance the service of his soul (*militia animae*) to the highest level. This made her a mother twice over: once for his body, the second time, for his soul (*mens*), and the result would be that William would be reborn every day in Christ.

> For a Christian person experiences two births: physical and spiritual. But the spiritual is nobler than the physical. In the human race the one cannot subsist profitably (*utiliter*) without the other. And in order that the physical and the spiritual may accord more worthily (*dignius*), someone says: [they are those] 'with which and without which we cannot live'. And although the meaning turns in another sense in that passage as originally written, I want you to accept it in the way I say, because of the clear reasons [for interpreting it as referring to] different things.

The New Testament notion of being born again was amplified by Augustine in his Commentary on John (and elsewhere) into an idea of *duae nativitates*.[81] Where St Paul had seen a conflict between flesh and spirit, requiring the believer to crucify the flesh,[82] Dhuoda saw tension but also

[77] In *LM* II, 3, 78–9, Dhuoda quotes from the Rule of Benedict 52, 4, on how to pray 'non . . . in longa pertrahendi verba, sed in summo et brevi affectu'. Did Dhuoda learn to pray as a child at the court Charlemagne, I wonder? On the distinctive *Sitz im Leben* of private prayer in this period, see now S. Waldhoff, *Alcuins Gebetbuch für Karl der Grossen*, Liturgiewissenschaftliche Quellen und Forschungen 89 (Münster, 2003), pp. 32–42; and Nelson, 'Did Charlemagne Have a Private Life?', and 'The Carolingian Cult of the Cross and the Civilising Process', both forthcoming.

[78] See G. W. Olsen, 'One Heart and One Soul (Acts 4: 32 and 34) in Dhuoda's "Manual"', *Church History*, 61 (1992), 23–33, at 30–1; Nelson, 'Was Charlemagne's Court a Courtly Society?'.

[79] *LM* VII, 1, 190–1.

[80] *LM* prologue, 48.

[81] John 3: 5–7; Augustine *Sermo* 121, 4, Patrologia Latina, ed. J.-P. Migne, XXXVIII (Paris, 1841), 38, 679; *Tractatus in Johannem* 11, 6, CC 36, 113–14.

[82] Galatians 5: 16–24.

the necessity of coexistence, and ultimately a kind of harmony. To convey this she looked to another source than the Apostle: in Dhuoda's mind, and at precisely this point, Augustine met Ovid. Dhuoda here alluded to Ovid's lines to his beloved in the *Amores*: 'Aversor morum crimina, corpus amo. Sic ego nec sine te nec tecum vivere possum' ('With or without you, life's impossible').[83] Compare Dhuoda on spiritual birth and fleshly birth: 'Cum quibus et sine quibus vivere non possumus.' Note the extra force of *vivere* in *her* context. Dhuoda clearly was not citing Ovid's tag at second-hand, for she knew its sense 'in the passage as originally written'. Furthermore, she offered her own interpretation of it, and told her son to accept that.[84]

> Hitherto I have been your *ordinatrix* as to your secular life; now, your mother a second time and in another sense, I admonish your soul, *ut in Christo cotidie renascaris* ('that you may be reborn every day in Christ'), and so that, though this body is mortal, you can escape spiritual death and live eternally with God.[85]

Dhuoda told her son to read works of Christian moral instruction, especially the Bible. She urged him to remain chaste while young, but she looked forward to his marriage and to his offspring.[86] She was comfortable on the subject of sexuality within marriage. She recognised that life at court had snares but she was more interested in its opportunities. She knew that a palace was not a building but the people who inhabited it.[87] And that was the audience she aimed to write for, beyond her immediate concern for her own 'beautiful boy'. She wrote, in short, not only as a bodily mother for her son but as a would-be giver of a second birth in the mind and spirit to other women's sons.

One great theme of the piety Dhuoda recommended was private prayer, as taught by Alcuin to Charlemagne, and as diffused from that court to subsequent generations of the Carolingian elite. She recommended prayers to the Cross to be said at bedtime. That the Cross became central to ninth-century theology is the key contention

[83] Cf. P. Dronke, *Women Writers of the Middle Ages* (Cambridge, 1984), 46, with the translation of Ovid's *Amores* by G. Lee (London, 1968), III, xi b, l. 7.

[84] For Ovid in Carolingian manuscripts, see R. J. Tarrant, 'Ovid', in *Texts and Transmission: A Survey of the Latin Classics*, ed. L. D. Reynolds (Oxford 1983), 257–84, and for knowledge of Ovid among those connected with Charlemagne's court, see Nees, *A Tainted Mantle*, 31, 122–3.

[85] *LM* VII, 1, 190.

[86] *LM* III, 3, 92.

[87] Letter sent on behalf of the bishops assembled at Quierzy in 858, to Kings Louis the German and Charles the Bald, MGH Conc. III, ed. W. Hartmann (Hannover 1984), no. 41, c. v, p. 412: 'The palace of the king is so called on account of the rational human beings who dwell therein, not on account of walls or courtyards that are insensible things.' For courtiers' consciousness of themselves as such even when they had left the court, see S. Airlie, 'Bonds of Power and Bonds of Association in the Court Circle of Louis the Pious', in *Charlemagne's Heir*, ed. Godman and Collins, 191–204, at 196.

of a recent fine book, Celia Chazelle's *The Crucified God*. The great ninth-century pastor Hrabanus Maurus wrote *In Praise of the Holy Cross* probably at the outset of Louis the Pious's reign, a work that combined image and text. It was copied at the author's behest for several recipients: a potent gift. Hrabanus's message was distilled in an image he himself produced, showing the crucified Christ, but with no cross visible. The figure-poem (*declaratio figurae*) says: 'Look, the image of our Lord, by the position of the limbs, consecrates for us the most saving, sweetest and most lovable form of the holy cross.'[88] Hrabanus's acrostic verse that forms the background to the image has meaning in its content as well as its form, and so 'makes a double appeal to the mind and to the eye'.[89] The body itself is the cross, and it is at once man and God. The central message is conveyed in the lines that fill the outstretched arms of Christ: 'Thus placed on the cross, God had given the crown in the high citadel. This God is the source, Emmanuel, and the end is the beginning.' Hrabanus follows the figure-poem with a detailed exposition. The body bears a series of messages:

> descending from his head are the words, 'Christus laxabit e sanguine debita mundo' ('Christ will pay from [his] blood debts for the world'). From his right hand runs this: 'In cruce sic positus desolvens vincla tyranni' ('On the cross thus placed dissolving the chains of the tyrant'). On his loincloth and across his thighs are written: 'Veste quidem parva hic tegitur qui continent astra, atque solum palmo claudit ubique suo' ('Yes, with this little garment he is clad who contains the stars, and encloses in the palm of his hand the earth and everywhere'). And this is written on his face and chin, his nipples and his navel: 'ordo iustus Deo' ('the way right for God').[90]

It is hard to think of a more exquisite application of human mind to divine body, or a profounder expression of the divine incarnate, than Hrabanus's inscribing on Christ's nipples and navel the letters D-E-O ('for God').

This was not just arcane theology for monastic scholars. Among the nine ninth-century recipients of manuscripts of Hrabanus's work (there are eighty-one manuscripts in all) were the emperor Louis the Pious and the magnate Eberhard. Another reader, almost certainly, was Dhuoda. More significant still, both Hrabanus and Dhuoda, and those taught by them, were inspired by the booklets of prayers that circulated among ninth-century lay and clergy. In fact, habits of private prayer such as those Dhuoda recommended to her son were acquired through the bringing of Insular (Irish and Anglo-Saxon) manuscripts to the Continent. The

[88] Hrabanus Maurus, *In honorem sanctae crucis*, ed. M. Perrin, Corpus Christianorum, Continuatio Medievalis 100, C 1 (Turnhout, 1997), C 1, 28–9. See M. C. Ferrari, *Il 'Liber sanctae crucis' di Rabano Mauro: Testo – Immagine – Contesto* (Bern, 1999), 128–9, 314–15, and *passim*; cf. Chazelle, *The Crucified God*, 99–131. I am grateful to Lynda Coon for help on Hrabanus's use of somatic allegory.

[89] P. Godman, *Poets and Emperors* (Oxford, 1986), 56.

[90] *In honorem*, 33.

late Donald Bullough had no doubt that in this wider dissemination Alcuin played 'a major part, with immeasurable and subtle effect on the hearts and minds of generations of readers'.[91] Thanks to Alcuin's work in composing, compiling and diffusing through a well-maintained communications-network, 'for more than a thousand years men and women to whom his name was unknown regularly spoke to God in Alcuin's words'.[92]

Behind Alcuin was the Psalter; and I want to end this lecture with another Anglo-Saxon reader and writer and translator, Alfred of Wessex. Only 50 out of the 150 psalms survive in the rather distinctively worded Old English translation. The case for Alfred's authorship, and for believing William of Malmesbury's claim (perhaps no more than an inference) that Psalm 50 was as far as Alfred had got when he died on the job, was made by Janet Bately on strong lexical grounds.[93] It has now been further strengthened by reference to the author's 'pragmatic approach to translating Scripture'.[94] Perhaps it could be added that a royal author who felt himself to have gone through many undeserved sufferings would have found David the psalmist, another royal author, a congenial model.[95] Where the Carolingian kings had to get their poets to make the parallel, Alfred did it for himself. While each psalm was prefaced with an interpretation using the traditional four levels of exegesis, literal, historical, Christological, moral, Alfred showed a strong preference for the historical and moral. Mind and body occur in several of these expositions, in the context of sufferings, and of enemies.[96] Alfred knew all about the interconnectedness of body and mind. Alfred was the man who had been struck down by a mysterious agonising pain at his wedding-feast in the company of many men and women, and who explained that pain as a divinely sent illness for which he himself had prayed, to save him from pride while allowing him still to remain useful as a king and to father children. Alfred was the man whose biographer likened him to the thief who was crucified alongside Christ, and saved by repentance.[97]

[91] D. Bullough, 'Alcuin and the Kingdom of God: Liturgy, Theology and the Carolingian Age', in his collection of papers, *Carolingian Renewal* (Manchester, 1991), 161–240, at 169.

[92] D. Bullough, 'Alcuin's Cultural Influence: The Evidence of the Manuscripts', in *Alcuin of York. Scholar at the Carolingian Court*, ed. L. A. J. R. Houwen and A. A. MacDonald (Groningen, 1998), 1–26, at 26.

[93] J. Bately, 'Lexical Evidence for the Authorship of the Prose Psalms in the Paris Psalter', *Anglo-Saxon England*, 10 (1982), 69–95, at 70, 94–5.

[94] P. P. O'Neill, *King Alfred's Prose Translation of the First Fifty Psalms* (Cambridge, MA, 2001), 73–96, at 94.

[95] *Ibid.*, 93, notes the translator's consistent rendering of *gratis*, 'without cause', in the context of suffering inflicted by enemies, as 'buton scylde' – blamelessly, innocently.

[96] *Ibid.*, for instance Psalms 3, 15, 30, 41, pp. 101, 114, 133, 150.

[97] Asser, *De Rebus Gestis Ælfredi*, cc. 74, 89, ed. W. Stevenson (Oxford, 1904), 54, 75.

Alfred was a thinking man, and a feeling man. In the main psalm-texts, he uses *mod* for mind, soul, spirit (*mens*, *anima*, *animus*, in Jerome's Vulgate Latin): for instance, of the conversion of the mind/spirit from trouble to joy in Psalm 22: 3.[98] When he translated the *Consolation of Philosophy*, Alfred chose to render Boethius's personified *Philosophia* by *Mod*.

To function well, minds and bodies both need time, and careful time-allocation is above all useful to the rationally restless for maximising 'the service to God of body and mind'. Alfred had thought wisely about this one too, says his biographer, and so he invented a clock.[99] Maybe, if David Pratt is right, the clock was used not just for the king's own personal time-management but for that of his faithful men even when they were not at court.[100] A Benedictine nun once said to me, with a smile, 'The Rule of St Benedict is impossible, but we live it anyway.' Ninth-century people, and not only nuns and monks (Weber's model time-keepers), would have understood that. These people kept body and soul together. They had to cope with religious requirements and bodily needs and desires, with existential angst, and with Christian restlessness. They lived, as we do, in a very imperfect world, and Augustine (whether read or heard explained) had taught them to face that pragmatically. The technology of ninth-century politics would not have permitted intrusive and extensive discipline and punishment on lines Michel Foucault discerned in modern states. Prayer and penance and fidelity necessarily involve *self*-discipline and a kind of self-assertion too. Perhaps we still have things to learn from the multifarious ways in which ninth-century people, even including some women, assumed a degree of agency in their own lives. Many continued to suffer, of course, for powerful men were not naturally restrained, and the trust of even noblewomen in the state's protection could be cruelly disappointed. Remember Northild as well as Dhuoda. Remember the many powerless ones whose lives, and the rights they claimed, often in vain, we can see only fitfully (though in last year's lecture, I offered a few glimpses). Nevertheless, these were not Dark Ages, in the sense either of being exceptionally nasty and hopeless, or of being exceptionally badly

[98] O'Neill, *King Alfred's Prose Translation*, 124: 'and min mod gehwyfde of unrotnesse on gefean'.

[99] Asser, *De Rebus Gestis Ælfredi*, cc. 103, 104, pp. 89–90.

[100] D. Pratt, 'Persuasion and Invention at the Court of King Alfred', in *Court Culture*, ed. Cubitt, 189–222, at 201–6, finally suggesting that 'further candle-lanterns may have been manufactured for Alfred's noble readers, in order that they might follow the disciplines of "court time" even when absent from their royal role model'. Pratt further notes, 213–16, Alfred's use of the expression 'the mind's eyes' (*modes eagan*) in his translations 'at every available opportunity': they are equated with such divine gifts as wisdom and righteousness through which minds themselves share immortality even while 'men's bodies grow old'.

documented. In this final lecture, I have offered some evidence for a brighter view. For I think that, in the end, through prayer and through laughter, through feasts and fasts, through engaging with rulers who, whatever their limitations, had the public good at heart, and last but not least through finding delight and solace in the works of poets from ancient Israel's to their own, ninth-century people coped, more or less, with the competing demands, the inseparable demands, the reconcilable demands, of bodies and minds.

Transactions of the RHS 15 (2005), pp. 29–49
doi:10.1017/S0080440105000290 Printed in the United Kingdom

MARMOUTIER AND ITS SERFS IN THE ELEVENTH CENTURY

By Paul Fouracre

READ 12 MARCH 2004

ABSTRACT. The 'Book of Serfs of Marmoutier' recorded the dealings the monastery had with its serfs in the eleventh century. The eleventh century itself is said to have been a time in which there was a collapse of political authority. Political and judicial institutions are alleged to have been 'privatised' as part of the so-called 'feudal revolution' that was caused by the collapse of Carolingian authority. This view has often been challenged. The Marmoutier material on serfs is discussed in relation to this debate. Do the monastery–serf relations reflect a privatisation of power? Or if the privatisation of power is an historical myth, how do we explain the highly contested nature of space, community, wealth and authority revealed in the 'Book of Serfs'? It is argued that authority had indeed fragmented but that this was a response to a conjunction of factors apart from the collapse of the Carolingian state. To the contrary, the Carolingian rulers had encouraged the kind of lord–serf relations that we see in the 'Book of Serfs'. What is different about our eleventh-century material is that there is more of it, and we are able to see details of social relations at a local level for the first time.

The monastery of Marmoutier lies on the north bank of the river Loire, slightly upstream from Tours. It was founded in *c.* 371 by the bishop and monk St Martin of Tours, as a retreat from the burdens of office. Like the monastery of St Denis near Paris, or the church of Rheims, Marmoutier is one of those treasured institutions which had a more or less continuous history from the later Roman period up to the French Revolution. It was the continuity of records from places like this that gave French medievalists a head start in describing the birth, growth and decline of medieval culture. For medieval Europe here read France. A glance at R. I. Moore's recent book *The First European Revolution c. 970–1215* reminds us of how strong this francocentric legacy remains.[1] Moore's Europe, like Southern's before him,[2] is located firmly between the rivers Garonne, Rhône and Rhine, and monasteries, such as that of Marmoutier, play a leading role in it. One of the greatest debates amongst medievalists has turned around the question of how, or even whether, European society was transformed at the end of the early middle ages. It

[1] R. I. Moore, *The First European Revolution c. 970–1215* (Oxford, 2000).
[2] R. W. Southern, *The Making of the Middle Ages* (1951).

is a debate that is centred on France and fuelled by the evidence of charters from monasteries. Charters from Marmoutier which deal with serfs are very much part of that evidence. In what follows I shall revisit the so-called 'feudal revolution' or 'mutation féodale' debate, because thinking about change determines how we regard the material from Marmoutier, and how we place it in historical context. Framing the material in such a way will also help us with the question of whether we can generalise from it. It is the case, moreover, that the most recent contributions to the 'feudal revolution' debate have deep implications for how we think more generally about the early middle ages as well as about this transitional period. The debate thus gives us the widest possible frame of reference for our material.

We begin with what R. I. Moore termed in a review article of 1984 'Duby's Eleventh Century'.[3] This is shorthand for George Duby's mid-twentieth-century account of how the Carolingian order in Europe was transformed at the end of the tenth century. The key to change in Duby's model was the way in which public justice, and institutions of justice, were privatised. For Duby, as earlier for J.-F. Lemarignier, M. Bloch and F.-L. Ganshof,[4] the fate of judicial institutions and in particular the *mallus*, the counts's court, came to stand for the whole of the Carolingian social, political and economic order. Those charters known as *placita* which recorded court cases, that is, cases involving dispute and judgement, became a major focus of investigation. Even though recent thinking has challenged the notion of a privatisation of justice, it has actually reinforced the focus on court records by arguing for continuities in the social processes at work in courts, whatever their institutional form. Dispute settlement and the *placita* have, like France, become core territory of the feudal debate.

Duby famously illustrated the structural change in society through the charters of the monastery of Cluny as they related to the county, and the county court, of Mâcon.[5] In his view, the Carolingian state had preserved and even strengthened institutions derived, ultimately, from Roman government. Through judicial institutions backed by royal authority, free

[3] R. I. Moore, 'Duby's Eleventh Century', *History*, 64 (1984), 36–54. Moore was reviewing three works by Duby which drew out the social and cultural consequences of structural change.

[4] The seminal work was G. Duby, *La société au XIe et XIIe siècles dans la region mâconnaise* (Paris, 1953). For earlier work emphasising the importance of judicial institutions in structural change, see Lemarignier's collected papers: J.-F. Lemarignier, *Structures politiques et religieuses dans la France du haut moyen âge. Recueil d'articles rassemblés par ses disciples* (Rouen, 1995). See also M. Bloch, *Feudal Society*, trans. L. Manyon (Chicago, 1961), and F.-L. Ganshof, *Feudalism*, 3rd English edn (1964). For a textbook account of this change according to what one might term the 'French school', J.-P. Poly and E. Bournazel, *La mutation féodale, Xe–XIIe siècles* (Paris, 1980).

[5] Duby, *Société mâconaise*.

people had a degree of protection from the arbitrary exactions of lords, and a forum in which disputes could be settled by definitive judgement. Grievances could thus be taken before the *mallus*, over which the count presided as the representative of royal authority. In these courts, cases were heard according to strict procedures, and judgements were arrived at according to accepted rules. It was a rule-based system. Its antithesis, in this view, was the world of feudal courts in which rules and judgements disappeared to be replaced by *ad hoc* argument and compromise, in courts which were run by lords and their followers rather than by counts and public witnesses and judges. This change reflected the privatisation of power in general; in a society in which royal authority had nosedived, lords had as much power as they could accumulate in any way they could, and peasants had lost the protection of judicial institutions. Enserfment followed.[6] Although there is a sub-set of debates about the origins of servitude in the central middle ages – did it derive from the slavery of Antiquity, or was it newly imposed upon a predominantly free peasantry by our now rampant lords?[7] – there is general agreement that the power of lords over the peasants in the districts they controlled was such that they were able to impose and maintain servitude over them. To the question of freedom, servitude and relative social power we shall return in the context of our Marmoutier material. But first let us examine more closely the issues at stake in challenges to 'Duby's eleventh century'.

Duby's particular contribution to this dialectical model was to argue for the abruptness of the change. Highlighting the rapid pace of change, that is, locating it in the half-century 980–1030, had the effect of making a sharper break between the Carolingian and the post-Carolingian, or

[6] For a classic 'French school' account of how this happened, see P. Bonnassie, 'From one servitude to another: the peasantry of the Frankish kingdom at the time of Hugh Capet and Robert the Pious (987–1031)', in P. Bonnassie, *From Slavery to Feudalism in South-Western Europe*, trans. J. Birrell (Cambridge, 1991).

[7] Bloch argued that ancient slavery had disappeared by the end of the tenth century. There was then a brief period of peasant freedom before serfdom was imposed by the seigneurial lords: M. Bloch, 'How and why ancient slavery came to an end', *Annales ESC* (1947), 30–43, 161–70. This article was unpublished at the time of Bloch's death, and although it advances what is a difficult proposition (that there was a 'privileged moment' of peasant freedom sandwiched between two ages of servitude), it was held in such high esteem by the generation of French scholars that followed Bloch that the proposition is still often accepted. See for instance Bonnassie's otherwise excellent account of the early medieval history of slavery: P. Bonnassie, 'The survival and extinction of the slave system in the early medieval West (fourth to eleventh centuries)', in Bonnassie, *Slavery to Feudalism*, 1–59. Even Dockès's radical account has all slaves liberated by the year 1000: P. Dockès, *Medieval Slavery and Liberation* (Paris, 1982). The alternative view is of the gradual emergence of medieval serfdom out of ancient slavery, with servitude constant enough to enable the continued use of ancient terminology, but flexible enough to adapt to new conditions, See, for instance, H.-W. Goetz, 'Serfdom and the beginnings of a "seigneurial system" in the Carolingian period: a survey of the evidence', *Early Medieval Europe*, 2 (1993), 29–51.

'feudal', worlds. In Bloch's view, by contrast, there had been a long period, from the later ninth to the eleventh centuries, in which the feudal had matured in the womb of the Carolingian.[8] According to Duby, the feudal was born out of a more precipitate crisis. His model was then taken up and crises and transformations discovered in other regions too, notably northern Spain and Latium in Italy, albeit with slightly different chronologies.[9] The model has nevertheless remained firmly francocentric, though discussion is increasingly anglophone. Nevertheless, those who study Anglo-Saxon England seem to regard the other side of the channel as quite other, characterised in the late Patrick Wormald's phrase as 'Professor White's Touraine', a decentralised, dysfunctional world serving only to point up the strengths of the Old English state.[10] The late Timothy Reuter's pleas to make sure that the experience of Germany was included in any assessment of the 'feudal revolution' have not yet been answered.[11]

Challenges to Duby's model have come first of all from a re-reading of his Cluny evidence. Several scholars have demonstrated, and with some ease, that he was simply wrong to claim that the Cluny charters show the Carolingian *mallus* functioning in traditional manner up to the 980s.[12] What charters from the mid-tenth century show is some continuity in court terminology but actual processes that were far from rule-based, in courts that were run without much reference to public authority and witness. In the face of this demonstration, the case for abrupt change has collapsed, although Pierre Bonnassie has argued more successfully for a 'feudal revolution' in Catalonia in the period 1020–60, the rapid transformation of political structures here being the result of a series

[8] Bloch, *Feudal Society*, 60ff.

[9] For south-western Europe, P. Bonnassie, 'From the Rhône to Galicia: Origins and Modalities of the Feudal Order', in Bonnassie, *Slavery to Feudalism*, 104–32. On Central Italy, with a view of more gradual change, P. Toubert, *Les structures du Latium médiévale: le Latium méridional et la Sabine du IXe siècle a la fin du XIIe siècle* (Rome, 1973). On Tuscany, with the proviso that 'privatised' power there would be countered by the rising power of the city-territories, C. Wickham, 'Property Ownership and Signorial Power in Twelfth-Century Tuscany', in *Property and Power in the Early Middle Ages*, ed. W. Davies and P. Fouracre (Cambridge, 1995), 221–44.

[10] P. Wormald, 'Giving God and King their Due: Conflict and its Regulation in the Early English State', in P. Wormald, *Legal Culture in the Early Medieval West* (1999), 333–57, at 341: 'There is . . . reason to believe that the English scene was quite unlike that in Professor White's Touraine: until, that is, conquest superimposed the French scene upon it.' It must be pointed out that Patrick Wormald was able to make this comparison (unflattering though it is) because, unusually for an Anglo-Saxonist, he had command of the Continental material.

[11] T. Reuter, 'Debate. The "Feudal Revolution". III', *Past and Present*, 155 (1997), 177–95.

[12] The most recent demonstrations are F. Cheyette, 'Some Reflections on Violence, Reconciliation and the "Feudal Revolution"', and S. White, 'Tenth-Century Courts at Mâcon and the Perils of Structuralist History: Re-reading Burgundian Judicial Institutions', both in *Conflict in Medieval Europe. Changing Perspectives on Society and Culture*, ed. W. Brown and P. Górecki (Aldershot, 2003), respectively 243–64 and 37–68.

of well-documented political crises.[13] A more profound objection to the whole notion of 'feudal revolution' challenges the sense of opposition between the Carolingian and post-Carolingian worlds. Taking his cue from work done by British scholars on dispute settlement in the early middle ages, Dominique Barthélemy suggested that the Carolingian order was not so public, and the seigneurial world not so private as had been assumed.[14] There was, in other words, not that much difference between them. A decade ago, Jane Martindale presented before this society a picture of courts in eleventh-century Aquitaine which seemed to her still to operate much as they had done under the Carolingians.[15] And in a departure from what has been (with the exception of Martindale) a debate largely between male historians, and about the nature of power, Pauline Stafford has questioned the 'mutation' of family structures that is supposed to have been part of the transformation of society. In parallel to the privatisation of power, family structures were said to have been transformed from the cognatic to the agnatic as the seigneurs consolidated their lineages around single family seats. On closer inspection, argues Stafford, these apparent structural differences evaporate.[16]

The latest phases of this debate were sparked by Thomas Bisson's strong statement about the realities of living in the changed political landscape of the eleventh century. With the collapse of public authority, argues Bisson, a regime based on violence came into being. It was a regime in which the peasants were trampled underfoot in the calvacade which thundered out from the castle.[17] To this picture, which rested on a conviction that there had indeed been a 'feudal revolution', there was a strong reaction on the basis that, like Duby's work, it drew too sharp a line between Carolingian order and 'feudal' disorder. Chris Wickham, however, has rallied to the defence of the 'mutation' model. He argues that structural change, that is from the public courts and judicial institutions of the Carolingian order to the privatised justice of the so-called 'feudal order', happened at different times, and in slightly different ways, in different regions across Europe,

[13] P. Bonnassie, 'The Formation of Catalan Feudalism and its Early Expansion (to c. 1150)', and 'The Noble and the Ignoble: A New Nobility and a New Servitude in Catalonia at the End of the Eleventh Century', in Bonnassie, *Slavery to Feudalism*, 149–69, 195–242.

[14] D. Barthélemy, 'La mutation féodale, a-t-elle eu lieu? (Note critique)', *Annales ESC*, 47 (1992), 767–77, and worked out in detail in D. Barthélemy, *La mutation de l'an mil, a-t-elle eu lieu? Servage et chevalerie dans la France des Xe et XIe siècles* (Paris, 1997).

[15] J. Martindale, '"His Special Friend"? The Settlement of Disputes and Political Power in the Kingdom of the French (Tenth to Mid Twelfth Century)', *TRHS*, sixth series, 5 (1995), 21–57.

[16] P. Stafford, "La mutation familiale": A Suitable Case for Caution', in *The Community the Family and the Saint. Patterns of Power in Early Medieval Europe*, ed. J. Hill and M. Swan, International Medieval Research 4 (Turnhout, 1998), 103–25.

[17] T. Bisson, 'The Feudal Revolution', *Past and Present,*142 (1994), 6–42.

but happen it did.[18] For Wickham, the key indication that change had taken place was the end of the *placitum* tradition, that is, the rule-based court, which issued definitive judgements framed by public authority. Most recently, Stephen White has returned to the attack on Duby, and has also concentrated his fire on Wickham as the last line of resistance of what he terms 'structuralist history'.[19] Apart from attacking Duby's reading of the Cluny charters, White's point is that the overstressing of binary oppositions in the structuralist tradition, i.e. the public versus the private, naturally leads to false impressions of radical transformation. It is not a safe assumption that there *must* be change, especially when we cannot locate the moment. The end of *placitum* tradition is not a good indicator of change because the *placitum* had never been the purely public, rule-based engine that Wickham imagines. Hardening his position from earlier work in which he largely endorsed the view held by British scholars on the nature of the *placitum*, White picks up on Janet Nelson's view of the Carolingian county court as having significant 'private' elements, so that there cannot have been much practical difference between the court of a Carolingian count and the court of the lord of seigneurie.[20] Compromise, the hallmark of more informal court processes in which no decision could be reached because both parties in a dispute were effectively more powerful than the court itself, is evident even in the records of the *placita* themselves. Earlier work on dispute settlement had insisted that even compromise was in the nature of a judgement imposed on the disputants.[21] This, implies White, is a misconception that came from false assumptions about the strength of the court's authority. If we think about dispute settlement as political and legal processes that involved a complex interaction of rules, norms, strategies and emotions, and which always ranged from the formal court to the informal settlement, says White, we can dissolve the public/private opposition, and, along with it, the notion of structural change.[22]

It is not immediately clear why White so fiercely attacks 'structuralism' in a way that sets up yet another opposition, this time between 'structuralism' and 'processual history', unless he is making a covert assault on what he might see as the last vestiges of Marxism. He never really defines 'structuralism', and certainly never 'processualism', which he does not take beyond the realm of dispute settlement. He and Wickham in fact have much in common, as do all the contributions to

[18] C. Wickham, 'Debate: The "Feudal Revolution" IV', *Past and Present*, 155 (1997), 196–208.

[19] White, 'Tenth-Century Courts', 58–62.

[20] *Ibid.*, 64–5, with reference to J. Nelson, 'Dispute Settlement in Carolingian West Francia', in *The Settlement of Disputes in Early Medieval Europe*, ed. W. Davies and P. Fouracre (Cambridge, 1986), 45–64.

[21] 'Conclusion', in *Settlement of Disputes*, ed. Davies and Fouracre, 219, 237.

[22] White, 'Tenth-Century Courts', 55 and n. 72, 64–6.

this debate. Despite White's assertion that 'structuralism' is theoretically over-determined, the discussion on both sides is essentially empiricist.[23] With the exception of Stafford, it homes in on dispute-settlement and the nature of judicial institutions; the essential testing ground remains France, and, strangely, economic change hardly features. It has always been a top-down model: in whichever view, the effects of the breakdown of the Carolingian state are what are at issue. Where does all this leave Marmoutier and its serfs, or vice versa?

We are relatively well informed about the serfs of Marmoutier thanks to a cartulary that is unique in being concerned solely with serfs. 'The Book of the Serfs of Marmoutier' (*Liber de Servis Majoris Monasterii*) consists of 127 notices recording the dealings Marmoutier had with its serfs. It seems to have been put together sometime around 1070, with the bulk of notices coming from the time of Abbots Albert and Bartholomew, that is, from 1032 to 1064. A further fifteen documents were added from 1070 to 1097.[24] The cartulary's second nineteenth-century editor, Grandmaison, also gathered together in an appendix another sixty-five charters from other cartularies on the basis that these were also concerned with Marmoutier's serfs.[25] Roughly the last fifteen of these documents fall well beyond our period. Where we have both a notice from the 'Book of Serfs' and a full charter from another cartulary dealing with similar material, we can see that the notices were shortened versions of originals, but that they contain the essential details.

Just over half of the documents in the 'Book of Serfs' record cases of 'auto-dedition', this being when people gave themselves to the abbey and became its serfs. There are also sales and gifts of serfs to the abbey by other lords; manumissions are very few, but there are several notices which detail disputes between Marmoutier and its serfs, these usually being about status, and disputes between Mamoutier and other parties about the ownership of serfs, and some of these cases too turn on the question

[23] I grateful to my colleague S. Rigby for pointing this out to me.

[24] The *Liber de Servis Majoris Monasterii* was first edited by A. Salmon (Paris, 1845), but Salmon apparently died before adding notes and commentary. The 1845 edition thus simply gives the texts of the 127 documents.

[25] *Liber de Servis Majoris Monasterii*, ed. Ch. L. Grandmaison, Publications de la Société archéologique de Touraine 16 (Tours, 1864). Grandmaison used Salmon's texts without alteration, but added introductory essays, notes and indices. The majority of the documents included in Grandmaison's appendix come from the monastery's cartulary for the Dunois. This, the Cartulary for the Vendômois and the *Liber de Servis* have all survived in the original. Other so-called 'Marmoutier cartularies' are modern reconstructions: *Cartulaire de Marmoutier pour le Dunois*, ed. M. Emille Mabille (Chateaudun 1874); *Cartulaire de Marmoutier pour le Vendômois* ed. M. de Trémault (Paris, 1893). On the composition of the various cartularies, see D. Barthélemy, 'Note sur les Cartulaires de Marmoutier (Touraine) au XIe siècle', in *Les cartulaires*, ed. O. Guyotjeannin, L. Morelle and M. Parisse (Paris, 1992), 247–59. The *Liber de Servis* documents are henceforth cited as *SM*, by number in the Salmon/Grandmaison edition. Documents from Grandmaison's appendix are cited as *SMA*.

of status. Unlike some of the documents in the other two eleventh- and early twelfth-century Marmoutier cartularies (for the Dunois and the Vendômois), the notices in the 'Book of Serfs' are concerned with ownership rather than with rights and services. What this gives us is a book which records who the serfs were. What the serfs actually did in terms of service, or paid in rent, we are not told, apart from the customary payment of four *denarii* which people were required to place on their heads as a public acknowledgement of their servile status. The context for the production of this unique cartulary seems to have been two generations of rapid expansion by Marmoutier, during which time it had acquired large numbers of serfs. The 'Book of Serfs' in effect told the coming generation of monks who their dependants were, giving proof of their status.

Grandmaison, mindful of a well-known and much earlier (eighth-century) Tours formula of commendation, in which destitute peasants gave up their freedom to landlords in return for basic sustenance, was convinced that serfdom was so dreadful that no one could wish it upon themselves unless they were in the direst straits.[26] The fact that there were so many auto-deditions in the Marmoutier cartulary pointed to the awfulness of life in eleventh-century Touraine. Dominique Barthélemy, however, has read the charters in a much more optimistic light. He noted that many of those giving themselves into serfdom had occupations that suggested that they were far from being desperate peasants, or even peasants at all. Some were cellarers, cooks, mayors or agents of the monastery, and some received land and or accommodation when they entered Marmoutier's *familia*.[27] In such cases, argued Barthélemy, the passage from freedom to servitude mattered less than the prospect of secure and possibly lucrative employment. Amongst the peasantry in general, there were complex relationships of dependence, family, patronage, service and rights which overshadow the basic opposition between freedom and servitude. Here Barthélemy was picking away at the idea of radical change around the year 1000, change which followers of Duby insisted had involved the imposition of new burdens of servitude on the peasantry. As a result, the latter had been transformed at the hands of the castellans. But, says Barthélemy, the kind of 'ministerial' serfs that one sees in the Marmoutier auto-deditions are already visible in Carolingian polyptychs; in short, there was no sudden transformation.[28]

[26] Grandmaison, *Liber de Servis*, xii–xvii. The 'commendation formula' is *Formulae Turonenses*, no. 47, in *Formulae Merowingici et Karolini Aevi*, ed. K. Zeumer, *Momumenta Germaniae Historica, Leges in quarto, sectio* 5 (Hannover, 1886), 158. The formula is well known because the act of commendation it outlines has been seen to prefigure the later act of so-called 'feudal commendation' that vassals made to their lords. Thus Ganshof made much of it in his account of the origins of feudalism: Ganshof, *Feudalism*, 5–9.

[27] Barthélemy, *La mutation*, 57–91, esp. 73–9.

[28] *Ibid.*, 160–70.

Barthélemy is clearly right that at least some of these Marmoutier serfs had property, families, jobs, prospects and even what we would call 'attitude'. But by concentrating on the auto-deditions he is privileging the happier and more successful relations between the abbey and its favoured dependants. Gifts, sales and disputes paint a less rosy picture, and here we can detect some of the tension between lords and peasants that advocates of the radical change argument have identified as evidence of brutal new conditions, often referred to as 'evil customs'. Those tensions may well also be a pointer to what was changing, or to what was perceived to be new, in eleventh-century Touraine. Disputes in the Marmoutier material were frequently about contested status. This comes down to disputes over rights, present and future, and what was at issue was human resources. Disputes could be highly complex and protracted, especially when several parties claimed rights, and compromise was common. Let us look at some cases.

Marmoutier was prepared to use coercion to force recalcitrant serfs back into line. One Gandelbert from the Vendôme married a woman called Gerberga who had once been free, but had become an *ancilla* of Marmoutier as the result of an earlier marriage to one of Marmoutier's serfs.[29] Gandelbert, says the notice, 'had been made a serf earlier', perhaps through marriage. Now he refused to accept that he was a serf. Prior Odo imprisoned him until he formally admitted his servile status. This is one of a number of cases where marriage raised the issue of status because any children subsequently born would inherit their parents' condition. The monastery was dogged in insisting that those who married the unfree would become serfs, and that all their descendants would retain the status. One Otbert, a free man, married an *ancilla* of the monastery and so became unfree. When she died, Otbert married again, this time a free woman, called Plectrude. Prior Odo asserted that he remained unfree. Otbert could not deny this, and so formally recognised his servile status. This now meant that Plectrude was unfree. Not wishing to leave her husband, she accepted her new status.[30] In the last piece in the 'Book of Serfs' we have a cross-reference to this charter, where we are given a different version of the Otbert story.[31] This time he was said to have burned down one of the monastery's barns, and since he could not pay

[29] *SM* 106.

[30] *SM* 108.

[31] As Barthélemy points out, *La mutation*, 61–3, it is not uncommon in this material to have slightly different accounts of the same events. This may reflect the different points of view of different parties. It also suggests that some accounts were highly contested. Since some disputes lasted for decades, it is not surprising that different parties to a dispute might have different memories of what had happened. But the inconsistencies remind us above all that we possess only fragmentary records of highly complex and contestable transactions, and that our reconstructions will usually remain incomplete.

compensation he was made a serf, which dragged Plectrude into serfdom too. After his death, Plectrude claimed that their son Vitalis was not a serf because he had been born before Otbert's enserfment. She agreed to undergo the ordeal of hot iron to prove her case, but when the iron was ready, she withdrew. Vitalis fought on as a fugitive. Eventually he was persuaded to come into the chapter to acknowledge his servitude, but then later denied that he had done so, and 'did much damage to us and our property', before finally being persuaded to acknowledge his and his son's servitude, presumably in return for some large sweetener. He finally came round when Pope Urban II came to Marmoutier to bless its new basilica, thus in 1096.[32] Entry into serfdom might be seen as a career move for some, but it seems that it could be regarded as a disability in the coming generations, even when the original enserfment had been voluntary. Another Otbert had been one of Marmoutier's mayors, and was a serf by virtue of land he held from it. After his death, his wife petitioned Abbot Bartholomew to free her daughter so that she could marry a freeman. Bartholomew agreed on the condition that the family leave Otbert's land, that the girl's brother should always remain a serf and that should she fail to find a free husband, she be returned to her servile condition.[33] Whatever immediate advantages of giving oneself as a serf to the monastery, it seems clear that they might be outweighed by the future disadvantages.

The charter evidence reveals that what was felt to be most disadvantageous was the impediment to the formation and prosperity of families. Servitude made inheritance difficult as lords still attempted to claim the serf's *peculium*, and inheritance could be blocked if serfs of the same descent had different lords. Marriage between serfs of different lords was therefore complicated, with the likelihood that both sets of lords would try to claim rights over the children. In one of the charters appended to the 'Book of Serfs' we hear of a case from 1087 in which Marmoutier and a Walter Rimand found that they had *servi* and *ancillae* in common. They thought that they ought to divide out the children of these people, and did so, apparently splitting the children of each couple, until 'just a little girl remained in a cradle', not worth dividing, but should she live, then she would be held in common until a decision could be made.[34] Even if such partitions did not mean the actual separation of parents and

[32] *SM* 127.

[33] *SM* 76.

[34] *SMA* 36. The children were all named, apart from 'una tantum puellula' who 'remansit in berceolo ad partiendum, quae si vixerit, communiter erit inter nostra et Galterii'. That children of the same parents were divided up, rather than whole families being assigned either to Marmoutier or Walter, is indicated by the phrase 'de infantibus' in conjunction with named parents. This must be the case, at least, when only a single child is named, for instance, 'de infantibus Rotberti Chiophardi: Adeliltia'.

siblings, but rather the assignment of future income and services, they would have made life difficult for the serf families. In a few cases, such as that of the mayor Otbert, servile status came with land, but more often it appears as personal, i.e. it moved with the person. In another appended charter, this time from 1077, one Waleran gives all his *servi* and *ancillae* from the *villa* of Nanteuil. The terms are worth quoting:

> Whatever rights I formerly had over them, or over their possessions, let them now belong to St Martin and the monks of Marmoutier. If any of the children of these serfs, male or female, should move to another place, be it near, be it far, and go and live in another *villa*, *vicus*, *castellum* or *civitas*, having been bound by the obligation of servitude, let it be held for them there.[35]

From the monastery's point of view one can see that it was essential to claim rights over posterity and to safeguard against future generations slipping out of dependence. From the serfs' point of view, one can see why this burden might seem intolerable. Nevertheless, as Barthélemy pointed out, the serfs of Marmoutier were, according to the charter evidence, doing relatively well. They at least have a voice in the charters, they have inheritances to try to defend, they have cash and they have the power to resist the monastery for long periods. One dispute in particular puts these issues in focus, as it shows the frustration on both sides as serfs tried to pass acquired wealth down the generations and the monastery tried to control their inheritances. And since it is a dispute, how it was settled is of great interest.

Sometime before 1084 three serfs called Hilduin, Guy and Herbert were in dispute with Marmoutier over lands, houses and vineyards which they wished to inherit from their grandparents.[36] The grandparents had been the monasteries' serfs, but these three were descended from one of their daughters, Gerlend, who had married a serf of the count of Anjou. The grandparents had had other unnamed sons and daughters who remained with Marmoutier. Hilduin, Guy and Herbert thus had lots of cousins who were Marmoutier's serfs, while they themselves were Angvein serfs. Now all the grandchildren wished to divide up their *communem hereditatem*. This was not allowed to them by law (the term is *lex*), so that Hilduin and co. made a complaint to Marmoutier's abbot, prior (Odo, again), chaplain and steward that their inheritance had been taken away from them. There was a hearing (*causa*) at which the monastery decided that they should not be allowed to inherit alongside

[35] SMA 31: 'Quisquis etiam ex ipsorum progenie servorum, vir sive femina, ad alia forte transierit loca, sive prope, sive longe, aliam inhabitet villam, vicum, castellum aut civitatem, eodem servitutis nexu obstrictus et ibi teneatur eisdem.'

[36] *SM* 116. The dispute is recorded in a single, relatively long notice, in which a definitive settlement seems to have been reached. Other disputes were reopened despite final settlements being recorded. This dispute may have been reopened, but of this there is no record.

their Marmoutier cousins, although the fact that they were cousins was recognised. This judgement they refused to accept. They then turned to their lord, Fulk the count of Anjou 'believing that they could get through the *violentia* of their lord the count what they had not been able to get in the *placitum*'. The counts of Anjou had often fallen out with Marmoutier, for the monastery had steadfastly resisted Angevin jursisdiction, but this was a particularly good time to call on Fulk of Anjou because he was himself in dispute with the archbishop of Tours, Ralph. This was part of a long-running struggle between the monks and archbishop that got caught up in the politics of reform.[37] Fulk drove Ralph out of Tours, and had been excommunicated as a result. The monks of Marmoutier and the canons of St Martin were also briefly excommunicated. Ralph returned in 1083. Abbot Bernard, who followed Bartholomew in 1084, and under whom this case was concluded, was a supporter of the archbishop and faced resistance from his own monks. It may have been this confused and volatile situation which encouraged Guy, Hilduin and Herbert to press their claims at this precise moment. The dispute now moved into the count's court (*curia*). The count heard the case along with four named people. They decided against the serfs, who again refused to accept the judgement, and threatened that 'they would seek justice for themselves'. How is not specified, but the threat moved Fulk to take up their case with the monastery. At a hearing presided over by Abbot Bernard, again Marmoutier refused to let them have any share in the inheritance, so the serfs returned to lobbying the count, arguing that he as their lord would lose out if they failed to secure the inheritance. Finally, after many words, threats and ill-deeds, there was a settlement. Guy, Hilduin and Herbert got 15 pounds of silver to waive all claims and grievances forever, and agreed that they would stop their children, grandchildren and any other relative from returning to the claim. In order to make them more faithful to the monks and their property, the three were also given membership of 'our benefits and society', which was conferred in the chapel. Fulk promised that if they should ever raise the grievance again he would drive them *de castellis et receptibus suis*. Crucially it is not clear to whom *suis* refers. Did these serfs really have *castella*? Or what were they doing in Fulk's? Either way, Guy, Hilduin and Herbert were clearly people of some standing. Being given the monastery's benefits and made members of its *societas* was a recognition of their importance. This and the considerable sum of 15 pounds of silver might even have been the real aim of the dispute. But

[37] On the struggles in Tours between the counts of Anjou, archbishops, canons, monks and popes, see S. Farmer, *Communities of Saint Martin. Legend and Ritual in Medieval Tours* (Ithaca and London, 1991), 38–51.

given that they were wealthy enough to own houses and vineyards, and had the standing to call on the count of Anjou to help them, it is all the more striking that Marmoutier was determined to stop them dividing the inheritance. The monastery would rather pay out cash and confer spiritual privileges than give up rights that would have jeopardised its future income.

This dispute record does not show settlement in the *placita* tradition, if we regard that as defined by a formal, rule-based process. Here there is reference to *lex*/law, but it could be either to local custom or to a body of written law. The two case hearings were in courts that were run respectively by the abbot and count and their close associates. Violence was threatened as part of the negotiations. The eventual settlement was out of court and based on compromise. It is useless to ask whether this was public or private justice at work. True, there is no royal authority acting as ultimate guarantor of the process, but there is plenty of authority there; namely, the authority that comes from law (*lex*), from office (that of abbot, prior and count), from the judgement of important people (who sat in court with the count) and, of course, from the record of the agreement itself. All of this we can identify in Carolingian Francia, and earlier. What is different is that authority, rights and judgements are being contested. A second dispute shows how they might be contested over generations, and again, there is an indication that the monastery was determined to maintain the servitude of serfs who had become relatively wealthy and influential. Indeed, the richer the serf families became, the more interest the monastery had in forcing them to acknowledge their servile status.

In two documents Grandmaison appended to the 'Book of Serfs', one undated, the other dated 1067, we hear of a protracted dispute over status and property.[38] To cut a long story short, a family of *milites* from Blois was in dispute with Marmoutier over the status of a woman called Hilducia. She had been freed, for a money payment. In the time of Count Odo of Blois (thus sometime 1004–37) she had married a Marmoutier sef, Ohelm. By virtue of her marriage Hilducia would have become a Marmoutier serf too, despite having recently been freed. Ohelm her husband had put up the money to free her, to make sure that her former owners did not trouble her further. They went so far as to draw up a charter of manumission. Ohelm clearly had money and influence. According to Marmoutier, he was always an *insidiosus* and rebellious serf. In an extraordinary charter of *c.* 1040, the monastery got Ohelm and Hilducia's son Ascelin to swear to future good behaviour, for the fear was that he would take on the bad habits of his father, especially if he married a free woman. In particular, the monks were worried that Ascelin would bring cases against them

[38] *SMA* 18 and 27. The impression is that the events of *SMA* 18 took place a few years before those of 27 in 1067.

backed by powerful people.[39] Ascelin did in fact associate with the locally powerful, and it is these people who were in dispute with Marmoutier over his property.

When all these parties were dead, apart from the ancient widow of Hilducia's original owner, William and Robert the sons of the two owners denied the manumission. If Hilducia had not been free when she crossed over to Marmoutier, they would have a claim on her son Ascelin's property, which was no doubt substantial. The monks got the charter of manumission from the widow, but Robert and William refused to acknowledge it, and refused to come to court, attacking the monastery's lands. Then William, who was a cleric, passed the dispute on to a *miles* called Landric, his sister's husband, because it would be easier for Landric, being a *miles* and not a cleric, to attack the monks. He did so with enthusiasm, until he forced the monks to a *placitum* in which the document was disregarded. Ordeal was offered and refused, and Robert and Landric accepted 16 pounds of *denarii* to end the dispute. In the next document we learn that later one Girard reopened the dispute on behalf of his wife Adelad who was Landric's daughter. Ascelin, who had been important enough to act as a witness, had earlier witnessed one of Adelad's charters.[40] Who had 'owned' Ascelin was clearly a complex matter. Girard did much violence to the monastery until Marmoutier paid out again, this time 100 *solidi* for Girard, 15 for Adelad, and 12 *denarii* for each of her five children. The agreement was made at Blois in the meadow that lies between the tower and the hall of the count. Ascelin was not mentioned. It is reasonable to suppose that it had been his death, probably around 1064, that had triggered the dispute.

Again, one wonders if the cash payment, made on two occasions, was the real aim of those pressing the dispute against the monastery, but Ascelin obviously had possessions worth fighting over. His wealth and influence did not help him out of servitude; indeed, they seem to have made his lords even keener to make sure that he was not emancipated. Once more, the status of one person (Hilducia), at one moment, determined the future of the serf family. As in the first case, we see people refusing to accept judgement, and resorting to violence in order to wear down the other party. It is also remarkable that the dispute could be settled and then reopened, with the monastery having to give way twice. The settlements involved informal meetings but also one *placitum* at which documents were presented and the ordeal offered. The final meeting and payment was in the open air, and again part of

[39] *SMA* 7.

[40] *Cartulaire de Marmoutier pour le Dunois* no. 49, pp. 45–6. Ascelin appears in no less than nine charters from the Dunois. He even witnessed one (no. 22, pp. 22–4) which was a *praeceptum* endorsed by the king.

the settlement was that the monks offered spiritual friendship. Girald was pardoned for all the harm he had done, he kissed the prior's hand and became a beneficiary of the community.

In these cases the variety of settlement procedures and the different ways in which claims were pressed, justified and answered reflects a society in which there were appeals to norms rather than authoritative rules.[41] The range of norms in these charters is broad: there were appeals to memory and family solidarity, and, as we have just seen, to formal written documents. Negotiations could call on both consent and coercion, on law, on custom, on the social power of superiors (the *violentia* of the count, for instance). And of course, in the case of Marmoutier, they could invoke a host of spiritual sanctions, above all, the prestige and power of St Martin himself, although, perhaps surprisingly, in the 'Book of Serfs' relics never make an appearance. One way of accounting for this variety, and also for the different kinds of venues in which disputes were settled, is to put it down to that privatisation of justice which was the supposed consequence of the collapse of royal authority. This, I shall argue, is an unhelpful approach. We can, of course, observe that political power in this region, north-western France, had fragmented, and we may argue that the consequence of this fragmentation was the emergence of the plurality of authorities, and variety of settlement procedures, that we have just witnessed. But to demonstrate that such plurality and variety was indeed the result of a change in the way in which power was distributed and organised, we must be able to show that lord–serf relations, and in particular the trajectory of disputes, would have been different at a time when political authority was less fragmented, i.e. at the height of Carolingian order. This we cannot do with certainty. Although Janet Nelson has drawn attention to cases in which peasants in the Carolingian period challenged their status and the services they owed in what might be termed public courts, there are very few of them.[42] They concern groups or communities rather than individuals, and one cannot be sure

[41] S. White, *Custom, Kinship, and Gifts to the Saints. The 'Laudatio Parentum' in Western France 1050–1150* (Chapel Hill and London, 1988), 70–85, is excellent on the relationship between law, rules, norms and custom in this society.

[42] Nelson, 'Dispute Settlement', 48–53. Where there is evidence of the public authority intervening to protect people against lords, we also find that there are complaints about officials abusing their powers, so that the 'state' appears in effect to be both protecting and abusing the people under its care. A good example is an early ninth-century case from Istra (Istria) in which locals appealed to Charlemagne to protect them from the 'oppressions' of their duke. The catalogue of 'oppressions' would not have looked out of place in any account of eleventh-century 'evil customs': *I Placiti del' Regnum Italiae*, ed. C. Manaresi (3 vols., Rome 1955–60), no. 17. On Carolingian justice and abuse, see P. Fouracre, 'Carolingian Justice: The Rhetoric of Improvement and Contexts of Abuse', in *La Giustizia nell' alto medioevo (secoli V–VIII)*, Settimane di studio del Centro Italiano di studi sull'alto Medioevo 42 (Spoleto, 1995), 771–803.

that what appears to be a dispute between peasants and an ecclesiastical institution might not be a vehicle for one institution or lord seeking to undermine another. The essential problem is that we cannot compare like with like here. We have no cases from the Carolingian period that are as detailed or as localised as our Marmoutier material, so we cannot be sure that the kind of issues we see in the 'Book of Serfs' were not common in an earlier period: they may have been, but were not recorded, or, perhaps (less likely) it may be that no trace of such records survived. If we cannot demonstrate that the fragmentation of political power did have an effect on lord–serf relations, and the way that disputes were settled locally (although one suspects that it did), can we point to any area of change that might have affected things? Or, to put it another way, can we get to at least some manifestations of the post-Carolingian order, such as the struggle by serfs to resist new exactions, the protraction of disputes, the prevalence of compromise and the apparent multiplication of authorities, by a route other than the assumed collapse of public power and authority?

Stephen White, in his acclaimed work *Custom, Kinship, and Gifts to the Saints*, published in 1988, analysed the norms underlying giving to the saints in eleventh- and twelfth-century north-western France, concentrating on the assent given by relatives, the so-called *laudatio parentum*.[43] Although White deals with the rise and fall of the *laudatio*, he sets it in a legal and anthropological rather than historical context. It seems to be from this perspective that he developed his conviction that notions of structural change should be subordinated to an understanding of the process of social negotiation. But as White himself demonstrates, the rise of the *laudatio* came with a massive increase in giving to ecclesiastical institutions amongst the lesser nobility.[44] It was precisely because families were moving into unfamiliar territory in making such donations that they began to seek the assent of kindred, and to draw upon the widest possible range of support for their actions. One reason why there is some sense of novelty and experimentation here is that in this region institutions were either newly founded, or newly reformed and re-invented. The period from the later tenth to the early twefth century was in R. I. Moore's words 'a time of hectic generosity', but also a time at which members of the nobility were 'competing desperately amongst themselves for land', giving, acquiring and competing all being part of

[43] White, *Custom*.

[44] *Ibid.*, Appendix, 212–27, has useful tables recording (amongst other things) the frequency of gifts to five north-western French monasteries, including Marmoutier. The general pattern is that gift-giving was most intense from around the middle of the eleventh century.

a ceaseless effort to improve local standing and to consolidate family influence.[45]

It is in the area of monastic reform that we can most clearly detect a sense of novelty, in what one might term the Cluniac rhetoric of waste and renewal. For once this is not limited to France, but can be seen throughout Europe.[46] Although in many cases it can be shown that institutions were not as wasted, nor lands as empty, as reformers claimed, it is nevertheless true that reform involved a massive turnover of land. In some areas of eastern England, for instance, it is argued that half of the land held in 1066 had changed hands during the monastic reform of the tenth century. Reform had its own history and internal logic, but it took place at a time of growing economic activity, from which it benefited and to which it contributed. From the later ninth century onwards references to cash in society increase, and ecclesiastical institutions, and indeed secular lords, are visible exploiting rights over a wider range of activities. As peasants moved around to take advantage of new opportunities, lords insisted on their personal dependence so that their productive resources could be tapped wherever they went. Of this we saw an example in the 'Book of Serfs',[47] but we can see that the problem of controlling a more mobile peasantry had come to the attention of the Carolingian rulers 200 years earlier. The Edict of Pitres was issued in 864 on the lower Seine. It dealt largely, and at great length, with the regulation of coinage, but it also empowered lords to demand the services of those of their serfs who had moved away from arable lands to find more lucrative work in vineyards. It insisted that marriages contracted by such migrant workers were invalid. Couples were to be separated, because people could marry

[45] Moore, *First European Revolution*, 82.

[46] The *eremus* (emptiness or waste) or *desertum* (deserted place) are concepts central to monasticism at all times, but they were particularly stressed in periods of reform. It was always useful to invoke notions of waste, destruction and emptiness in the old, in order to justify the new, whether in terms of territorial occupation, or the imposition of a new regime. Local narratives were devised to explain how things had gone to waste: Viking and Saracen destruction, sin, luxury and laziness were favoured explanations. Historians have often taken such narratives rather too literally. Cluniac reform, which broadcast this rhetoric to an unprecedented degree, was only one part of the tenth- and eleventh-century expansion. For careful discussion of how the concepts were used in Spanish contexts, and of how they have confused historians, see J. Escalona Monge, 'Communidades, territorios y poder condal en la Castilla de Duero en el siglo X: Communities, Territories and Power in Tenth-Century Castille', *Studia Historica: historia medieval*, 18–19 (Salamanca, 2001), 85–120, and J. Jarrett, 'Power Over Past and Future: Abbess Emma and the Nunnery of Sant Joan de les Abadesses', *Early Medieval Europe*, 12 (2003), 229–56. For caveats on taking the statements of Benedictine reform in tenth-century England too literally, see C. Cubitt, 'The Tenth-Century Benedictine Reform', *Early Medieval Europe*, 6 (1997), 77–94.

[47] See n. 35, above.

only if they had the same lord.[48] When in the 'Book of Serfs' Marmoutier told Hilduin, Guy and Herbert that 'the law' did not allow them to inherit in common with the serfs of the monastery, the reference might have been to an edict or 'capitulary' such as that of Pitres, for we can find other examples of Carolingian legislation which helped lords to retain control over their *servi*.[49] The power of lords over serfs as we see it in the eleventh century had not been brought into being as a consequence of the collapse of Carolingian authority, but rather it had evolved in tandem with that authority. That model of change which sees lords taking for themselves powers once the preserve of the 'state' tends to forget that the state was itself formed out of the collective power of lords, and that throughout its history, Carolingian government had sought to strengthen the power of lords over their dependants. It had also tried to get lords to shoulder more of the burden and responsibility of government at local level. From this perspective, the plurality of authorities we see in the 'Book of Serfs' did not spring up as newly privatised powers, but had evolved as all manner of lords had been pressed into service in the keeping of order.

Marmoutier itself was one of those institutions that had been reformed and reinvented at the end of the tenth century. There are competing narratives of how this had happened, but the result is clear: a massive inflow of donations, peaking around the middle of the eleventh century.[50] Thus whenever we see the monastery dealing with its lands, clients and dependants, it is quite likely that lands and rights had been acquired fairly recently. This may help us to understand why the monastery struggled so

[48] *Edictum Pistense* c. 31, *Monumenta Germaniae Historica, Capitularia Regum Francorum* II, ed. A. Boretius and V. Krause (Hannover, 1897), 324. If such people did marry, 'illud coniugium, qui non est legale neque legitimum, . . . dissolvatur'. According to the law and to 'our ancient custom' any children would follow the mother.

[49] In seeking to maintain social order, Carolingian legislation tended to reinforce the division between free and unfree while at the same time speaking out against oppression. The rulers were particularly concerned with their own rights and resources, including the management of *beneficia*. Restrictions placed on the movement, marriage and inheritance of serfs on royal lands and *beneficia* provided a model for other lords. See, for examples of legislation from the reign of Charlemagne, *Monumenta Germaniae Historica, Capitularia Regum Francorum* I, ed. A. Boretius (Hannover, 1883) no. 33 c. 4, 92: lords are told not to conceal *fiscali* who flee and claim to be free; no. 43, c. 11, 122: numbers of *servi* and *ancillae* entering the church to be restricted so that there are not labour shortages on estates; no. 46, c. 18: lords with benefices to feed their dependants at times of famine; no. 58, c. 1, 145, where *servi* and *ancillae* with different lords have married, the lords are to decide between themselves about the ownership of any future children. Children of mixed free/serf marriages cannot hold an intermediate social position, because 'non est amplius nisi liber et servus'.

[50] There were two narratives of the monastery's re-foundation and growth which gave prominence to the comital houses of Anjou and Blois respectively: see Farmer, *Communities*, 78–116. On the growth of the abbey's possessions in the eleventh century, see White's tables, cited above n. 44, and C. Lelong, *L'Abbaye de Marmoutier* (Tours, 1989), 24–31.

hard to establish its rights over the children of serfs, that is, in order to make sure that recently acquired resources were made permanent. Growing prosperity meant greater opportunities for dependants to move and build up their own wealth. It also meant that a wider social range of people joined in the 'hectic giving', with the result that the monastery acquired a mosaic of different kinds of resources, the gift of a dependant here, rights in a mill there or rights over fish traps in different locations and so on.[51] At the same time there was intense competition for resources. As Sharon Farmer has pointed out, even for a highly successful monastery such as Marmoutier rising costs outpaced income,[52] and the same must have been true for families striving to establish or consolidate their local standing. For Marmoutier, as we have seen, cash flowed out as it bought off challenges to its rights. This is the background to the high level of contestation that we see in the 'Book of Serfs', and also in Marmoutier's other cartularies. That families such as that of the *milites* Robert, Landric and Girard made the most of any opportunity to get cash out of Marmoutier is in this context quite understandable. Cash, never ending disputes, the struggle to control *servi*, and their resistance, the spread of *castella*, that is, fortified residences, the growing prominence of people termed *milites* and not least a rhetoric of renewal and reform, combine to make this world of the 'Book of Serfs' look very different from, say, the world of the Carolingian polyptychs which simply listed peasant holdings and services without a hint that these were ever contested.

The 'mutationists' are quite right to say that things had changed, but one can dispute the view that it was the collapse of the Carolingian order that drove the change. The view advanced here is that it was the response of that order to a conjunction of economic, religious and political stimuli that produced new conditions. It is important here to remember that people had adapted to particular pressures throughout the early middle ages: this was not a caste society, nor a society where nothing ever happened to power relations until the 'mutation féodale' came along. The fierce dividing line between free and unfree in the early Frankish laws masks differentiation and movement within, and across, both groups. There is no reason why the kind of exchange mobility that W. G. Runciman postulated for Anglo-Saxon England should not be

[51] To manage these scattered plots of lands and rights the monastery established a series of priories, and, as we have seen, priors such as Odo played a key role in the maintenance of servitude. On the development of the priories as a response to the rapid acquisition of lands and rights, O. Gantier, 'Recherches sur les possessions et les prieuries de l'Abbaye de Marmoutier du Xe au XIIe siècle', *Revue Mabillon*, 53 (1963), 93–110, and maps after 136.

[52] Farmer, *Communities*, 128–34. The particular problems were the growth of expensive liturgical commemoration and the supervision of priors to ensure that the abbey realised all of its potential income.

found elsewhere too in the early middle ages.[53] In the will of Bertramn of Le Mans, for instance, which comes from the early seventh century, we find the kind of ministerial serfs that Barthélemy identified in the 'Book of Serfs'. They were even termed *ministeriales* in a milieu in which, interestingly, there was a lot of cash around. In Bertramn's will they received horses.[54]

In the mid-eighth century we hear of *servi* who were traders at the fair of St Denis who were charged higher tolls than free people.[55] From the late eighth century onwards we see an increasing number of *servi* given to churches (as well as free people giving themselves) to provide particular services, such as the provision of wax for lighting, or the payment of rent (*censum*) which was dedicated to the upkeep of the church.[56] Groups of such people also appear in the polyptychs. As in the 'Book of Serfs' their dependant status is ritually acknowledged, but the nature of their service, and its relatively easy terms, marked them out as superior to those serfs burdened with heavy labour service. In Germany these kind of people grew into a substantial rural class, the *Zensualität*, or *cerocensuales*, which in many regions were numbered in the thousands by the later middle ages,[57] not to mention the *ministeriales* who famously shot up the social scale in the eleventh century by virtue of their service as horsemen.

Chris Wickham has argued that at the height of the Carolingian order there were across the Frankish dominated lands recognisably similar ways of holding courts, settling disputes and mediating between different interests.[58] This is what is in his mind when he says that the end of the

[53] W. G. Runciman, 'Accelerating Social Mobility. The Case of Anglo-Saxon England', *Past and Present*, 104 (1984), 3–30.

[54] *Testamentum Bertramni Cenomannis*, ed. J. M. Pardessus, *Diplomata, Chartae, Epistolae Leges aliaque Instrumenta ad Res Gallo-Francicas spectantia* (2 vols., Paris, 1843–9), 197–215, here 208: 'volo et jubeo ut ex omnibus servientibus sanctae ecclesiae, qui ministeriales noscuntur, vel meis tam clericis quam secularibus qui mecum conversari videntur, singulos caballos, tam ingenui quam liberi vel servientes'.

[55] *Monumenta Germaniae Historica, Diplomata Karolinorum* I, ed. E. Mühlbacher (Hannover, 1906), nos. 6, 9–11. This charter is from 753, and preserved in the original.

[56] Those dedicated to providing wax for lighting were often termed *luminarii*. Numbers varied from polyptych to polyptych, but the variations have not been systematically mapped. *Luminarii* are particularly prominent in the mid-ninth-century polyptych of St Bertin. See *Le Polyptyque de l'Abbaye de St Bertin*, ed. F. Ganshof (Paris, 1975), *passim*, but with comments at 29 and 83–4.

[57] The key article on the *Zensualität* is K. Schulz, 'Zur Problem der Zensualität im Hochmittelalter', in K. Schulz (ed.), *Beiträge zur Wirtschafts- und Sozialgeschichte des Mittelalters* (Cologne and Vienna, 1976), 86–127. Also useful is M. Matheus, 'Forms of Social Mobility: The Example of the *Zensualität*', in *England and Germany in the High Middle Ages*, ed. A. Haverkamp and H. Vollrath (Oxford, 1996), 357–69. I am grateful to Dr Julia Barrow for drawing my attention to these works.

[58] Wickham, 'Property Ownership and Signorial Power', 221–6, and Wickham, 'Feudal Revolution', 202–5.

rule-based *placita* signifies the end of that order. But he too accepts that these rules were always applied pragmatically in ways that allowed the courts to be used within strategies of social negotiation. This is a point that White tends to ignore. And as Patrick Geary has pointed out, it is reasonable to assume that informal settlements always outnumbered the formal.[59] Whatever the regime, the capacity for dealing with new conditions was always there, reflected even in the formularies, which are, after all, books of rules. The 'Book of Serfs' is situated in a milieu of change and novelty: its very compilation was part of one institution's strategy to manage in new conditions. It gives us insights into how serfdom could be maintained despite the improving lot of many serfs, and it gives us glimpses of the personal relationships, frictions and dramas involved in the competition for resources at a very local level. It is a quality of information that we lack for earlier periods. This, finally, is a rather important factor that we should take into account when we judge the difference between the Carolingian world and what came after it.

[59] P. Geary, 'Extra-Judicial Means of Conflict Resolution', in *La Giustizia nell'alto Medieovo (secoli V–VIII)*, 569–601.

Transactions of the RHS 15 (2005), pp. 51–74 © 2005 Royal Historical Society
doi:10.1017/S0080440105000332 Printed in the United Kingdom

HOUSEWIVES AND SERVANTS IN RURAL ENGLAND, 1440–1650: EVIDENCE OF WOMEN'S WORK FROM PROBATE DOCUMENTS*

By Jane Whittle

READ 30 APRIL 2004 AT THE UNIVERSITY OF KENT AT CANTERBURY

ABSTRACT. This essay examines the work patterns of housewives and female servants in rural England between the mid-fifteenth and mid-seventeenth centuries. Despite the fact that such women expended the majority of female work-hours in the rural economy, their activities remain a neglected topic. Here probate documents, wills, inventories and probate accounts are used alongside other types of sources to provide insight into women's work. The three parts of the essay examine the proportion of female servants employed in different households and localities, the types of work that servants and housewives undertook and the scale and level of commercialisation of four common types of women's work.

Robert Loder, the seventeenth-century Berkshire farmer who kept a particularly informative set of farm accounts, described the work of his two maid servants as 'the doing of the thinges, that must indeed be donne', and concluded that apart from making malt, they brought him little profit.[1] On a similar note, Thomas Tusser, in his *Five Hundred Points of Good Husbandry*, wrote, 'Though husbandry semeth, to bring in the gains; yet huswifery labours, seeme equall in paines.'[2] Men's work appeared to create the profits, although women worked just as hard. What were 'the things, that must indeed by done' that occupied women in rural households and did their work really bring in little profit? Service and housewifery in rural households was the majority experience of working women in England between the mid-fifteenth and mid-seventeenth centuries. In 1600, an estimated 70 per cent of the English population

* This essay was researched and written during an ESRC research fellowship. The collection and analysis of Kent probate inventories was undertaken during an earlier Leverhulme-funded project jointly with Mark Overton, Darron Dean and Andrew Hann, who I would like to thank for their contributions and help. I would also like to thank Ian Mortimer for introducing me to the Kent probate accounts and providing a subject index.

[1] *Robert Loder's Farm Accounts 1610–1620*, ed. G. E. Fussell (Camden Society Third Series 53, 1936), 71.

[2] Thomas Tusser, *Five Hundred Points of Good Husbandry United with as Many of Good Huswiferie* (1573), sig. S2r.

relied on agriculture for its livelihood, while a further 22 per cent lived in rural areas but carried out other occupations.[3] According to Kussmaul, servants 'constituted around 60 per cent of the population aged fifteen to twenty-four' in early modern England.[4] Despite the proportion of the population never marrying reaching a high point in the mid-seventeenth century, marriage, and therefore housewifery, remained the experience of the great majority of adult women. Some rural women worked as day labourers in agriculture, carrying out as much as a third of routine day labouring work on certain farms.[5] On the whole, however, only women from poorer households worked for daily wages, and only large farmers and gentlemen relied heavily on such workers. The great bulk of women-hours expended on work in rural economy and society was undertaken by housewives and servants.

Yet this majority experience has received little serious historical attention. Although there is a well-known list gleaned from various literary sources of activities commonly allotted to women in rural households, tasks such as spinning, dairying, caring for poultry, cooking, housework, child care and helping in the fields at harvest time, this is only a starting point. The nature of women's work has remained hidden behind generalisations and misconceptions. A lack of documented occupational designations for the great majority of women seems to have led to an assumption that there is little documentary evidence of women's work, and perhaps also that many women had no occupations, neither of which is the case. Also implicit in historians' neglect of the work of housewives and female servants is an assumed insignificance of women's work, often accompanied by its designation as 'domestic', without any detailed consideration of what domestic might mean in an economy in which most production was located in or near the home. Additionally, the idea of what Vickery has described, with irony, as an early modern 'wholesome "family economy" in which men, women and children shared tasks and status', has discouraged historians to looking more carefully at the division of labour between men and women within the household, assuming women's work complemented that of men, and could be subsumed within male occupations.[6]

This essay challenges all of these assumptions, and it does so using probate documents, a source familiar to early modern economic and

[3] E. A. Wrigley, *People, Cities and Wealth: The Transformation of Traditional Society* (Oxford, 1987), 170.

[4] Ann Kussmaul, *Servants in Husbandry in Early Modern England* (Cambridge, 1981), 3. Problems with Kussmaul's sources are discussed below.

[5] For example see L. R. Poos, *A Rural Society after the Black Death: Essex 1350–1525* (Cambridge, 1991), 214 and 217; A. Hassell Smith, 'Labourers in Late Sixteenth-Century England: A Case Study from North Norfolk [Part 1]', *Continuity and Change*, 4 (1989), 29.

[6] Amanda Vickery, 'Golden Age to Separate Spheres? A Review of the Categories and Chronology of English Women's History', *Historical Journal* 36 (1991), 402.

social historians. Wills record bequests made to servants, while probate accounts record wages owing to them. Wills and accounts also contain information about the age structure of the household. The lists of moveable goods in probate inventories provide evidence of the work carried out. Comparisons between wills, accounts and inventories allow the social structure of particular households, in terms of age, gender and servant employment, to be matched with their economic structure, in terms of production and housework. Probate documents have drawbacks: most notably, they provide only positive rather than negative evidence. If a servant is given a bequest in a will, we know that servant was employed by the household of the testator, but if no servants are given bequests we do not know that no servants were employed. Comparisons with literary descriptions of rural work patterns, household and farm accounts, and other sources remain vital. In terms of sheer numbers and their stretch down the social structure, however, no other type of document from this period can equal the reach of wills and inventories.

The exploration of women's work in this essay is split into three sections. The first examines gendered patterns of servant employment in various types of household. Although it is not possible to deduce the total number of servants employed in this period, the types of households that employed servants, and the types of servants they employed, can be observed. The employment of female servants has been seen as an indicator of the amount of work available for women in rural economies, for instance that pastoral regions employed more female servants than arable areas, because dairying provided more work for women. Thus although rural housewives were found everywhere, the number of female servants provide an indicator of the value of women's work to particular households and economies. This assumes that female servants and housewives carried out the same types of work. In the second section evidence of the types of work carried out by female servants and housewives is examined in detail. The final section argues that key forms of women's work, such as dairying, brewing, baking and spinning, should be understood as by-employments within the household, treated as distinct occupations rather than integral elements of a vaguely defined domestic economy. Although they did not necessarily constitute full-time occupations for women, each has its own history in terms of levels of commercialisation and change over time, effecting women's overall work patterns.

Servants

Surprisingly little is known about the employment of rural servants in the period between 1440 and 1650.[7] In her classic account Kussmaul used

[7] Although see also Jane Whittle, 'Servants in Rural England c. 1450–1650: Hired Work as a Means of Accumulating Wealth and Skills before Marriage', in *The Marital Economy of Scandinavia and Britain 1400–1900*, ed. Maria Agren and Amy Erickson (2005), 89–107.

100 parish listings, dating from 1574 to 1821, to examine patterns of servant employment. She found that 'the overall ratio of male to female servants is 107:100' although the ratios in farmers' and craftsmen's households were more biased towards men, at 121:100 and 171:100.[8] However, Kussmaul's data-set is heavily skewed to the period after 1650: of the 100 listings, only five date from before 1650, of which three relate to rural communities, and only one of these, the 1599 listing from Ealing, records the occupation or status of servant employers.[9] Unlike Kussmaul's analysis, Wall's study of the Marriage Duty Act data of *c.* 1700 records regional differences in the sex ratio of servants.[10] Goldberg, comparing this with late fourteenth-century evidence from the Poll Tax returns, suggest a threefold division of servant employment patterns, 'which saw service to be more feminised in urban and pastoral communities than rural, arable communities'. In towns and cities female servants typically outnumbered male servants, in rural pastoral regions there were equal numbers, while in arable areas males outnumbered females in service by as much as two to one.[11]

In the absence of useable tax returns or parish listings, other than that for Ealing, Table 1 takes bequests to servants in wills as an indication of servant employment patterns. These wills were made by rural householders, yet they record a dominance of female servants: male servants are outnumbered by female servants at a ratio of 78:100. Only one collection of wills, that from Lincolnshire, showed a male predominance. There are hints of regional contrasts. Two small collections, from Swaledale in Yorkshire and Uffculme in Devon, both areas where pastoral farming and textile production were combined, show the highest proportion of female servants, with three or more women to each man employed. Other regions strongly represented here, such as Suffolk and Halifax, as well as north-east Norfolk, also combined dairying with cloth production, although in Suffolk and Norfolk arable farming was carried out as well. Only the small sample from King's Langley, Hertfordshire, comes from an arable region with large farms.[12] The selection of wills

[8] Kussmaul, *Servants in Husbandry*, 4.

[9] The 100 are listed in P. Laslett, 'Mean Household Size in England since the Sixteenth Century', in *Household and Family in Past Time*, ed. P. Laslett and R. Wall (Cambridge, 1972), 130–1. Those giving occupational details are listed in Kussmaul, *Servants in Husbandry*, 12–13.

[10] Richard Wall, 'Regional and Temporal Variations in English Household Structure from 1650', in *Regional Demographic Development*, ed. J. Hobcraft and P. Rees (1977), 100–10. Wall compares parishes from East Kent, East Wiltshire, Southampton, Shrewsbury and London.

[11] P. J. P. Goldberg, *Women, Work and Life Cycle in a Medieval Economy: Women in York and Yorkshire c. 1300–1520* (Oxford, 1992), 160.

[12] For agricultural regions see Joan Thirsk, *England's Agricultural Regions and Agrarian History, 1500–1750* (Basingstoke, 1987), particularly 28. For north-east Norfolk see Jane Whittle, *The Development of Agrarian Capitalism: Land and Labour in Norfolk 1440–1580* (Oxford, 2000), 259.

Table 1 *Bequests to servants in wills, 1439–1650*

	Number of wills or accounts	Percentage mentioning servants	Number of servants with gender specified	Percentage of servants female
1. West Suffolk wills 1439–61	887	7.6	87	55
2. North-east Norfolk wills 1440–1579	234	13.2	60	57
3. Wills from Halifax, Yorks. 1500–59	534	8.8	61	61
4. Lincolnshire wills 1504–32	1,024	12.0	182	45
5. Wills from King's Langley, Herts. 1498–1650	109	8.3	8	50
6. Wills from Swaledale, Yorks. 1522–1600	205	7.3	19	80
7. Wills from Uffculme, Devon, 1545–1649	133	10.5	16	75
8. East Suffolk wills 1620–6	1,136	6.5	106	62
9. West Suffolk wills 1630–5	894	5.1	62	65
Total	5,156	8.4	601	56
10. Essex gentry wills 1558–1603	271	55	–	–
11. Kent probate accounts 1611–25	734	15.0	189	47

Sources: 1. *Wills of the Archdeaconry of Sudbury, 1439–1474*, I, ed. Peter Northeast (Suffolk Records Society 44, 2001). 2. Norfolk Record Office, Norwich: all surviving wills for the parishes of Brampton, Corpusty, Hevingham, Marsham, Saxthorpe and Scottow, 1440–1580, from the Norwich Consistory Court, Norwich Archdeaconry Court, and Norfolk Archdeaconry Court. 3. *Halifax Wills: Part 1, 1389–1544*, ed. J. W. Clay and E. W. Crossley (privately printed, undated), and *Halifax Wills: Part 2, 1545–59*, ed. E. W. Crossley (privately printed, undated). 4. *Lincoln Wills*, I, ed. C. W. Foster (Lincoln Record Society 5, 1912); *Lincoln Wills*, II, ed. C. W. Foster (Lincoln Record Society 10, 1914); and *Lincoln Wills*, III, ed. C. W. Foster (Lincoln Record Society 24, 1927). 5. *Life and Death in Kings Langley: Wills and Inventories 1498–1659*, ed. Lionel Munby (Kings Langley, 1981). 6. *Swaledale Wills and Inventories 1522–1600*, ed. Elizabeth K. Berry (Yorkshire Archaeological Society Record Series 152, 1995 and 1996). 7. *Uffculme Wills and Inventories: Sixteenth to Eighteenth Centuries*, ed. Peter Wyatt (Devon and Cornwall Record Society New Series 40, 1997). 8. *Wills of the Archdeaconry of Suffolk 1620–1624*, ed. Marion E. Allen (Suffolk Records Society 31, 1988/9), and *Wills of the Archdeaconry of Suffolk 1625–1626*, ed. Marion E. Allen (Suffolk Records Society 37, 1995). 9. *Wills of the Archdeaconry of Sudbury 1630–1635*, ed. Nesta Evans (Suffolk Records Society 29, 1987). 10. *Elizabethan Life: Wills of Essex Gentry and Merchants Proved at the Prerogative Court of Canterbury*, ed. F. G. Emmison (Chelmsford, 1978). 11. Centre for Kentish Studies, Maidstone [hereafter CKS], Archdeaconry Court of Canterbury account papers, PRC2/16, PRC2/18, PRC2/23 and PRC2/24.

in Table 1 is biased towards eastern England, in later centuries a region dominated by arable farming. Yet before 1650 England's rural economy was less specialised than it became by the eighteenth century.[13] The predominance of mixed farming, as well as smaller farm sizes, seems to have favoured the employment of female servants.

It is possible that there is a bias towards female servants in bequests, either because women earned less and were seen as more deserving recipients of gifts, or because female servants developed closer relationships with employing families, but this is difficult to prove. Kent probate accounts, which record wages owing to servants at time of death, rather than bequests, record larger numbers of servants, and contain a lower proportion of women than most of the will collections. Without an identical sample of wills, however, we cannot separate the effect of differences in documentation from regional variations. Accounts, like wills, under-record servants, as not all servants had wages owing that had to be paid by an administrator. Evidence from bequests in wills is problematic in other ways. Obviously, will-makers were under no obligation to leave bequests to servants. Henry Best, whose famous *Farming and Memorandum Books* records a household of eight servants, left no bequests to servants in his will of 1645.[14] Employment of servants was almost universal amongst the gentry, yet only 55 per cent of wills of Essex gentry record such bequests. Unfortunately, it was impossible to look at the gender balance of gentry servants, as the majority of these wills had general clauses, such as bequests 'to all my manservants' or 'maidservants' or 'the servants resident in my household'. Nor can it be certain that ordinary will-makers necessarily described servants in a way that allows them to be distinguished from other beneficiaries. For these reasons, the incidence of bequests to servants in wills is only a minimum level of servant employment, not the true level. However, when servants are mentioned, it does allow servant employment to be observed in a wide spectrum of household types.

The evidence from wills is set in context by comparisons with other types of document. Farm and household accounts record wage payments to servants. Such accounts are both relatively rare, and atypical of rural households. With farms of between 250 and 700 acres, in a period when the majority of farms were under 50 acres in size,[15] the households of the wealthy yeomanry and gentry represent a more smaller, wealthier, section of society than wills. Wealthy households employed large numbers

[13] Ann Kussmaul, *A General View of the Rural Economy of England, 1538–1840* (Cambridge, 1990), 3.

[14] *The Farming and Memorandum Books of Henry Best of Elmswell 1642*, ed. Donald Woodward (Oxford, 1984), 247–9.

[15] See Whittle, *Agrarian Capitalism*, 190; Robert Allen, *Enclosure and the Yeoman: The Agrarian Development of the South Midlands 1450–1850* (Oxford, 1992), 73.

of servants: all the households in Table 2 employed at least four or five servants per year, while four had more than ten. On average, these ten households employed eight servants per year: two women and six men; only one in four servants was female.[16]

The Ealing 'census' of 1599 records the occupation or status of heads of household as well as listing household members including servants. Although Ealing is now part of west London, at the end of the sixteenth century it was a rural community dominated by farming, some eight miles from the City. Nonetheless, like many parishes just outside London, it had a large number of wealthy households, with nine belonging to gentlemen, merchants and wealthy professionals, and this affected its profile of servant employment. Elsewhere in England many villages had no gentry households at all.[17] Correspondingly there was an unusually high proportion of servants in Ealing, making up 24 per cent of its population. Of these servants, 41 per cent were female, giving a gender ratio of 141:100.[18] However, servants, male and female, were not evenly spread between households. All wealthy households and households of yeomen employed servants, while only 20 per cent of other households did. In yeomen's households, 25 per cent servants were female, compared to 39 per cent in the households of gentlemen and other wealthy farmers, while in the households of ordinary farmers, 57 per cent of servants were women. Taken together, evidence from wills, household accounts and the Ealing census demonstrate that patterns of servant employment were influenced by a household's wealth as well as its production regime. Wills representing ordinary rural households of moderate wealth indicate that such households more often employed women than men, as did husbandmen in Ealing. Household accounts show a strong bias towards male servants, as did Ealing's yeomen. For the gentry the picture is more mixed, and we can speculate that patterns on servant employment varied according to the balance between farming and running a large household.

Further confirmation of this pattern is provided by probate accounts from Kent, which allow patterns of servant employment to be compared to inventoried wealth.[19] The employment of a lone female servant

[16] These numbers are approximate due to variations in employment patterns from year to year.

[17] In the 1520s, thirty-nine parishes studied in north-east Norfolk, with an estimated population of 4,350, contained only twenty-three resident gentry households. Wealthy non-gentry concentrated in market towns. Whittle, *Agrarian Capitalism*, 203 and 210–11.

[18] A 1562 communicant list from Romford, on the other side of London, indicates a similar servant gender ratio of 138:100: M. K. McIntosh, *A Community Transformed: The Manor and Liberty of Havering, 1500–1620* (Cambridge, 1991), 37.

[19] Inventoried wealth was the total value of moveable goods owned by the deceased, including debts owing to that person. The final balance of the probate account, after funeral expenses, debts owed and various other payments had been made, was considered a less accurate measure of previous wealth. See also Mark Overton, Jane Whittle, Darron Dean and Andrew Hann, *Production and Consumption in English Households, 1600–1750* (Abingdon, 2004), 138.

Table 2 *Servants recorded in farm and household accounts*

Owner, location, date	Size of farm and type of agriculture	Female servants (number and any work details)	Male servants (number and any work details)
1. John Capell: Porter's Hall, Stebbing, Essex: 1483–4.	300 acres of crops + several dozen cattle and other livestock.	1, no description.	10, no description.
2. Humphrey Newton: Newton, Cheshire: 1498–1520.	Approx. 100 acres of arable and 150 of pasture.	2–3, brewed, made cheese, spun flax and hemp.	2–3, no description.
3. Peter Temple: Burton Dassett, Warwickshire: 1543–8.	665 acres of enclosed pasture, fattening cattle, sheep and a few milk cows.	0–3, no description (records incomplete).	2–6, also at least one shepherd (records incomplete).
4. Roberts family: Boarzell, Sussex: 1568–70.	300 acres of pasture, arable and woods. Beef cattle and sheep, some cows.	2–3, no description.	7–8 male servants of whom 2 were boys.
5. Nathaniel Bacon: Stiffkey, Norfolk: 1587–97.	Approx. 600 acres; mixed, mainly arable farming including saffron and hops.	2–3, all dairy maids.	8–10, including a bailiff, sub-bailiff and stockman.

6. Robert Loder: Harwell, Berkshire: 1610–20.	Approx. 150 acres of arable and 100 acres of pasture.	2 usually, did malting.	2 usually, as well as a carter and a shepherd.
7. Henry Best: Elmswell, East Riding Yorks.: 1617–44.	360 (+) acres of arable and 100 acres of pasture. 14 milk cows.	1–3, washing, milking, brewing and baking.	4–6, foreman, 3 other men, 2 boys, details of work given.
8. Nicholas Toke: Godinton estate, near Ashford, Kent: 1626–8.	'An estate of considerable size.'	1, no description.	8, no description.
9. Reynell family: Forde, south Devon: 1627–33.	No information.	5, including a chamber maid and a dairymaid.	8, including a cook, coachman, buttery boy and ploughman.
10. Willoughby family: Leyhill, east Devon: 1644–6.	No information, but in 1644 sold butter and 800 lb of cheese.	4, including one dairymaid.	6 male servants.

Sources: 1. L. R. Poos, *A Rural Society after the Black Death: Essex 1350–1525* (Cambridge, 1991), 212–18. 2. Deborah Youngs, 'Servants and Labourers on a Late Medieval Demesne: The Case of Newton, Cheshire, 1498–1520', *Agricultural History Review*, 47 (1999),145–60. 3. *Warwickshire Grazier and London Skinner 1532–1555. The Account Book of Peter Temple and Thomas Heritage*, ed. N. W. Alcock (Oxford, 1981). 4. *Accounts of the Roberts Family of Boarzell, Sussex, c. 1568–1582*, ed. Robert Tittler (Sussex Record Society 71, 1977–9). 5. A. Hassell Smith, 'Labourers in Late Sixteenth-Century England: A Case Study from North Norfolk [Part I]', *Continuity and Change*, 4 (1989), 11–52. 6. *Robert Loder's Farm Accounts 1610–1620*, ed. G. E. Fussell (Camden Society Third Series 53, 1936). 7. *The Farming and Memorandum Books of Henry Best of Elmswell 1642*, ed. Donald Woodward (Oxford, 1984). 8. *The Account Book of a Kentish Estate 1616–1704*, ed. Eleanor C. Lodge (Oxford, 1927). 9 and 10. *Devon Household Accounts, 1627–59, Part 1*, ed. Todd Gray (Devon and Cornwall Record Society New Series 38, 1995).

Table 3 *Servant employment in the Ealing 'census' of 1599*

	Number of households	Percentage of households with servants	Number of servants	Percentage of servants female
All	85	34.1	104	41.3
Farming	52	40.4	87	36.7
Non-farming	33	24.2	17	64.7
Wealthy	9	100.0	52	44.2
Yeomen	6	100.0	32	25.0
Others	70	20.0	20	60.0
Wealthy farmers	6	100.0	41	39.0
Yeomen	6	100.0	32	25.0
Husbandmen	40	22.5	14	57.1

Source: K. J. Allison, *An Elizabethan 'Census' of Ealing* (Ealing, 1962).

Table 4 *Kent probate accounts mentioning servants, 1611–25*

	Households with servants		Female servants		Male servants		Average inventoried wealth of household
	(No.)	(%)	(No.)	(%)	(No.)	(%)	
One female servant	36	33	36	41	–	–	£68
One male servant	19	17	–	–	19	19	£141
Two servants	16	15	15	17	15	15	£113
Three or more servants	28	25	37	42	67	66	£199
Servants, number unspecified	11	10	–	–	–	–	£262
Total	110	100	88	100	101	100	(average £140)

Source: CKS, Archdeaconry Court of Canterbury account papers, PRC2/16, PRC2/18, PRC2/23 and PRC2/24.

was the most common pattern, found in 33 per cent of accounts mentioning servants. These households had an average inventoried wealth of £68, less than half of that of households who employed a lone male servant, with an average wealth of £141, while, as we would expect, households with three or more servants, and with unspecified numbers of servants, were wealthier still. Again, these findings also suggest that female servants were more likely to be employed in poorer households than men, and were more often employed on their own, as the lone servant.

All the documents examined here have weaknesses, but considered together they start to build a representative picture of servant employment in rural England in the period 1440–1650. They demonstrate that servant employment was widespread both geographically and socially. Nonetheless, the levels of wealth and occupational structures created by local economies affected both the number of households employing servants and the number and type of servants, male or female, that households employed. The households of gentry and wealthy yeomen farmers always contained servants in this period: normally four or more such employees. These almost always included women as well as men, but more men than women were employed. Lower down the social scale servant employment remained quite common, but typically only one, or at most two, servants were employed and many households did not have a servant. When a lone servant was employed, such a person was more often a woman than a man. It seems likely that in some localities, such as Uffculme in Devon and Swaledale in Yorkshire, where small farms predominated, and dairying and spinning were important elements of the local economy, female servants outnumbered their male counterparts. The gender of servants employed was determined not only by the productive activities of the household, and therefore of a region, but also within regions and localities, by the wealth of the particular household concerned.

Work

Just as male servants in rural households gained a training in husbandry, the work of a male farmer, so, in theory, female servants gained a training in the various arts of housewifery, the work of a housewife.[20] Exactly what types of work female servants and housewives really did in particular households, however, needs investigation.[21] Wage assessments set the legal maximum rates of pay that could be given to any hired worker, including servants. Thirty-six wage assessments dating from between 1444 and 1651 were examined for job descriptions of female servants. Most gave no information about the types of work female servants might

[20] Kussmaul, *Servants in Husbandry*, 34.

[21] Some of the material in the following section is discussed in more detail in Whittle, 'Servants in Rural England'.

do, differentiating wage rates in terms of age or general descriptions such as 'best woman servant' and 'common servant'. However, eight did provide details, listing the skills more experienced female servants might be expected to have: cooking, baking, malting, brewing, dairying, overseeing other servants and being 'able to take charge of a household'.[22] Specialist jobs mentioned for female servants were dairy maid, malt maker, wash maid and chamber maid, although out of the assessments studied, the last two specialisms were only listed in Essex in 1651. Dairying, mentioned specifically in six assessments, was the most common form of specialist female farm service listed.

Henry Best's *Farming and Memorandum Books*, describing the running of his large farm in east Yorkshire in the first half of the seventeenth century, notes that his two female servants were responsible for milking fourteen cows. When he hired a maid servant, Best asked if she had 'beene used to washinge, milkinge, brewinge, and bakinge' and assumed that every maid knew how to clean and tidy a house. As with his male servants, he expected his maids to be strong and able to do hard physical work.[23] Another well-known source from the early seventeenth century, already quoted, is Robert Loder's farm accounts. Loder had a large arable farm in Berkshire, and like Best, he employed two female servants each year. He regarded malt-making to be their most profitable task. It was certainly an important aspect of Loder's farm economy, as he sold between £76 and £122 worth of malted barley each year. However, Loder's accounts also record his maids doing other types of work: each year they made hay and helped with the grain harvest, one year the maids picked and sold his cherries, in other years they only sold them and other women were hired to pick them. In 1619 Loder calculated that one of his maids spent twenty-one days selling cherries, travelling to market with a horse each day.[24] A maid was also responsible for selling apples. In 1618, when Loder expanded his dairy, the maids helped with the milking, supplementing workers employed by the day.[25]

Additionally, Loder's maids also carried out those tasks he described as 'the doing of the thinges, that must indeed be donne'. What these were requires speculation. Loder records that his household, which comprised

[22] These were assessments from Northamptonshire 1560: B. H. Putnam, 'Northamptonshire Wage Assessments of 1560 and 1667', *Economic History Review*, 1 (1927), 131–2; Worcester 1560: D. Woodward, 'The Background to the Statute of Artificers: The Genesis of Labour Policy 1558–63', *Economic History Review*, 33 (1980), 42–3; Rutland 1563, and Colchester, Essex, 1583: *Tudor Royal Proclamations*, II, ed. P. L. Hughes and J. F. Larkin (New Haven, 1969), 215–18 and 499–501; East Riding of Yorkshire 1593, Oakham, Rutland 1610 and Essex 1651: F. M. Eden, *The State of the Poor* (1966), xc–xcii, xcv–xcvii and xcviii–ci; and Suffolk 1630: W. A. J. Archbold, 'An Assessment of Wages for 1630', *English Historical Review*, 12 (1897), 307–11.

[23] *Henry Best*, ed. Woodward, 138–42.

[24] *Robert Loder*, ed. Fussell, 169.

[25] *Ibid.*, 154.

himself, his wife, five servants and his young children, was fed primarily from his farm's own produce. Not only was cheese made on the farm, but wheat was consumed, presumably as bread; malt and hops were consumed, presumably in beer; and hogs were fattened.[26] Someone made the cheese, baked the bread, brewed the beer, fed the pigs and preserved and prepared their meat. It is likely that this was done by Loder's wife and the two maid servants, although this is never stated. It is worth noting that the majority of adults in the household were paid employees, and Loder notes that day labourers also consumed as much food and drink as one more resident adult, so the bulk of this food processing work was undertaken to feed workers rather than to provide for a nuclear family.

Literary evidence has often been used to provide basic descriptions of rural women's work. Four well-known literary works from this period which provide such descriptions are the anonymous late fifteenth-century *Ballad of the Tyrannical Husband*;[27] Fitzherbert's early sixteenth-century *Boke of Husbandry*;[28] Thomas Tusser's *Five Hundred Points of Husbandry* from later that century;[29] and Gervase Markham's *The English Housewife* published in 1615.[30] The *Ballad of the Tyrannical Husband* takes the form of an argument between husband and wife over who does the most work. While the husband's work is satirised as consisting solely of ploughing, the wife's list of tasks is long: she milked cows, made butter and cheese, cared for poultry, baked, brewed, processed flax, spun wool and made cloth, as well as preparing meals and keeping the house tidy. Her burden of farm and craft work came on top of child care: she complains that her 'sleep is but small' as she lies 'all night awake with our child' but still tidies the house and milks the cows each morning before her husband gets up. The image of women's hard work and many tasks was not restricted to the genre of satirical popular songs. It is a point also made in Fitzherbert's and Tusser's farming advice manuals. Fitzherbert offered advice on time management to the housewife rather than the husbandman, recognising that she was frequently faced with multiple tasks and had to make difficult decisions about which was most urgent, and most likely to profit the household.[31] Tusser noted that while the husbandman had seasonal respites when less work needed to be done, the housewife's tasks 'have never an end', combining a daily cycle with seasonal work.[32]

[26] For example, *ibid.*, 44–5.

[27] *Women in England c. 1275–1525: Documentary Sources*, ed. P. J. P. Goldberg (Manchester, 1995), 169–70.

[28] John Fitzherbert, *The Boke of Husbandry* (1533).

[29] Tusser, *Five Hundred Points.*

[30] Gervase Markham, *The English Housewife*, ed. Michael R. Best (Montreal, 1994).

[31] Fitzherbert, *Boke of Husbandry*, sig. K4r–v .

[32] Tusser, *Five Hundred Points*, sig. S2r. Tusser's advice to husbandmen follows a seasonal routine, but includes tasks carried out by women; his advice to housewives follows a daily routine.

Both Fitzherbert and Tusser admit a degree of ignorance about women's work. The parts of their books which refer to women's work are not so much advice as lists of tasks a husband could expect his wife to undertake, lists which are much the same as that in the *Ballad*. Markham's *The English Housewife* was a new departure in offering detailed advice about a range of women's tasks. Some of these seem more appropriate to gentlewomen than the average housewife. Chapters describe medicinal remedies, elaborate cookery, the distillation of vinegars and perfumes and keeping wine, as well as the more common 'offices' of housewifery: processing wool, hemp and flax, dairying, malting, brewing and baking and, rather strangely, 'the excellency of oats'. Children are not mentioned, nor is laundry or other forms of cleaning, and poultry only appear as the recipients of oatmeal. Markham is also silent about the generation of income. Fitzherbert suggests a wife should keep her own accounts, but should report her financial affairs to her husband, just as he should report to her. She should generate her own income by going 'to the market, to sell butter, chese, mylke, egges, chekyns, capons, hennes, pygges, gese, & al maner of cornes'.[33] That the housewife should make money by selling products as well as saving money by producing things at home is a point repeated by both the *Ballad* and Tusser.

Literary evidence provides a list of tasks women might be expected to do in a rural household, but it should not be mistaken for representative evidence of what rural women actually did. It is both incomplete, and too comprehensive, as a picture of what real women did. On the one hand some obvious tasks are omitted or only briefly mentioned, such as child care, fetching water and fuel, and laundry. On the other, it would be a mistake to imagine that all rural women carried out all these tasks. There were differences according to types of farming and the wealth of the household, and, presumably, differences in particular women's aptitude and enthusiasm. There was also change over time, particularly in the opportunities to earn money.

The nature of women's work in particular households is described in probate documents. Less wealthy rural households commonly employed one female servant: what work did such women do? Cross-referencing wills or probate accounts which mentioned servants with probate inventories which list the moveable goods owned by a household gives an indication of the work activities carried out. Wills and accounts also contain information about household structure, for instance, whether the family contained young children or the elderly who required extra care. Given that female servants were so often employed in relatively poor households, with a sparse domestic environment, it seems unlikely they were primarily concerned with cooking and cleaning. Ordinary rural

[33] Fitzherbert, *Boke of Husbandry*, sig. K4v–5r.

households would not have been able to afford such a luxury. Roger Alderson of Grinton in Swaledale, north Yorkshire, left a milk cow to his servant, Katherine Alderson, when he made his will in 1541.[34] It is possible Katherine was a relation; however, Roger described her simply as 'my servant'. He also left bequests to his wife and children, so he was not without close family. Architectural evidence and sixteenth-century probate inventories indicate a very basic living environment in Swaledale's upland farms.[35] Most dwellings consisted of a single living room, and inventories demonstrate that the majority of moveable wealth consisted of livestock rather than household goods. It seems likely that Katherine helped care for cows and sheep, milking and making cheese and butter, as well as spinning wool: the main elements of the local economy. She may also have helped care for the family's children. Sarah Thompson, a Kent widow, was wealthier than Roger Alderson, but, with seven children under the age of eleven, must have needed help with child care. She employed one female servant. Nonetheless, Sarah's inventory also records 'cattle, horses, kine, sheep, hogs and husbandry instruments' worth £80, indicating that there was farming work to be done.[36]

Records of inheriting children's ages in probate accounts correlated with servant employment show that female servants were more likely to be employed if there were children under the age of six in the household, although the sample is very small.[37] Out of sixty-five households leaving accounts mentioning servants, seventeen could be identified as containing young children. Fourteen, or 82 per cent, of these employed female servants, compared to 65 per cent in the whole sample as a whole.[38] It is often assumed that the location of women's work in or near the home in early modern England made child care easily compatible with other forms of work, but was this really the case? Surely there were difficulties in combining work in the fields, dairying (which required careful timing and a high degree of cleanliness), brewing or laundry (which required large quantities of heated water) with the care of small children. Cases of accidental death from sixteenth-century Sussex coroners' inquests suggest that there were sometimes problems. For instance, Alice Tuckenes, a

[34] *Swaledale Wills and Inventories 1522–1600*, ed. Elizabeth K. Berry (Yorkshire Archaeological Society Record Series 152, 1995 and 1996), 56.

[35] *Ibid.*, 3.

[36] CKS, Archdeaconry Court of Canterbury: Sarah Thompson of Wye: Inventory 11.9.193 (1642); Account PRC1/7/68 (1645).

[37] The sample used here is the sixty-five Kent probate accounts that could be cross-referenced with probate inventories, described in more detail below.

[38] The effect disappears if older children are included: 64 per cent of households with children under fifteen had female servants, compared to 62 per cent of the sample more generally.

servant of John Neve, left his daughter Susan sitting in a small chair in his house while she went out to milk the cows. While she was out Susan fell into the fire and died soon afterwards. Mary Water, aged one and a half, was in the kitchen of her father's house in the care of two servants. One went outside to empty a tub of hot water, while the other went to settle a swarm of bees; while they were gone Mary fell into a tub of water and drowned.[39]

Another context of female servant employment was in the households of single or widowed men, carrying out the work tasks normally allotted to a wife. William Read of Ashell in Uffculme, Devon, was widowed, with grown up children and grandchildren, when he made his will in 1576. He nevertheless had a small working farm with three cows, three sheep, three pigs and growing corn, as well as cheese, butter, bacon, lard, corn and hay stored in the house and barn. William left his servant Katherine Landman a small bequest of two shillings. Unless other servants were employed, but not remembered in the will, Katherine must have worked hard, cooking, cleaning, caring for livestock and processing farm products into preserved foodstuffs.[40] Unmarried men of whatever age were likely to need the assistance of female servants to run a household. John Buntyng of Tostock in mid-Suffolk, who made his will in 1440, left bequests to two female servants. One received 'a bullock, a brass pot holding a gallon and 8 bushels of barley', while the other received 'four bushels of barley'; the main beneficiary of his will, however, was his niece, who received '20s. and a cow two years old'. The range of the bequests suggests a farm producing barley and livestock, as well as malting, brewing and dairying on a small scale.[41]

These examples can be supplemented by a more systematic analysis of probate documents. Sixty-five Kent probate accounts from the first half of the seventeenth century which recorded servants' wages were matched with probate inventories from the same households, to compare servant employment patterns with material evidence of four common forms of women's work: dairying, spinning, baking and brewing.[42] Comparisons have to be restricted to contrasting households with female servants to those with only male servants, as households without servants at all cannot be identified, thus the numbers are quite small; however, the results were unexpected. We might predict that households with evidence of the classic women's occupations – milk cows for dairying, spinning wheels,

[39] *Sussex Coroners' Inquests 1558–1603*, ed. R. F. Hunnisett (Kew, 1996), 12 and 24.

[40] *Uffculme Wills and Inventories: Sixteenth to Eighteenth Centuries*, ed. Peter Wyatt (Devon and Cornwall Record Society New Series 40, 1997), 4. Reade's inventoried wealth came to a modest total of £21 11s 4d.

[41] *Wills of the Archdeaconry of Sudbury, 1439–1474*, I, ed. Peter Northeast (Suffolk Records Society 44, 2001), 53.

[42] CKS, Archdeaconry Court of Canterbury probate inventories and accounts.

Table 5 *Evidence of women's work in Kent probate inventories, 1600–49*

	Spinning (%)	Dairying (%)	Brewing (%)	Baking (%)	Number of inventories
All	47	55	39	34	1,852
Female	40	31	22	19	299
Male	48	60	42	37	1,553
Gentleman	38	43	43	36	42
Yeoman	51	83	65	49	206
Husbandman	54	79	38	33	104
Agricultural	55	91	54	46	867
Crafts	59	58	49	43	326
Waged	43	52	26	29	42

Source: CKS, Archdeaconry Court of Canterbury probate inventories. For methods used for sampling and analysis see Mark Overton, Jane Whittle, Darron Dean and Andrew Hann, *Production and Consumption in English Households, 1600–1750* (Abingdon, 2004), 28–31, 34–9, 181–4.

baking and brewing equipment – would be more likely to contain female servants. Only nine households had clear evidence of all four of these activities, and of these only four employed female servants compared to 65 per cent of the whole sample. Of households with servants, 40 per cent had spinning wheels, and 69 per cent of these households did contain a female servant. However, servant-employing households with female servants and no spinning wheels were nearly twice as common as those with wheels and female servants. The majority (72 per cent) of households with servants had milk cows or 'kine', although none had more than ten cows. Yet households without cows were slightly more likely to contain female servants, and servant-employing households with three or more milk cows were less likely to employ a female servant than those with just one or two cows.[43]

More light is shed on these matters by a wider survey of probate inventories. Table 5 draws evidence from a large sample of Kent inventories from the first half of the seventeenth century.[44] Spinning, dairying, baking and brewing were identified from equipment owned,

[43] The calculations for spinning and milk cows assume that households with servants of unspecified gender contained female servants. There were thirty-two households with three or more cows, of which twenty-two had female servants (69 per cent), fifteen households had one or two cows, of which fourteen had female servants (93 per cent).

[44] This data was collected as part of an earlier project, the results of which are published in Overton *et al.*, *Production and Consumption*. See 29–31 for details of the Kent inventory sample. Only those dating from 1600 to 1649 were used in this analysis.

such as brewing vats and spinning wheels, and from specialist rooms, such as dairies or bake-houses.[45] As ever, this evidence needs to be treated carefully. Activities go unrecorded when they relied only on very cheap or non-specific equipment, or on equipment that was not owned by the user. Distaffs for spinning were rarely listed because they were so cheap, although spinning wheels were reliably recorded. Milk cows, milk pails, butter churns, kneading troughs and brewing vats are recorded; but, for instance, if a woman produced soft cheese or butter with non-specialist equipment having leased a cow, or baked non-wheat bread on a stone by the fire, her activities leave no record. Nevertheless, as long as we bear in mind the fact that non-recording could indicate small-scale, lower-quality production rather than no production, the data relate some important points about women's work.

Evidence of spinning, dairying, brewing and baking on a significant level was far from universal. Goods relating to these activities were more common in inventories for men than inventories for women. This is not because men undertook these activities: most male inventories relate to the households of married men which contained women, while 'female inventories' were left by widows and unmarried women, some of whose collections of goods did not always relate to a full household, but rather the possessions of someone who lived within a larger household. Status designations given in the inventory heading, such as gentleman, yeoman and husbandman, allow the inventories to be ranked very roughly in order of wealth. Yeomen's households were the most likely to carry out all these activities except spinning, which was slightly more common in the households of husbandmen. Occupational designations, of agriculture on a commercial scale, crafts and wage earning, were attributed from evidence within the inventory.[46] Dairying, as would be expected, was more common in households involved in commercial agriculture, but surprisingly common in craft and waged households. The waged sample is very small, but does hint at an important pattern of production, with such households being the least likely to brew and bake. Spinning was the activity least sensitive to differences of status, occupation or gender of the inventoried person, but many households show no evidence of this form of women's work, so often portrayed as universal.

By-employment

The realisation that various archetypal forms of women's work were not universal in this period is not entirely new. Shammas noted a similar pattern in another large sample of rural English inventories, dating

[45] *Ibid.*, 181–4.
[46] For methodology see *ibid.*, 34–42.

from 1550–1650.[47] She was concerned with measuring the extent of home-based production, rather than examining patterns of work, and saw this as evidence of proletarianisation among poorer households. Viewed from the opposite perspective, it could also be seen as evidence of commercialisation. That not all households contained women who spun, brewed, baked and made butter and cheese implies that items made in this way were purchased, and that other households or businesses produced these items for sale. The scale of production, relationship of each activity to the market and how it changed over time requires investigation, as well as the gender of workers. Further, given the variations in the incidence of these types of work, elements of women's work such as dairying, spinning, brewing and baking should not be regarded as a single occupation of 'women's work'. Each had a degree of independence. Nor is dairying integral to other types of farming, or spinning necessarily located in the same household as weaving. Commercial brewing and baking did not arise naturally out of the provisioning of a household, nor did provisioning a household necessarily require these activities to be carried out. So rather than assuming that women's work was uniform, and giving it a vague label such as 'domestic production', it is more helpful to regard these activities as different occupations and treat them as an element of rural by-employment. Women's activities are noted in existing studies of by-employment, but this has not always filtered into our understanding of women's work. For instance in her classic article Thirsk writes that when mining and pastoral farming were combined, the householder mined 'while his family attended to the land and animals',[48] and Skipp notes that in the Forest of Arden, spinning 'was easily the area's most important domestic by-employment'.[49] What neither historian spells out is that by-employment, in these cases, consisted of men and women specialising in different production activities in order to support the household.

Milking and dairying were among a small number of agricultural tasks that were exclusively female, as they had been in the medieval period, and would remain until the late eighteenth century.[50] Although by the seventeenth century there is evidence of 'dairyman' and 'cheeseman'

[47] Carole Shammas, *The Pre-Industrial Consumer in England and America* (Oxford, 1990), 20–40.

[48] Joan Thirsk, 'Industries in the Countryside', in *Essays in the Economic and Social History of Tudor and Stuart England in Honour of R. H. Tawney*, ed. F. J. Fisher (Cambridge, 1961), 73.

[49] Victor Skipp, *Crisis and Development: An Ecological Case Study of the Forest of Arden 1570–1674* (Cambridge, 1978), 57.

[50] B. M. S. Campbell, 'Commercial Dairy Production on Medieval English Demesnes: The Case of Norfolk', *Anthropozoologica*, 16 (1992), 107–18; Christopher Dyer, 'Changes in Diet in the Later Middle Ages: The Case of Harvest Workers', *Agricultural History Review*, 26 (1988), 22; John Broad, 'Regional Perspectives and Variations in English Dairying, 1650–1850', in *People, Landscape and Alternative Agriculture: Essays for Joan Thirsk*, ed. R. W. Hoyle (British Agricultural History Society, 2004), 93–112.

being given as male occupations, it seems likely that these were men who managed dairy farms and marketed dairy produce, rather than doing the milking, or making butter and cheese themselves. Strong cultural taboos meant that only women worked directly with milk.[51] The best-quality butter and cheese produced for the market was made largely in the wealthy farming households of yeomen and gentry, which had the space and equipment to do so. As many other households did not produce their own dairy products, or could only make products of low quality which needed to be eaten fresh, much of the dairy products made by women on the larger farms must have been destined for sale. The farms of Robert Loder, Henry Best, the Tokes of Kent and the Willoughbys in Devon all produced more dairy products than they needed, and sold the excess.[52]

By the eighteenth century 'it was generally agreed that one woman could milk and process the liquid of up to ten cows'.[53] Bartholomew Dowe's *A Dairie Booke for Good Husewives*, published in 1588, purports to describe the advanced methods of Suffolk dairying, which he observed his mother practising, to a woman from Hampshire, where he was then living. Dowe claims that on a large Suffolk dairy farm, each female servant could care for and milk twenty cows: 'for every score of kine a maid'. The Hampshire woman replies, 'eight or nine kine is enough for one maide servaunt to milke in this Countrie'.[54] We might dismiss Dowe's claim for Suffolk as hyperbole, if it were not for the fact that his mother's dairy enterprise can almost certainly be traced to Sibton Abbey in east Suffolk via surviving accounts for 1507–13. During this period the abbey's dairy was managed by one Katherine Dowe, the name of Bartholomew's mother. In 1509, the dairy had sixty-three cows, and the abbey employed Katherine and three maids to milk them, make butter and cheese, as well as keeping pigs and poultry and making linen: which works out at fifteen or sixteen cows per worker.[55] Kent inventories do not record dairying on this scale. Of the 1,852 inventories sampled, those mentioning milk cows had an average of three per household in the period 1600–49.[56] The maximum number owned by one household in this period was thirty-four, but this was an isolated case; even the larger herds rarely contained more than ten

[51] Deborah Valenze, 'The Art of Women and the Business of Men: Women's Work and the Dairy Industry c. 1740–1840', *Past and Present*, 130 (1991), 142–69.

[52] See Table 2. *Robert Loder*, ed. Fussell, 153–4; *Henry Best*, ed. Woodward, 172 and 175; *The Account Book of a Kentish Estate 1616–1704*, ed. Eleanor C. Lodge (Oxford, 1927), 81; *Devon Household Accounts, 1627–59, Part 1*, ed. Todd Gray (Devon and Cornwall Record Society New Series 38, 1995), 151–63.

[53] Nicola Verdon, ' " . . . Subjects Deserving of the Highest Praise": Farmers' Wives and the Farm Economy in England, c. 1700–1850', *Agricultural History Review*, 51 (2003), 29.

[54] Bartholomew Dowe, *A Dairie Booke for Good Huswives* (1588), sig. A3r.

[55] *The Sibton Abbey Estates: Select Documents 1325–1509*, ed. A. H. Denney (Suffolk Records Society 11, 1960), 38–9 and 142.

[56] Sample as used in Table 5, above.

cows. Herds of this size could be managed by one woman, as long as she was not overburdened with other types of work. This explains the lack of direct correlation between the employment of female servants and dairying in the Kent inventories cross-referenced with accounts. Small dairy herds did not necessarily require female labour beyond that of the housewife. Farmers who produced butter and cheese commercially, even if this was only a small part of their farming enterprise, such as Loder, Best, Toke and Willoughby, employed at least one female servant.

In the medieval period ale was brewed and sold by women from poor, middling and wealthy households. Ale did not keep well, so it was more economical to make a large batch and then sell much of it to one's neighbours, and thus circulate the task of brewing around the community. In the fifteenth and sixteenth centuries brewing became increasingly concentrated and professionalised, and simultaneously a male occupation. The innovation of beer brewed with hops prolonged the time the beverage could be stored before sale, accentuating these trends. In southern and eastern England where wheat bread was consumed, baking had been a specialised male occupation by at least the fourteenth century. Once brewing became specialised particular households began to take up 'victualing': baking, brewing and running an ale-house. Small towns had a number of such victualers whose products were peddled to households in nearby communities. Women were certainly still involved in these activities, in partnership with their husbands and as peddlers, but brewing had ceased to be the female preserve it once was.[57] Inventories show that by the seventeenth century households with the space and equipment to do so produced beer and bread at home, catering for their staff of servants and other workers as well as the family.[58] However, excess bread or beer from these households was not sold on in the same way as dairy products. Poorer households which lacked the necessary equipment, and households in which women were too busy to brew and bake, now relied on specialist victualers and peddlers.

Spinning, although universally female, was not carried out by all women.[59] The identification of spinning in probate inventories relies on the presence of a spinning wheel, or on the listing of raw wool or flax together with finished yarn. Kent inventories indicate that although spinning was found in households of all levels of wealth, it was not evenly spread geographically: the proportion of households showing evidence of

[57] Judith M. Bennett, *Ale, Beer and Brewsters in England: Women's Work in a Changing World, 1300–1600* (Oxford, 1996); Mavis E. Mate, *Daughters, Wives and Widows after the Black Death: Women in Sussex, 1350–1525* (Woodbridge, 1998), 59–71.

[58] See Table 5, above; also Shammas, *The Pre-Industrial Consumer*, 35 and 39.

[59] Male 'spinners' were middlemen who purchased and sold on yarn: Alice Clark, *Working Life of Women in the Seventeenth Century* (1919), 113.

spinning varied a great deal between communities. Out of twenty-eight Kent communities surveyed for the period 1600–49, ten revealed evidence of spinning in more than 50 per cent of inventories, although in no community did the proportion exceed 58 per cent.[60] On the other hand, in five communities, including Canterbury, the proportion was under 30 per cent: Milton had the lowest incidence at 17 per cent. Interestingly, there was no clear pattern of geographical distribution. As might be expected, communities such as Goudhurst, in the Wealden broadcloth area, showed a high incidence of spinning, but so did Minster in Thanet, in the north-east of the county, perhaps due to its proximity to Sandwich, which specialised in the New Draperies.[61]

In *The Ballad of the Tyrannical Husband*'s fictional account of women's work, the housewife wove cloth as well as spinning the yarn, producing clothing for her family from raw materials. In the late fourteenth and fifteenth centuries, Goldberg found that female weavers were commonly found in rural areas and small towns as part of the cloth trade, as well as occasionally in larger cities.[62] The exclusion of women from weaving as a specialist trade in the late fifteenth and sixteenth centuries is documented by Clark.[63] Probate inventories from the first half of the seventeenth century show that loom ownership was quite rare, and very largely confined to specialist cloth-producing areas. Not only had women been excluded from professional weaving, but weaving for home use seems also to have died out. Thus, in the sixteenth and seventeenth centuries, women who spun did so as a cash-earning activity, as part of the commercial cloth production system. Only a minority of spinners lived in households where weaving was also carried out. Spinning is more laborious than weaving: Zell's figures for Kent broadcloth suggest six spinners were needed to supply each weaver in the late sixteenth century, if they all worked full time, which was unlikely.[64] Spinning was notoriously poorly paid: Clark thought full-time spinning could just support a woman if she worked on high-quality yarns, as long as she had no dependants.[65] Kent inventories indicate that 44 per cent of widows had spinning equipment. Somewhat ironically, the same was true of only 26 per cent of spinsters, while over 50 per cent of husbandmen's and

[60] The twenty-eight communities are listed and mapped in Overton *et al.*, *Production and Consumption*, 31.

[61] C. W. Chalklin, *Seventeenth Century Kent: A Social and Economic History* (1965), 124–6.

[62] Goldberg, *Women, Work and Life Cycle*, 97–9, 120 and 146–7.

[63] Clark, *Working Life of Women*, 102–6.

[64] It took eighty-five to ninety days to spin enough yarn for one broadcloth and fourteen days to weave it: Michael Zell, *Industry in the Countryside: Wealden Society in the Sixteenth Century* (Cambridge, 1994), 166 and 176. Sara Mendelson and Patricia Crawford, *Women in Early Modern England 1550–1720* (Oxford, 1998), 271, suggest four spinners to each weaver in the cloth industry more generally.

[65] Clark, *Working Life of Women*, 115 (although her evidence is mostly from 1650 to 1750).

yeomen's inventories record evidence of spinning.[66] In Kent at least, it appears that in the early seventeenth century spinning was rarely a full-time occupation undertaken by independent women, probably because earnings were so low. Instead it was a money-earning activity that housewives, widows and female servants worked on when they were free from other tasks. Trends in spinning in the century after 1650 show that decline in Kent's cloth industry led to a decline in the ownership of spinning wheels, and thus of spinning as a female by-employment.[67]

Conclusion

This brief summary perhaps serves best to indicate the need for more research on these topics, following the example of Bennett's excellent study of brewing.[68] The lack of detailed research on women's work is often excused by lack of documentation. Yet some of the most common and well-known types of document that survive for the mid-fifteenth to mid-seventeenth centuries, wills and inventories, together with probate accounts, contain a great deal of evidence about women's work. They are not straightforward to interpret, and need to be used in conjunction with other types of sources, but they do provide a means to getting beyond a static, oversimplified view of what female servants and housewives did in rural households. Women's work varied regionally and according to a household's wealth. Different occupations were commercialised in different ways: women's work was not isolated from the market. Some forms of women's work generated income through sale of products; others were part of a larger profit-orientated household structure, such as the wives and female servants on yeomen's farms who processed food, cooked and cleaned for paid employees as well as family members.[69] Housewives and female servants also spent time caring for young children, a task often omitted in descriptions of women's work.

The employment of female servants demonstrates that on a practical level at least, women's work was valued: why else bother to pay for an extra woman's labour? Yeomen's households normally employed one or two female servants, but might employ as many as six male servants. The occupations of female servants on these farms remained small scale: malting, brewing and baking became male professions, carried out away from the farm when undertaken on a large scale, while spinning was not profitable enough for full-time work in these households. In contrast,

[66] The low rate for spinsters does not mean that unmarried women were least likely to spin, simply that they did not spin on their own equipment: they were not independent spinners.

[67] Overton *et al.*, *Production and Consumption*, 48.

[68] Bennett, *Ale, Beer and Brewsters*.

[69] Using family here in its modern sense, to mean those related to the household head and resident.

the male-dominated occupations on such farms, arable and livestock agriculture, were expanding in scale over the period. Commercial dairy farming is one possible exception, but most dairies remained small enough for one woman to manage. Katherine Dowe's subcontracted dairy in Suffolk was unusual.

A large proportion of female servants in rural England were employed as lone servants in the less wealthy households of husbandmen. The irony is that these smaller farms were less likely to carry out all of the four female occupations we have measured, so appear to have had less work for women. Yet a close analysis of probate inventories and accounts of twenty-six Kent households that employed only one female servant reveal that there was work to be done. Of the householders represented, seven were widows or widowers, at least five of whom were elderly; eight had young children under six years old; seventeen had at least one cow that needed to be milked; eight had one or more spinning wheels. Each household employing one female servant had a unique combination of activities normally allotted to women: Thomas Willard of Benenden with goods worth £84 was a married victualer whose household brewed and baked as well as selling the products. Roger Baker of Chartham with goods worth only £26 was also married and his household kept a cow, geese and hens, spun linen and wool, grew hemp and baked bread. John Garrett of Goudhurst, worth £29, was married with six children aged between two and sixteen: his household made malt and cheese. Gabriel Morland of Wye worth £58 was widowed and elderly, a faded gentleman with a house full of stuff, much of it old, and one female servant to run it.[70] The servants in these households 'did the things that must indeed be done', a mixture of farm work, housework and caring for the young and old, reflecting the varied work patterns of maid servants and housewives across rural England.

[70] CKS, Archdeaconry Court of Canterbury probate documents: Thomas Willard inventory 10.36.326 (1609), account PRC2/16/200 (1612); Roger Baker inventory 10.33.223 (1609), account PRC2/15/30 (1610); John Garrett inventory 10.44.5 (1611), account PRC2/18/66 (1613) and Gabrael Morland inventory 10.49.196 (1616), account PRC2/22/35 (1619).

Transactions of the RHS 15 (2005), pp. 75–95 © 2005 Royal Historical Society
doi:10.1017/S0080440105000319 Printed in the United Kingdom

PUTTING THE ENGLISH REFORMATION ON THE MAP

The Prothero Lecture

By Diarmaid MacCulloch

READ 7 JULY 2004

ABSTRACT. The essay examines how the international Protestant identity of the English Church came to be in tension with the later assertion of sacramentalist or Catholic values within it. It chronicles how the Reformation in England came to align not with Lutheranism but with Reformed Protestantism, and compares Henry VIII's reforms with contemporary Reformations in mainland Europe seeking a 'middle way'. Edward VI's Church is contrasted with the temperature perceptible in Elizabeth I's religious settlement – which nevertheless asserted Protestant values with no concessions to Catholicism. The anomalous role of the cathedrals in England is identified as a major source of the English Church's later deviation from mainstream European Reformed Protestantism, which itself produced attempts to recreate a Reformed Church in the English north American colonies.

I had two agendas in mind in constructing this title. The first is the ongoing task of asserting that England did indeed have a Reformation in the sixteenth century. This might seem superfluous: after all, we have all heard of Henry VIII and his marital troubles, and we have all heard of bloody Mary and good Queen Bess defeating the Spanish Armada with a fine speech and a dose of English bad weather laid on by the Almighty. But the Church of England has over the last two centuries become increasingly adept at covering its tracks and concealing the fact that it springs from a Reformation which was Protestant in tooth and claw.[1] This labour of obfuscation began with the aim of showing that Anglicans were as good if not better Catholics than the followers of the pope. It then continued with the perhaps more worthy aim of finding a road back to unity with Rome, in the series of ecumenical discussions which began in 1970, known by the

[1] One can sample mature Anglo-Catholic distortions and obfuscations throughout the entries relating to the English Reformation in the first edition of an otherwise excellent reference work, *The Oxford Dictionary of the Christian Church*, ed. F. L. Cross (Oxford, 1957). This is emphatically not the case in the *Dictionary*'s present incarnation, edited by Dr E. A. Livingstone, 3rd edn (Oxford, 1997, and subsequent revisions). An up-to-date compendium of 'in-house' Anglican historiographical attitudes in scholarly form is embodied in Paul Avis, *Anglicanism and the Christian Church: Theological Resources in Historical Perspective* (rev. edn, 2002).

acronym ARCIC (Anglican-Roman Catholic International Commission). The participants in these discussions have not been anxious to emphasise difference, and very often they have fallen back on the Anglo-Catholic rewriting of English church history pioneered by John Keble and John Henry Newman in the 1830s, as the Oxford Movement took shape. A good deal of my career has been spent trying to undo the Anglo-Catholic view of history, not because I think that Anglo-Catholics are bad people, but simply because within their ranks over a century and a half, there has been a troupe of historians who have been too clever for their own good.[2]

Yet even before the Anglo-Catholics turned their talents to rewriting the English Reformation, something strange had happened to the Protestant Church of the Reformation in England. After the Restoration of Charles II in 1660 it became something distinctive, and whatever that was, was in the nineteenth century christened Anglicanism.[3] One of the fascinations of practising English church history is to see how this unique Anglican synthesis of Western Christianity evolved, and how it relates to the Reformation which went before it. There are still areas within that map on which there are dragons and unknown territories. It has been one of the exciting experiences of my academic career to see church history become once more a crowded area of exploration, where many young scholars without any confessional axes to grind feel that it is worthwhile to become familiar with the theological jargon and the agonies and ecstasies of early modern religion.

Perhaps after two decades of plugging away at this theme, I might feel (and others might feel still more strongly) that the point has been made, if not done to death. But then my second mapping task becomes important. So often even those who were not inhibited in talking about a Reformation in England took up that peculiar English assumption that England is by definition different and special, and that therefore even if it did have a Reformation, an English Reformation could not have all that much to do with the noises off across the English Channel, let alone whatever noises filtered southwards over the border with Scotland or across the Irish Sea. This attitude is a reflection of that English habit of talking about the rest of Europe as 'the Continent', something which the English have even persuaded Americans to do, in a thoroughly illogical

[2] P. Nockles, 'Survivals or New Arrivals? The Oxford Movement and the Nineteenth-Century Historical Construction of Anglicanism', in *Anglicanism and the Western Christian tradition*, ed. S. Platten (2003), 144–91. I also discuss this further in my 'Judging the English Reformation: Biographical Perceptions of Archbishop Thomas Cranmer', *Proceedings of the Anglo-Spanish Conferences, Valencia* (forthcoming).

[3] For discussion of the fugitive use of the term 'Anglicanism' before the nineteenth century, and its possible origins in the mouth of King James VI of Scotland, see *The Short Oxford History of the British Isles: The Sixteenth Century*, ed. Patrick Collinson (2002), 110–11.

way. That will not do. England's Reformation was remarkably barren of original theologians, at least until the coming of that quietly wayward figure Richard Hooker. The insularity of the English story might be said to begin with Hooker, and not just because of his own cooling attitudes to the Reformations of the rest of Europe. What is remarkable about Hooker is that none of his writings were translated into Latin. In other words, no one in any other European region could be bothered to read him, so Hooker was left languishing in that baffling and marginal European language, English (which it must be said is particularly baffling when Hooker writes it).[4] Otherwise, the flow of ideas in the Reformation seems at least at first sight to be a matter of imports from abroad, with an emphatically unfavourable English balance of payments.

If England had a Reformation, and an emphatically Protestant Reformation, and apparently it borrowed most of its ideas from elsewhere, what sort of Reformation was it? How should we relate it to the Reformations which sprang from Martin Luther's fury over indulgences in 1517 and Huldrych Zwingli's championing of Lenten sausage-eating in 1522? Can we apply labels like 'Lutheran' or 'Reformed' in an English context, and what might they mean here? When I was telling myself the story of the whole European Reformation so that I could write a big fat book on the subject, this issue was always on my mind, and it is that on which I propose to concentrate today – with just a few kicks at the twitching corpse of High Church Anglican history.

We will start our mapping in royal palaces: the Reformations of kings and queens both English and overseas. First let us meet Henry VIII. Henry was a king fascinated by theology, because he was convinced that his crown brought him a unique relationship with God. God had put his family on the throne, even though (as Henry knew full well but would never admit) they had a remarkably weak claim by blood to be kings of England. His father had won the crown by God's favour in a battle at Bosworth in 1485. So it mattered what God thought of his actions, and all his life Henry was determined to get this right. His first instinct in the Reformation was that it was a blasphemy against God. He read Martin Luther, another man who felt a one-to-one relationship with God and was passionately determined to get the relationship right. Henry's reaction to Luther's encounter with God was, however, wholly negative, and expressed in his ghost-written *Assertio Septem Sacramentorum*, earning both papal gratitude and a riposte from Luther which was rightly taken as *lèse-majesté*.

Luther and Henry never laid aside their mutual loathing through their remaining quarter-century of life, particularly since Luther disapproved

[4] On Hooker's later impact in England, see Diarmaid MacCulloch, 'Richard Hooker's reputation', *English Historical Review*, 117 (2002), 773–812.

of Henry's repudiation of Katherine of Aragon with a good deal more genuine moral fervour than Pope Clement VII. Yet Henry was still the first king in Europe fully to declare against Rome; all those rulers who had previously done so were mere princes or city councils. Not even the newly minted King Gustav Vasa of Sweden made such a clean break with the Holy See when he set up his untidy alliance with the Reformation from the late 1520s. Inevitably Henry must decide what this break had to do with the Reformations in progress in central Europe. There is much that is puzzling about the decisions which Henry made, and one can easily catalogue the puzzles.[5]

Henry VIII made his Reformation a complicated matter. His Church has often been called 'Catholicism without the pope' – recent scholars have seen it more as 'Lutheranism without justification by faith', for the king never accepted this central doctrine of the Reformation.[6] Henry was part both of the old religious world and the new. Throughout the king's reign, the Latin mass remained in all its splendour, and all his clergy had to remain celibate, as did the monks and nuns whose lives he had ruined. On the other hand Henry ceased to pay much attention to the doctrine of purgatory, he destroyed all monasteries and nunneries in England and Wales (and, where he could, in Ireland) and he was positively proud of closing and destroying all the shrines in England and Wales.

It is worth seeing this mixture in a wider context, in a way that classically Anglican historians were never inclined to do. Several northern European monarchs were not necessarily enthused by Luther and Wittenberg, yet still made their own pick and mix Reformations, sometimes without breaking with Rome. I have already mentioned Gustav Vasa of Sweden, but an equally interesting case is the Elector Joachim II of Brandenburg, who had a Lutheran brother-in-law but also a Catholic father-in-law, the king of Poland. Joachim's uncle was Luther's enemy the indulgence-peddling Cardinal Albrecht of Mainz, so it is perhaps not surprising that the elector had no excessive reverence for the old Church hierarchy. He took it upon himself to enact his own religious settlement for Brandenburg. He specifically declared the settlement to be temporary until there could be a general settlement throughout the empire. The elector made no break with Rome, but he confiscated much of the Church's lands and dissolved monasteries, just as Henry VIII was doing at the same time in

[5] For further discussion, see Diarmaid MacCulloch, 'Henry VIII and the reform of the Church', in *The Reign of Henry VIII: Politics, Policy and Piety*, ed. Diarmaid MacCulloch (1995), 159–80.

[6] This is a formulation invented by Peter Marshall: cf. A. Ryrie, 'The Strange Death of Lutheran England', *Journal of Ecclesiastical History* [hereafter *J. Eccl. H.*], 53 (2002), 64–92, at 67.

England, and with almost as much lack of concern to reinvest his winnings in good causes.[7]

Equally interesting were the policies of Duke Johann III of the united duchies of Jülich–Cleves–Berg. In 1532–3 he enacted a Church Ordinance without consulting his clergy, and yet equally without breaking with Rome. Duke Johann's son succeeded as Duke Wilhelm V in 1539: he was not only brother-in-law of Luther's protector the elector of Saxony, but more importantly for England, he was Anne of Cleves's brother. So the English political and religious leadership would be particularly aware of what was going on in Jülich–Cleves at the end of the 1530s, when for instance Henry VIII pushed a new doctrinal statement through parliament, the Six Articles of 1539.[8] Just as in the changes in Cleves, these reaffirmed the traditional liturgical ceremonies of the Church, and yet they did not reverse any of the changes that had so far occurred in England.

Yet equally a keynote of the Cleves changes as embodied in Duke Johann's 1532/3 *Kirchenordnung* was that preaching should be based on scripture and the early Fathers and should be free of polemics. This was of course also the constant cliché of the Henrician Reformation. Many will be familiar with its encapsulation in the great pictorial title-page of the Great Bible of 1539, which shows Henry handing down his Bible to his grateful subjects, but historians have neglected an exactly contemporary artefact associated with the king. This was a literal witness to the Anne of Cleves marriage, and also a fascinating witness to the official mood on the eve of that disastrous marital adventure: the ceiling of the chapel of St James's Palace, installed at the time of Anne of Cleves's arrival in 1540. What is noticeable about this emphatic statement of Henry's religious policy is that the only motif apart from royal emblems and the initials of Anne of Cleves is the repeated motto *Verbum Dei* – 'the Word of God'. There is not a trace of any traditional Catholic symbolism.[9]

As always, King Henry VIII managed to confuse his subjects about his views on the Bible. In 1543 he forced an act through parliament which overlooked King Canute's lesson to his courtiers and tried to limit Bible-reading on the basis of social hierarchy. It is not always remembered that exactly at that time in Scotland, there was very similar legislation about Bible-reading in the Scottish parliament, but this Scottish legislation was not restrictive but permissive in its effect. An act of 1543 for the first time

[7] J. Estes, 'Melanchthon's Confrontation with the "Erasmian" *Via Media* in Politics: The *De Officio Principum* of 1539', in *Dona Melanchthoniana*, ed. J. Loehr (2001), 83–101, at 93–5.

[8] *Ibid.*, at 96–7.

[9] T. String, 'A Neglected Henrician Decorative Ceiling', *Antiquaries Journal*, 76 (1996), 139–52, at 144–5. For an illustration of the Great Bible and discussion, see Diarmaid MacCulloch, *Thomas Cranmer: A Life* (London and New Haven, 1996), 238–40.

allowed lieges, that is landowners, to possess the Bible.[10] The Scots were thus newly *allowed* an access to the Bible approximately equivalent to its newly *restricted* access in England: a symptom of a regime which for a moment had decided to undermine the old Church in Scotland and come closer to the religious settlement south of the border. What we are seeing alike in Brandenburg, Jülich–Cleves, England and the Scotland of 1543 is a whole series of attempts to find a 'middle way' – that phrase which meant so much to King Henry, let alone to others like Archbishop Cranmer who often radically disagreed with him as to precisely what it might mean.[11]

Because Henry VIII's own personal Reformation was not the only Reformation on the map of Henry's England. There were at least two others. First let us note the Reformation from below, which was also a Reformation before the Reformation: that of Lollardy. Without saying too much about the Lollards, I would reaffirm against some of my colleagues that in terms of the theological future of the Church of England, they mattered a great deal.[12] Admittedly Lollardy was never a unified force, and in the fifteenth and sixteenth centuries it was certainly not identical with the views of John Wyclif: given the way that it had been so effectively persecuted out of the universities and positions of power, that was hardly surprising. Nevertheless, on the eve of the Reformation, one can assemble an array of core beliefs which were common to most of those who would have thought of themselves (and who were recognised by neighbours and the old Church authorities) as having a distinctive and dissident identity or outlook within English religion: the identity which their detractors labelled Lollardy.[13] Equally, when a definite shape emerged for the Protestant Church of England's thought in the reign of Elizabeth, it had three major characteristics: a distrust of assertions of the real presence in the eucharist, a deep animus against images and shrines and a reassertion of the value of law and moral systems within the Reformation structure of salvation. All these three were also characteristic of mainstream early Tudor Lollardy, and all three clashed with Luther's style of Protestantism. I am not saying anything as silly or as simple

[10] Gordon Donaldson, *The Scottish Reformation* (Cambridge, 1969), 30.

[11] For useful discussion, see George Bernard, 'The Making of Religious Policy, 1533–1546: Henry VIII and the Search for the Middle Way', *Historical Journal*, 41 (1998), 321–51.

[12] See a very different argument throughout Richard Rex, *The Lollards* (Basingstoke, 2002), esp. ch. 5 and Conclusion.

[13] Amid the great mass of literature on Lollardy, see especially Margaret Aston, *Lollards and Reformers: Images and Literacy in Late Medieval Religion* (1984); A. Hudson, *Lollards and their Books* (1985); A. Hope, 'Lollardy: The Stone the Builders Rejected?', in *Protestantism and the National Church in 16th Century England*, ed. P. Lake and M. Dowling (1988), 1–35. There is still much to discover about the theology of post-Wyclifite Lollard groups; in particular, we await the completed research of Patrick Hornbeck on this subject.

as to assert that the English Reformation was home-grown, or nothing but Lollardy writ large. Nevertheless, the Lollard inheritance cannot be ignored when seeing the choices which the English Reformers now made, constrained as they were by the existence of Henry VIII and of competing Reformations on the other side of the North Sea.[14]

There was then yet another English Reformation: the programme sought and put into effect as far as they dared by the group of politicians and senior clergy who had been rallied by Queen Anne Boleyn, Thomas Cromwell and Thomas Cranmer. I have labelled them evangelicals in previous writings, and I will not labour the point as to why I think this a better word than Protestant in the conditions of early Tudor England.[15] Thanks to Boleyn, Cromwell and Cranmer, there was something of an evangelical establishment in Church and royal court, with constant if precarious access to power from 1531 right up to the old king's death. This group started close to the beliefs of Martin Luther, because to begin with, as news of the Reformation filtered into England in the early 1520s, Luther seemed to be the only act in town. There were always anomalies, such as the marked hostility of the English evangelicals to imagery in church: that was apparent already in the 1530s when the evangelicals tortuously smuggled their views on various matters of doctrine into the Church's official doctrinal statements. They made sure that Henry VIII's Church renumbered the Ten Commandments in such a way as to stress the command against graven images, something which Luther did not do, any more than did the pope, but which had been newly revived in Zürich. It is too simple to see this momentous little change simply as a borrowing from the Swiss Reformation. It suggests the tug of a Lollard agenda already at work even on those who were now bishops and politicians.[16]

However, the Lutheranism of these establishment evangelicals remained strong on the vital matter of the eucharist throughout the 1530s. It began weakening after a symbolic moment in 1540 when King Henry burned England's most prominent and self-conscious Lutheran spokesman, Robert Barnes – Barnes was one of the very few major magisterial Reformers to be executed anywhere in the European Reformation, and in one of history's great ironies, he was executed by the pope's chief enemy in Europe.[17] Now the future of England's Protestantism turned out to lie not with Wittenberg, but somewhere else. To find out where

[14] I develop these ideas at greater length in Diarmaid MacCulloch, *The Later Reformation in England 1547–1603*, revised edn (Basingstoke, 2000), 55–65.

[15] See e.g. Diarmaid MacCulloch, *Tudor Church Militant: Edward VI and the Protestant Reformation* (1999), 2, 4.

[16] MacCulloch, *Cranmer*, 192.

[17] For a masterly recent treatment of the 1540s, see A. Ryrie, *The Gospel and Henry VIII: Evangelicals in the Early English Reformation* (Cambridge, 2003).

this future lay and what it turned out to be, we must meet some more European rulers trying to find a middle way.

One of the most important is Archbishop Hermann von Wied of Cologne; after gradually moving from Roman obedience, he tried to create an autonomous Protestant Church in the lower Rhineland, but he was evicted by Charles V in 1546 after vigorous opposition to his plans from the canons of his own cathedral. Von Wied has often been casually characterised in English-speaking historiography as a Lutheran in his later years, but he did not at all conform to Lutheran doctrinal tramlines (particularly on the matter of images), and he became an inspiration for theologians who equally kept outside the Lutheran fold. One of them was his fellow-archbishop Thomas Cranmer, who seems to have kept in touch with the former archbishop even in von Wied's years of retirement in the 1550s.[18] Von Wied's proposals to reform the liturgy were highly influential on the construction of the Book of Common Prayer. He represented one possible future direction for the European Reformation, snuffed out on the mainland by the Holy Roman Emperor's action against him.

Besides von Wied, there is the story of the little imperial territory of East Friesland. This tiny corner of Europe has a disproportionate significance for the course of northern European Reformations in many ways, not least for the early Reformation in England. When its ruler Count Enno II died in 1540, he left his widow Anna von Oldenburg with three young sons. Countess Anna was a resourceful and cultured woman: she brushed aside opposition and assumed regency power on behalf of her children, planning to build them a secure and well-governed inheritance in East Friesland which might form the basis of greater things for the dynasty. It was not her fault that none of her sons proved her equal in capability or strategic vision. In politics she sought out alliances with rulers who like herself wanted to keep out of religious or diplomatic entanglements.[19]

In her own domestic religious policy, Countess Anna likewise sought to avoid total identification with either Lutherans or papalist Catholics, just as Henry VIII generally did after his break with Rome. When she began her efforts in East Friesland, she chose as principal pastor in her little port-capital at Emden an exotic and cosmopolitan figure from the Polish noble caste, Jan Łaski (usually known in his international travels as Johannes à Lasco by non-Polish Latin-speakers trying to get their tongues

[18] MacCulloch, *Cranmer*, 393–4, and other index refs. s.v. von Wied, Hermann. See also J. K. Cameron, 'The Cologne Reformation and the Church of Scotland', *Journal of Ecclesiastical History*, 30 (1979), 39–64; and R. W. Scribner, 'Why Was There No Reformation at Cologne?', *Bulletin of the Institute of Historical Research*, 49 (1976), 217–41.

[19] H. E. Jannsen, *Gräfin Anna von Ostfriesland: eine hochadelige Frau der späten Reformationszeit (1540/42-1575)* (Munich, 1988).

around Polish pronunciation). Łaski was a humanist scholar, friend and benefactor of Erasmus. When he broke with the old Church in the late 1530s, he remained an admirer of Archbishop von Wied of Cologne. Łaski was also in friendly contact with Swiss Reformers, and he had views on the eucharist diametrically opposed to Luther – the sort of views which Cranmer was about to develop for himself in England. The remarkable career of this cosmopolitan Pole is a symbol of how effortlessly the non-Lutheran Reformation crossed cultural and linguistic boundaries. It is arguable that by the end of his life in 1560, he had become more influential in the geographical spread of Reformed Protestantism than John Calvin. The two men were in any case never soul-mates.[20]

But how might we label the theology which Łaski represented? In the 1540s it is anachronistic to call this movement Reformed Protestantism, though that is what it became. What we are seeing in these beginnings is the conscious creation (in a variety of different contexts and shapes) of what might perhaps too topically be termed a 'third way', avoiding Wittenberg and Rome. In doing so, enthusiasts for a 'third way' were naturally drawn to various other great reforming centres, which in the 1540s meant Zürich, Basel and Strassburg. And it was this triangle which chiefly influenced what happened next in England, the decisive moment in shaping the actual structures of the English Reformation. No longer was Wittenberg the chief inspiration for England's evangelical religious changes.

In 1547 Henry's Reformation was swept away when his little son Edward inherited the throne. Little legacy of that first Henrician Reformation remains in the Church of England with three very considerable exceptions: the break with Rome, the royal supremacy and the cathedrals which he had either preserved, refounded or founded for the first time (a matter to which we will return). Edward was the figure-head for the evangelical-minded clique of politicians both lay and clerical, including the now veteran evangelical Archbishop Cranmer as a prominent member. This clique, now freed from the murderously watchful eye of the old king, immediately began accelerating religious changes.

All this was against the background of the subtle shift in theological stance among the English evangelical leadership which we have begun exploring. To recapitulate: in general in Henry VIII's time they had been broadly Lutheran in sympathy, mostly for instance continuing to

[20] Andrew Pettegree, *Marian Protestantism: Six Studies* (Aldershot, 1996), 80–4. The best overall treatment of Łaski is to be found in *Johannes à Lasco: Polnischer Baron, Humanist und europäischer Reformator*, ed. Christoph Strohm (2000), particularly, on his eucharistic views, C. Zwierlein, 'Der reformierte Erasmianer a Lasco und die Herausbildung seiner Abendmahlslehre 1544–1552', in *ibid.*, 35–100.

accept the real presence in the eucharist (one has to point out that this made their relations with the king a good deal less dangerous than otherwise might have been the case). Around the time of the old king's death in 1547, Archbishop Cranmer became convinced that Luther was wrong in affirming eucharistic real presence. One might cynically call this a convenient moment to change his convictions, but we should never underestimate the psychological effect of suddenly being released from the hypnotic power of Henry's extraordinary personality.

The king's death came at a crucial moment in another way: a military and political disaster for central European Protestants. In 1547 the Emperor Charles V defeated leading Protestant German princes in the Schmalkaldic Wars. England was suddenly poised to act as a refuge for prominent European Protestants, but not Lutherans, who generally either accepted the compromise imposed by the emperor or stayed and fought it (and each other) from comparatively safe refuges like Magdeburg. Accordingly from late 1547 Cranmer welcomed to England many overseas reformers displaced by the Catholic victories. The refugees whom he found most congenial were now non-Lutherans; indeed some of the most important were from the then vanishing Reformation of Italy, which was for the most part now finding refuge in non-Lutheran strongholds, especially Zürich and Strassburg. Two of the refugees, the great Italian preacher Peter Martyr Vermigli and some time later the leader of the Strassburg Reformation Martin Bucer, were given the leading professorial chairs in Oxford and Cambridge respectively. In their wake came hundreds of lesser asylum-seekers.

In 1550 came a significant step: the official foundation of a London 'Stranger Church' intended to embrace all those various refugees, whatever their cultural or linguistic background. Its superintendent – in effect, its bishop – was none other than Jan Łaski, who had likewise eventually been forced out of East Friesland in the wake of the Interim. The English government was anxious to use his leadership skills to curb religious radicalism among the refugees, so they gave him a handsome salary and one of the largest churches in the city, Austin Friars. Łaski administered his congregation to show how England might gain a pure Reformed Church (this was clearly the intention of several leading English politicians).[21] So Edward's Reformation was marked both by its awareness of being part of international Protestantism, and by its now open move towards the Churches which were consciously not Lutheran – the Churches which would soon come to be called Reformed. The English break with Lutheranism was destined to be permanent. At the very end of Edward's reign, the English government tried to entice

[21] Andrew Pettegree, *Foreign Protestant Communities in Sixteenth Century London* (Oxford, 1986), chs. 2–4.

Philip Melanchthon from Wittenberg to succeed Martin Bucer as Regius Professor at Cambridge. Indeed they got to the point where they sent him his travel expenses and had set a date for him to arrive, in late June 1553 – but the young king's death intervened, and Melanchthon had enough warning that he could quietly drop the whole idea (what happened to the English money is not clear). But it is unlikely that Melanchthon would have brought a Lutheran future with him to England. It is more probable that Cambridge would have proved the escape-route from hard-line Lutheranism which he sought for much of his career, and that he would have found a new home in Reformed Protestantism.[22]

Before this melancholy coda, the short reign of Edward VI had created many of the institutions of the Church of England which survive to the present day. Cranmer transformed the liturgy by masterminding two successive versions of a Prayer Book in English, the first in 1549. He was generally cautious in orchestrating the pace of change, and his caution was justified when a major rebellion in western England in summer 1549 specifically targeted the religious revolution, specifically his first Prayer Book. Not just Catholics objected to the book: no one liked it. It was too full of traditional survivals for Protestants, and it was probably only ever intended to be a stopgap until Cranmer thought it safe to produce something more radical.[23] In dialogue with Peter Martyr and Martin Bucer, Cranmer produced a second Prayer Book in 1552 far more radical than 1549; the theology of the eucharist which its liturgy expressed was close to a major agreement on the eucharist which Zürich had just agreed in 1549 with John Calvin of Geneva, the *Consensus Tigurinus*. The creation of the *Consensus* was a crucial moment in the European Reformation. It provided a rallying-point for non-Lutherans and also a point of attack for hard-line Lutherans such as Joachim Westphal of Hamburg, thus making permanent the division between the Lutherans and the Reformed. When England aligned with the *Consensus Tigurinus*, it was clear that the English evangelical establishment was by now fully ready openly to reject consciously Lutheran stances in theology.

Cranmer also presided over the formulation of a statement of doctrine (the forty-two articles) and the drafting of a complete revision of canon law. This revision was a remarkable witness to Cranmer's vision of England as leader of Reformation throughout Europe: Peter Martyr and Łaski were both active members of the working-party which drafted the law reform – even though Łaski had often vocally disapproved of the slow pace at which England was implementing religious change. With this combination of authors, it is not surprising that the draft scheme of

[22] MacCulloch, *Cranmer*, 538–40.
[23] *Ibid.*, 461–2, 504–8.

canon law was vocally hostile to Lutheran belief on the eucharist as well as to Roman Catholicism and to radical sectaries like Anabaptists.[24]

The canon law reform is admittedly one of the great might-have-beens of English history. It was defeated in parliament out of sheer spite, because the secular politicians in the regime had badly fallen out with leading Protestant clergy, who accused them of plundering the Church not for the sake of the Reformation but for themselves. So in spring 1553, the duke of Northumberland blocked a procedural motion which would have extended the life of the law reform commission and would therefore have allowed its work to be considered for parliamentary enactment.[25] As a result, the carefully drafted scheme fell into oblivion – Elizabeth I never revived it when she restored Protestantism. In one of the great untidinesses of the Reformation, the Protestant Church courts of England went on using the pope's canon law. There was an effort to tidy it up fifty years later to remove its worst popish features, but the next great effort did not come until the time of Archbishop Geoffrey Fisher in the 1950s. And crucially, the lost legislation had provided for the introduction of procedures for divorce. Because those provisions fell, the Church of England was left as the only Protestant Church in Europe not to make any provision for divorce – for no more elevated theological reasons than a politician's malice and Elizabethan inertia. This was the first respect in which the English Reformation diverged from the European-wide norm.

Let us lay aside the interval of Mary's reign, despite the major significance which historians now realise that it had for the Counter-Reformation throughout Europe.[26] We only need to note that Mary made her own vital contribution to the Protestant Reformation by restoring the heresy laws, and burning Cranmer and his various colleagues. That bitter experience became a central part of English consciousness in succeeding Protestant centuries. It tied Protestant England into an active and deeply felt anti-Catholicism which was the particular forte of Reformed Protestant Christians. If anything was the glue which fixed the kingdom into a Reformed Protestant rather than a Lutheran mould, this was it.

[24] See especially the *Reformatio*'s section on heresy in *Tudor Church Reform: The Henrician Canons of 1535 and the Reformatio Legum Ecclesiasticarum*, ed. Gerald Bray (Church of England Record Society VIII, 2000), 186–213.

[25] On this, see MacCulloch, *Cranmer*, 531–5, and on the precise circumstances and nature of the defeat, J. F. Jackson, 'The *Reformatio Legum Ecclesiasticarum*: Politics, Society and Belief in Mid-Tudor England' (D.Phil. thesis, Oxford University, 2003), 222–4.

[26] Two of the most important recent contributions to opening up this field have been Eamon Duffy, *The Stripping of the Altars: Traditional Religion in England 1400–1580* (New Haven and London, 1992), 524–63; and T. F. Mayer, *Cardinal Pole: Priest and Prophet* (Cambridge, 2000), 203–301.

Those later centuries proved to be Protestant because Mary's greatest contribution to the English Reformation was to die after only five years. Yet never again did the kingdom of England play the captaining role which Cranmer had planned for it among the Reformed Churches, and that was thanks to the next queen on the throne, Mary's younger half-sister Elizabeth. Indeed it is worth noting that the shape of the English Reformation was unique in Europe, because it owed so much to two women, Henry VIII's Queen Anne Boleyn and her daughter Queen Elizabeth. Mischievously, one might say it owed a good deal to a third, Queen Mary I, as well.

The young Queen Elizabeth was marked out in 1558 as a Protestant, not least because she was her mother's daughter. She faced a formidable array of Catholic power in Europe, and she had to make careful choices about how to structure the religion of her traumatised and rudderless kingdoms of England and Ireland. She did so in a settlement steered through her parliament in 1559, which has formed the basis of the Church of England (and therefore of worldwide Anglicanism) to the present day. It has been the subject of much argument, which is of course an argument about the nature of Anglicanism. In much traditional historical writing about English religion, the emphasis has been on the religious compromises which Elizabeth made in this 1559 religious settlement. It would be more sensible to note how little compromise the queen made in swiftly and decisively setting up an unmistakably Protestant regime in Westminster.

The new queen proved expert at making soothing noises to ambassadors from dangerous Catholic foreign powers, but few people could be deceived about the nature of her programme. There was no question of offering the settlement for the inspection or approval of the overwhelmingly Catholic clerical assemblies, the Convocations of Canterbury and York. Its enactment in parliamentary legislation faced stiff opposition from the Catholic majority in the House of Lords. This meant a delay in implementing it until April 1559, when two Catholic bishops were arrested on trumped-up charges, and the loss of their parliamentary votes resulted in a tiny majority for the government's bills in the Lords. It could be said that the 1559 settlement was based on ruthless politicking and a complete disregard for the opinions of the senior clergy who were then in post. Revolutions usually cut corners, and this was a revolution, however much it was finessed.[27]

The shape of the resulting parliamentary settlement was in fact a snapshot of King Edward VI's Church as it had been in doctrine and

[27] The construction of the settlement is described in detail (including a thorough-going and effective demolition of Sir John Neale's reconstruction of events in 1558–9) in N. L. Jones, *Faith by Statute: Parliament and the Settlement of Religion, 1559* (1982).

liturgy in autumn 1552.[28] That meant bringing back the 1552 Prayer Book, not the 1549 Book, which enjoyed virtually no support from anyone, and which not even the queen attempted to revive.[29] The 1559 legislation made a number of small modifications in the 1552 Book and associated liturgical provisions, centring on liturgical dress and the eucharist. Traditionally in Anglican history, these were called concessions to Catholics. That is absurd. How would these little verbal and visual adjustments mollify Catholic-minded clergy and laity, whom the settlement simultaneously deprived of the Latin mass, monasteries, chantries, shrines, gilds and a compulsorily celibate priesthood? Clearly they did have a purpose and significance: the alterations were probably aimed at conciliating Lutheran Protestants either at home or abroad. At home, Elizabeth had no way of knowing the theological temperature of her Protestant subjects in 1559, while over the North Sea, the Lutheran rulers of northern Europe were watching anxiously to see whether the new English regime would be as offensively Reformed as had been the government of Edward VI.[30] It was worthwhile for Elizabeth's government to throw the Lutherans a few theological scraps, and the change also chimed with the queen's personal inclination to Lutheran views on eucharistic presence.

Nevertheless, the new Church of England was different in tone and style from the Edwardian Church. Edward's regime had wanted to lead militant international Protestantism in a forward-moving revolution. Many Edwardian leaders had gone into exile under Mary to parts of Europe where they saw such militant change in action, and they expected

[28] MacCulloch, *Cranmer*, 620–1.

[29] *Pace* arguments to the contrary in Roger Bowers, 'The Chapel Royal, the First Edwardian Prayer Book, and Elizabeth's Settlement of Religion, 1559', *Historical Journal*, 43 (2000), 317–44. The centre of his case is the assertion that some particularly sumptuous musical settings of the 1549 liturgy could not possibly have been written in 1549–52, and must post-date musical innovations in the Catholic restoration of Queen Mary. This *a priori* assumption is rather undermined by the fact that one of Bowers's examples, a 'Second Service' by John Sheppard, is most unlikely to have been written for Elizabeth, since Sheppard made his will a fortnight after Elizabeth's accession and died a fortnight later (Bowers has mistaken his date of death). Sheppard probably had other concerns in his dying weeks than providing music for the Chapel Royal. If Sheppard's elaborate music can thus be reassigned to the period 1549–52, there is no reason why any of the other supposed 1559 settings of the 1549 texts should not be likewise, and no reason to assign any of them to 1559.

[30] The atmosphere is well captured in the letters of the period 1559–61 between Zürich reformers and leading English returned exiles, printed in two paginations in Latin and English translation, *The Zürich Letters* . . . , ed. H. Robinson (2 vols., Parker Society, 1842, 1845), *passim*. See also Diarmaid MacCulloch, 'Peter Martyr Vermigli and Thomas Cranmer', in *Peter Martyr Vermigli: Humanism, Republicanism, Reformation*, ed. E. Campi *et al.* (2002), 173–201, at 199–200. For an interesting argument from an unexpected quarter that the eucharistic adjustments may perfectly plausibly be seen as an effort to update the liturgy to developments in Reformed Protestant thinking, see C. S. Carter, 'The Anglican 'Via Media': A Study in the Elizabethan Religious Settlement', *Church Quarterly Review*, 97 (1924), 233–54.

to carry on the good work now that God had given them the chance to come home. Elizabeth begged to differ. She took particular exception to returning exiles associated with Geneva: she excluded them from high office in the new Church, because she was furious with the Scots Edwardian activist and Genevan enthusiast John Knox – he had written the famously titled *First Blast of the Trumpet against the Monstrous Regiment of Women*, claiming that it was unnatural (monstrous) for a woman to rule. Knox had intended it against Elizabeth's predecessor Mary, then found that unfortunately the arguments applied to her as well.[31]

Elizabeth's own brand of Protestantism was peculiarly conservative. And in one respect, the new queen gathered around her like-minded people as she planned the religious future. Neither she nor any of her leading advisors (including her new archbishop of Canterbury, Matthew Parker, and her first nominee for archbishop of York, William May) had gone abroad under Mary. They had conformed outwardly to the traditional Catholic Church: in other words, they were what John Calvin sneeringly called 'Nicodemites' – like the cowardly Nicodemus, who only came to Jesus Christ under cover of darkness. Elizabeth and her advisors knew the specialised heroism of making choices about concealing opinions and compromising in dangerous times, rather than the luxury of proclaiming their convictions in unsullied purity. No other Protestant Church in Europe had such a beginning. It meant that the queen had a sympathy for traditionalist Catholics whose religious convictions she detested, but who kept similarly quiet in her own Church – towards the end of her reign, Sir Nicholas Bacon's lawyer and philosopher-son Francis said admiringly that she did not seek to make windows into men's hearts.[32]

Elizabeth was a subtle and reflective woman who had learnt about politics the hard way. She showed no enthusiasm for high-temperature religion, despite the private depth and quiet intensity of her own devotional life. Many of her Protestant subjects, including many of her bishops, found this extremely frustrating, particularly when it became clear in the 1560s that she would permit no change in the 1559 settlement. There were idiosyncratic features of this settlement which were randomly preserved in her fossilisation of the Edwardian Church. Notable were the traditionally shaped threefold ministry of bishop, priest and deacon,

[31] The full extent of the queen's fury has now been revealed in Pettegree, *Marian Protestantism*, 144–8, 197–9.

[32] This remark so often misquoted and so often attributed to Elizabeth herself is to be found in *The Works of Francis Bacon*, ed. James Spedding, Robert Leslie Ellis and Douglas Denon Heath (14 vols., 1857–74), I: *Lord Bacon's Letters and Life*, 178. It occurs in Bacon's 'Observations on a Libel' of 1592, but is also to be found word for word with its surrounding material in a letter of Francis Walsingham to M. de Critoy, written between 1589 and Walsingham's death in 1590: *ibid.*, 98. Spedding is almost certainly correct in postulating that Bacon had ghost-written this letter of Walsingham's.

together with the preservation of the devotional life and endowments of cathedrals. Neither at the time bore much ideological freight.

As far as the threefold ministry was concerned, Archbishop Cranmer had preserved separate ordination services for the three orders of ministry in constructing his Ordinal of 1550, despite advice to the contrary from his friend Martin Bucer, but it is difficult to discern in Cranmer any sense of apostolic succession of the ministry or any idea that ministers of God's word and sacraments differed materially from other servants of the Tudor monarchy.[33] On 17 December 1559, Matthew Parker was consecrated archbishop of Canterbury by four colleagues in episcopal orders: William Barlow, John Scory, Miles Coverdale and John Hodgkin. These bishops represented a certain spectrum of Protestant theological perspectives, indicated by the interesting variety of clerical garments which they chose to don at various moments of the ceremony, but it is unlikely that anyone regarded any of the quartet as more significant than another: the common factor was that they had all been bishops in the reign of King Edward VI.

Victorian Anglo-Catholics became very excited by the fact that back in 1536, Barlow had been consecrated under the pre-Reformation Catholic Ordinal, albeit after the Roman schism, and they devoted an inordinate amount of ink to investigating this, because of a frustrating lack of exact documentary corroboration of the original consecration (which certainly had taken place). It is likely that Barlow would have told them not to bother: it was not a matter which he would have regarded as of any importance in 1559. His ministry was validated by its discreet witness to evangelical reform under Henry VIII and its more ample exercise under Edward VI. Neither did anyone else make an issue of Barlow's consecration at the time, despite the bitter controversies between Catholics and Protestants which were already raging around Parker's consecration from the later years of Elizabeth I.[34] The notion of apostolic succession dependent on a line of bishops was not something which appealed to early Elizabethan bishops, although by the early seventeenth century, the situation was changing, as we will see.

The other fossils from Edward's interrupted Reformation, the cathedrals, were particularly important in the unexpected developments of the English Church in subsequent generations. Cathedrals were a hangover from King Henry's Reformation which had no parallel

[33] See MacCulloch, *Cranmer*, 278–9, 460–1.

[34] For an interesting late seventeenth-century discussion of the consecration, innocent of later High Church preoccupations, but clearly setting out the pre-Oxford Movement issues in controversy with Roman Catholics about Parker's consecration, see J. Strype, *The Life and Acts of Matthew Parker*... (3 vols., Oxford, 1821), I, 112–22. On the Barlow controversy, see A. S. Barnes, *Bishop Barlow and Anglican Orders: A Study of the Original Documents* (1922).

anywhere else in Protestant Europe. Not even the more conservative Lutherans preserved the whole panoply of cathedral deans and chapters, minor canons, organs and choristers and the rest of the life of the cathedral close as did the English. Most northern European Protestant cathedrals survived (where they survived at all) simply as big churches, sometimes retaining a rather vestigial chapter of canons in Lutheran territories. Why the English cathedrals were not dissolved like the monasteries is not clear, but it has a lot to do with the personal preferences of Queen Elizabeth. In any case, dissolved they were not, and that made the Church of England unique in the European Reformation. Within their walls, they made of Cranmer's Prayer Book something which he had not intended: it became the basis for a regular (ideally, daily) presentation of a liturgy in musical and ceremonial form.

Other than in the cathedrals, this choral exploitation of the Prayer Book was practised very rarely in Elizabethan and Jacobean England. It was to be found in Westminster Abbey and in Queen Elizabeth's Chapel Royal (plus the little brother of the Chapel Royal at Ludlow, headquarters of the Council in the Marches of Wales).[35] Otherwise only a minority of Oxbridge college chapels adopted this tradition, perhaps accompanied (and probably in vestigial form during Elizabeth's reign) by a small clutch of churches which had come through the Reformation still collegiate, through one or other accident of history. The parish churches of England, all 9,000 of them, would hear very little music at all, beyond the enormously popular congregationally sung metrical psalms created in the mid-Tudor period by a variety of hands: these were part of the great outpouring of metrical psalmody which was the common property of the European-wide Reformed Protestant family. That remained the case down to the late seventeenth century, and then the replacement psalmody collection of 1696 popularly known as 'Tate and Brady' only marginally extended the parochial musical repertoire, until the coming of Methodism set new standards of popular hymnody for its mother Church in the eighteenth century.[36]

[35] On Westminster Abbey, see particularly J. F. Merritt, 'The Cradle of Laudianism? Westminster Abbey, 1558–1630', *J. Eccl. H.*, 52 (2001), 623–46, and various essays in *Westminster Abbey Reformed 1540–1640*, ed. C. S. Knighton and R. Mortimer (2003), 38–74. I have gone so far as to argue for a 'Westminster Movement', on the analogy of the nineteenth-century Oxford Movement: MacCulloch, *Tudor Church Militant*, 210–13.

[36] The foundational work on the divergence between cathedral and parish church music is N. Temperley, *Music in the English Parish Church* (2 vols., Cambridge, 1980), and very important also is R. A. Leaver, *'Goostly Psalmes and Spirituall Songes': English and Dutch Metrical Psalms from Coverdale to Utenhove, 1536–1566* (Cambridge, 1991). On the wider European phenomenon of psalmody, see Diarmaid MacCulloch, *Reformation: Europe's House Divided 1490–1700* (2003), 146, 307–8, 326, 352, 460, 511, 536, 588, 590–1.

The cathedrals, those great and glorious churches, with their choral foundations, pipe-organs and large staff of clergy, were an ideological subversion of the Church of England as re-established in 1559. Otherwise it was Reformed Protestant in sympathy. If it was Catholic, it was Catholic in the same sense that John Calvin was Catholic, and up to the mid-seventeenth century it thought of itself as a part (although a slightly peculiar part) of the international Reformed Protestant family of churches, alongside the Netherlands, Geneva, the Rhineland, Scotland or Transylvania. It had long left Lutheranism behind. Lutherans had not helped their cause by some egregious examples of harassment of Protestant exiles from England in Mary's reign. For example, marked inhospitality had been shown in Scandinavia to Jan Łaski's Stranger Church exiles, and the little English exile congregation suffered expulsion from the town of Wesel in 1556 because of their Reformed eucharistic beliefs: in the latter case, Switzerland offered the twice-exiled English from Wesel a safe refuge at Aarau, thanks to the good offices of the government of Bern. The Elizabethan episcopal hierarchy, so many of whom had themselves been Marian exiles, would not forget that Lutheran inhospitality.[37]

Back in the 1970s and 1980s historians spent a lot of time arguing about whether there was a 'Calvinist consensus' in the Elizabethan Church.[38] That was a necessary debate which produced much fruitful thinking, but it was the wrong question to ask. John Calvin had virtually no effect on the Church of Edward VI: in no sense had it been Calvinist, although that description is still sometimes misleadingly found in textbooks. Cranmer, Łaski, Bullinger, Bucer and Martyr were the great names of that Edwardian Church, and Calvin's hour had not yet come; he was not well informed about affairs in England.[39] By 1558, however, times had changed. What about Elizabeth's Church of England? It was certainly a Reformed Protestant Church, and certainly, also, Calvin emerged on the English scene as important.

[37] On Łaski's troubles in Scandinavia in 1553, see O. P. Grell, 'Exile and Tolerance', in *Tolerance and Intolerance in the European Reformation*, ed. O. Grell and B. Scribner (1996), 164–81. On Wesel and Aarau, *Original Letters Relative to the English Reformation* . . . , ed. H. Robinson (2 vols. in single pagination, Parker Society, 1846–7), I, 160–8.

[38] P. Lake, 'Calvinism and the English Church 1570–1635', *Past and Present*, 114 (1987), 32–76: another useful perspective on that debate is provided by Nicholas Tyacke, 'The Ambiguities of Early-Modern English Protestantism', *Historical Journal*, 34 (1991), 743–54. For a contrasting perspective, see Peter White, *Predestination, Policy and Polemic: Conflict and Consensus in the English Church from the Reformation to the Civil War* (Cambridge, 1992), usefully reviewed by P. Lake, 'Predestinarian Propositions', *J. Eccl. H.*, 46 (1995), 110–23. For a statesmanlike afterview, S. F. Hughes, '"The Problem of 'Calvinism"': English Theologies of Predestination *c.* 1580–1630', in *Belief and Practice in Reformation England*, ed. S. Wabuda and C. Litzenberger (1998), 229–49.

[39] MacCulloch, *Tudor Church Militant*, 173–4, 176.

But we have to remember that Calvin never became a Reformed pope. The effect of his example and his writings was greatest in those Churches created during the popular upheavals of the 1560s – Scotland, France, the Netherlands – also in the attempted Reformations by certain princes and civic corporations in Germany's 'Second Reformation' later in the century and into the seventeenth century. Even in such settings, the other great non-Lutheran Reformers were read and honoured, and their thought was influential. Everywhere there was nuance and eclecticism: a spectrum. Just as in England, everywhere in Europe, Heinrich Bullinger, Peter Martyr, Jan Łaski and also Luther's former colleague Philip Melanchthon had as much shaping effect as Calvin. What emerges from detailed scrutiny of the Elizabethan Church of England is a Church on this European-wide spectrum of Reformed Protestantism, with a tendency to sympathise with Zürich rather than with Geneva – where Bullinger's *Decades* were made compulsory reading for the less-educated clergy of the Province of Canterbury by Archbishop Whitgift, and where the sort of sacramental theology espoused in Geneva was regarded as rather over-sacramentalist by the majority of English divines.[40]

Then around 1600, some English theologians, such as Richard Hooker, or his friend and admirer, Lancelot Andrewes, began questioning various aspects of the theological package which I have described. Hooker remained very individual in what he chose to criticise or defend, and it was Andrewes who was the chief shaper of the theological sea-change which now began taking shape in the English Church. Andrewes and his associates felt distressed by the Reformed assertion of predestination, and they listened sympathetically to the objections to it which were being vigorously voiced by self-consciously Lutheran theologians in Germany and Scandinavia.[41] As they formulated a new approach to the problem of grace and salvation, they began feeling that there must be more to God's sacramental gift of eucharist than the carefully balanced formulations of the Reformed theologians in the *Consensus Tigurinus*, and so they began to look again at how to describe the nature of eucharistic presence. Often in parallel with their new thoughts on predestination, they initially took their cue from Lutheran writers on the real presence, though this explicit interest in Lutheranism gradually lessened among them and their successors: the name of Luther was too much part of the Reformation.[42]

[40] For Samuel Ward of Sidney Sussex's opinion to this effect, see B. D. Spinks, *Two Faces of Elizabethan Anglican Theology: Sacraments and Salvation in the Thought of William Perkins and Richard Hooker* (Lanham, 1999), 164.

[41] On this, see Nicholas Tyacke, *Anti-Calvinists: The Rise of English Arminianism* (Oxford, 1987), especially 20, 39, 59.

[42] I am very grateful to Dr Peter McCullough for drawing my attention to Lancelot Andrewes's use of Martin Chemnitz's *Examinis Concilii Tridentini* (Frankfurt, 1574), which McCullough notes in particular in relation to Andrewes's sermon on Isaiah 6.6–7, preached

Unlike Luther, these English 'revisionists' began valuing bishops to the extent that they asserted episcopal government as the only divinely approved form of church government. They even valued cathedrals and their elaborate devotional life.[43]

All these ideas came together in what one might call a second revolutionary theology. This was a theology increasingly important to one party within the Church of England: those who have been variously labelled Arminians, Laudians, 'avant-garde conformists', call them what you will. In the early seventeenth century, that party, a sacramentalist, hierarchically minded party, gradually gained power in the Church, thanks in particular to some nimble political footwork on the part of Lancelot Andrewes, and a subsequent alliance with King Charles I.[44] The party eventually included the archbishops of Canterbury and York, William Laud and Richard Neile. In the seventeenth century, few of them were prepared to reject the word Protestant – that would be the achievement of the later Non-Jurors and the Oxford Movement – but the more mischievous of them were certainly prepared to borrow a Roman Catholic joke and call the Reformation a 'Deformation'.[45] In terms of the wider Reformation, they came to see their Church of England as more and more separate from the general story of the Reformations through the rest of the European continent, and so they anticipated the younger Pitt in deciding that it was time to roll up the map of Europe as far as English religion was concerned. Most telling was the campaign of conformity which Archbishop Laud waged in the 1630s against the Stranger Churches – those same Churches which under Jan Łaski had once been a template for a future Church of England.[46]

The immediate result was that many central theologians of the Reformed Protestant English tradition became increasingly unhappy and angry. The same anger motivated many during the 1630s to flee across

---

on 1 Oct. 1598 and published in L. Andrewes, *Αποσπασμάτια Sacra* (1657), 515–22. Andrewes is clearly also silently drawing on Luther's analogy of eucharistic presence as like heat in red-hot iron in this sermon. We await Dr McCullough's biography of Andrewes and his edition of Andrewes's sermons. For Luther's uneasy place in English Reformation polemic and self-defence, see R. H. Fritze, 'Root or Link? Luther's Position in the Historical Debate over the Legitimacy of the Church of England, 1558–1625', *J. Eccl. H.*, 37 (1986), 288–302.

[43] For more extended discussion, see MacCulloch, *Later Reformation*, ch. 6.

[44] On Andrewes's successful operation to gain control of the Chapel Royal of Charles as prince of Wales and hence of the theological future of the court, see Peter McCullough, *Sermons at Court: Politics and Religion in Elizabethan and Jacobean Preaching* (Cambridge, 1997), 194–209.

[45] MacCulloch, *Tudor Church Militant*, 173.

[46] Anne Oakley, 'Archbishop Laud and the Walloons in Canterbury', in *Crown and Mitre: Religion and Society in Northern Europe*, ed. W. M. Jacob and N. Yates (1993), 33–44.

the Atlantic, to form a true Church of England in New England.[47] One might argue that the subsequent history of the Church of England in the old country is an unpredictable deviation from this story – that the real story of the English Reformation was to be told in New England, and not in Lambeth Palace. That is one reason why in order to understand the dynamic of the English Reformation, it is so important to keep an eye on a still wider map: the patterns which English people created when they travelled across the Atlantic. Even in southern American colonies like Virginia, the version of the episcopal Church of England which southern colonists had established by the end of the seventeenth century was not quite that which was to be found in the old country.[48]

The Church of England has never decisively settled the question of who owns its history, and therefore of what its colour might be on the world map of Christianity. Within it remain two worlds: one, the sacramental world of theologians like Lancelot Andrewes, William Laud, the world that still values real presence, bishops and beauty, and the other, the world of the Elizabethan Reformation, which rejects shrines and images, which rejects real presence, which values law and moral regulation based on both Old and New Testament precept. These two worlds contend for mastery within English tradition, and they have created that fascinating dialogue about the sacred which the world calls Anglicanism. Long may the fight continue. It will be better for the sanity of the Anglican tradition if neither side manages to win.

[47] See F. J. Bremer, *John Winthrop: America's Forgotten Founding Father* (Oxford, 2003).

[48] For a subtle and sensitive overview of English religion in the American colonies, see P. Bonomi, *Under the Cope of Heaven: Religion, Society and Politics in Colonial America* (Oxford, 1986). On the continuing links between Old and New England, F. J. Bremer, *Congregational Communion: Clerical Friendship in the Anglo-American Puritan Community, 1610–1692* (Boston, 1994).

Transactions of the RHS 15 (2005), pp. 97–116 © 2005 Royal Historical Society
doi:10.1017/S0080440105000344 Printed in the United Kingdom

THE TRIUMPH OF THE DOCTORS: MEDICAL ASSISTANCE TO THE DYING, *c.* 1570–1720

The Alexander Prize Essay

By Ian Mortimer

READ 21 MAY 2004

ABSTRACT. This essay examines the frequency of medical interventions paid for on behalf of the dying in provincial southern England through a study of approximately 18,000 probate accounts in three dioceses (Canterbury, Chichester and Salisbury). Very substantial increases in the propensity to obtain medical relief are noted for all status groups in almost all areas. It seems that, depending on status, individuals in the south-east *c.* 1705 were between four and twelve times more likely to seek a medical strategy when faced with a serious, life-threatening illness or injury than their counterparts *c.* 1585. This increase in the use of medical strategies in the face of life-threatening ailments was not accompanied by a commensurate increase in the number of practitioners serving the population, but it was accompanied by a rise in the number of practitioners who were described as 'doctor' by their clients. It would appear that the medicalisation of the dying in southern England came about through surgeons and physicians more frequently supplying medicines, more regularly acting as general medical practitioners and more often travelling to see their seriously ill patients, regardless of the nature of their qualifications. Finally, the implications for general attitudes to medicine among the seriously ill and dying are discussed, with the conclusion that, by 1700, a form of medical individualism had developed whereby individuals came to see medicines as a natural means of supplementing divine healing power and even a way of facilitating the healing power of God.

In 1640, Robert Curtis, a wealthy gentleman from Tenterden, fell from his horse while riding through the parish of New Romney. Badly injured, he was taken to an inn run by one Mr Tooke. A local woman, Goodwife Wells, was summoned to attend him while a man called Beeching was sent to fetch various surgeons and physicians. Beeching first rode to Tenterden where he found Mr William Devison, surgeon, and Mr Richard Relfe, physician, and they hastened to the injured man. Beeching then rode on to Canterbury to request the attendance of another surgeon, Mr Peter Peters, and two physicians, Dr Edmund Randolph and Mr Charles Annoott. Meanwhile, back in New Romney, Robert Curtis's condition was worsening. Another local woman, Anne Brackfield, was brought in to help attend. But despite the ministrations of all these surgeons, physicians and female attendants, Robert Curtis died.[1]

[1] Centre for Kentish Studies (CKS), Maidstone: CKS PRC19/1/36 (probate account of Robert Curtis of Tenterden).

This sounds like one of those serendipitous discoveries that happen in the course of archival research. Medical history is full of them. But what makes the above document so interesting and important is that its discovery was not wholly accidental; it is one of more than 13,500 administrators' and executors' accounts (hereafter collectively referred to as 'probate accounts') which survive for the diocese of Canterbury.[2] Of this total, no fewer than 3,531 record details of medical and nursing assistance. The collection as a whole represents about 8–10 per cent of all the adult males dying across a period representing five or six generations, plus about 1.5 per cent of the adult females. It allows us to reconstruct the changing patterns of medical terminology and consumption across a period that begins when Elizabethan astrological medicine was at its height and ends not long before the establishment of the first county hospitals. Moreover, not only is this by far the largest collection of accounts to survive for a single diocese, it also consists of the most detailed examples.[3] Such was the scrupulousness of the Canterbury clerks that they frequently included names of payees and specific reasons for payment. For example: of the 941 payments to physicians, the practitioner's name was included in 609 cases. Coupled with the full records of medical licences for the diocese and the records of the freemen of Canterbury, we have a unique opportunity to examine the medical treatment of serious and fatal illnesses across a whole diocese not only from the point of view of the practitioner and his qualifications but also from that of his patients, with clear knowledge in almost every case about their geographical location and inventoried wealth.

That is the good news. As every user of probate material will be aware, methodological pitfalls abound. Indeed, one could write an entire thesis on problems in the use of probate accounts.[4] This is not the place to

[2] The author wishes to express his gratitude to the Wellcome Trust for a grant to obtain microfims of CKS PRC1 and PRC2 (archdeaconry court probate accounts 1569–1728) and PRC20 (consistory court probate accounts 1605–91), and to the Wellcome Trust and the Royal Historical Society for further grants to be able to consult the unfilmed series, PRC 21 (consistory court probate accounts 1569–1605) and PRC19 (consistory court probate accounts 1635–1729).

[3] The East Kent collections together account for about one third of all surviving probate accounts for the whole country. Other large collections include an indeterminate number, perhaps in the region of 10,500, for the Prerogative Court of Canterbury, about 6,000 for the diocese of Lincoln and about 3,300 for the diocese of Sarum (including the archdeaconry of Berkshire). The collection for the archdeaconry of Chichester is fourth largest, with about 1,200 extant accounts. See A. L. Erickson, 'Using Probate Accounts', in *When Death Do Us Part*, ed. Tom Arkell, Nesta Evans and Nigel Goose (Oxford, 2000), 103–19.

[4] On this subject see Amy Louise Erickson, 'An Introduction to Probate Accounts', in *The Records of the Nation*, ed. G. Martin and P. Spufford (Woodbridge, 1990), 273–86; Erickson, 'Using Probate Accounts'; Ian Mortimer, *Berkshire Probate Accounts 1583–1712* (Berkshire Record Society, Reading, 1999), introduction.

do that; the intention of this essay is rather to demonstrate the most important findings of a detailed examination of these accounts. It is clear that there was a huge increase in medical assistance purchased by, or on behalf of, the dying in provincial southern England over the course of the seventeenth century. Moreover, it appears that in the course of this process of medicalisation, the responsibility for directing the care strategies of the majority of the dying people attended by those from outside their household passed from local female carers to urban-based medical practitioners. This tells us much about medical availability, obviously, but it also allows us to see a wider spectrum of attitudes to death and extreme physical suffering reflected across a wide range of social and geographical groups.

It is important at the outset to mention a few of the methodological issues alluded to above. First, there is a significant disparity between the measurable wealth of those represented in the accounts. The average 'charge' on the accountant – or gross estate value of the deceased – recorded in the late sixteenth century is very much less than in the late seventeenth. Moreover, this was not merely a shifting range of wealth: there are very few individuals represented in the decades around *c.* 1700 whom one could regard as 'poor'. The average gross estate value of those who died after 1685 is well above £250 whereas prior to 1650 a number of accounts were made for low status people with estates of less than £6. The average of the entire sample was at a low point of about £50 in the 1590s. One of the reasons for this increase in recorded wealth of probate account subjects was no doubt inflation, especially in the late sixteenth and early seventeenth centuries;[5] but a more important reason was the legislative framework. Prior to 1685, church courts had called for accounts in a number of circumstances (mostly relating to perceptions of indebtedness), but in that year parliament passed the Act for the Reviving and Continuance of Several Acts of Parliament.[6] Henceforth accounts were only made where called for by the relatives and creditors of the deceased, not at the court's instigation. In most counties, accounts ceased to be presented in any great numbers. In East Kent, where the probate account tradition was strong, they continued to be produced but largely only for wealthier individuals whose estates were liable to be swallowed up by debt.

In order to accommodate this bias in the data, and to avoid the problem that irregularities between quantifiable wealth and status are

[5] Probate inventory-derived prices for the seventeenth century reveal a relatively low level of inflation. A few commodities actually fell in price. See Mark Overton, 'Prices from Probate Inventories', in *When Death Do Us Part*, ed. Arkell, Evans and Goose, 120–43.

[6] Mortimer, *Berkshire Probate Accounts*, viii.

most frequently found in accounts relating to women,[7] the entire sample of dying males has been divided into four wealth groups, those with gross estate values of £200 or more, £100–£199/19/11, £40–£99/19/11 and under £40. Examination of the results then reveals certain men with high status descriptors in the lowest wealth group. Some of these were older men whose wealth had been distributed previously and who were resident in relatives' houses, others were younger brothers living in the parental home inherited by an elder brother and some were adult sons of gentlemen living at home. These low wealth but high status men's accounts regularly display indications of their having access to very considerable resources – out of proportion with their own wealth – when perceived by their kinfolk to be in need of medical assistance. Furthermore, it may be observed that it was usually the relatives of the deceased who paid the medical bills, and who may have called in the physicians and surgeons who assisted the dying patient. As a result, it is essential to find a way of pooling those who had access to extensive and high status medical care on account of their relatives' wealth with those who had access on account of their own wealth. Four 'status groups' for deceased males have accordingly been drawn up, based partly upon wealth and partly upon social distinctions, as follows:

Status: A = All males with a gross estate value of £200 or more (including, where this figure is not extant, those with a balance of account of £200 or more), or with debts of more than £300 (i.e. balance in excess of £300 in the red, which usually requires debts of considerably more than £300),[8] and those with lower charges and smaller debts described as 'knight' or 'gentleman'.[9]

Status: B = All males with a gross estate value of £100–£199/19/11 and two individuals worth less than £100 who are described as 'esquire'.[10]

[7] Women represented in these accounts were predominantly widows, who had previously disposed of much of their household wealth and lived in more modest circumstances than their male counterparts.

[8] The reason for pulling this highly indebted section out of the rest is that most individuals with this level of debt who are described in the accounts are described as gentlemen; a number have no epithet however. Also with this level of debt it is possible that certain of their chattels had been sold before their deaths to pay creditors, or had been passed to family members to avoid them being taken by creditors, and thus their inventories are underestimates of their moveable wealth.

[9] In the cases of a few documents, where neither charge nor balance is available, expenditure in excess of £300 has been used as an indication of status A.

[10] It is not clear in these two cases whether 'esquire' was meant as a high status designation or merely reflects the deceased's family claiming he was armigerous.

Status: C = All males with a gross estate value of £40–£99/19/11 and those worth less described as 'Mr', 'clerk', 'yeoman' or 'doctor'.

Status: D = All males with a gross estate value of £0– £39/19/11 except those designated as falling into the above categories.

The next problem that must be mentioned is that of under-recording. For present purposes, this significant issue may be addressed very simply. There is no reason to suppose that there was a tendency to record medical and nursing services more in any one period than another. Therefore we may proceed on the assumption that the accounts record minimum levels of medical intervention. What we are attempting to do is not so much to register an absolute level of medical involvement as to measure rates of change. Thus the minima which these accounts offer allow us to proceed to chart changing levels of medical involvement relative to previous and later levels for similar status groups.

The third and final methodological problem that needs to be stressed here is more basic. What was medical assistance? What, for that matter, was nursing assistance? The latter question is especially relevant for the period before 1650, when the term 'nurse' meant wetnursing more frequently than sicknursing. Can one even differentiate between nursing help (by which we usually mean constant palliative care) and medical help (by which we usually mean occasional or intermittent care with a remedial objective)? How can we be sure that women attending a patient were or were not acting in a medical capacity? In facing all these questions one can only progress with an analysis based on the exact language used. We may reasonably associate all named and nondescript practitioners paid for 'physic' and medicines with 'medical care', together with all occupationally defined medical practitioners who were paid for care in the time of the sickness, or paid a specific debt for physic. If we also associate all instances of sicknursing and 'attendance', or 'keeping', or 'watching' or 'helping in the time of the sickness whereof he died' with 'nursing care', we may draw up graphs in respect of each status group (see Figures 1–4).

One of the most striking aspects of these graphs is that nursing care was the most common form of assistance purchased on behalf of all status groups in the late sixteenth century, and for status C and D individuals the predominant form of paid assistance for the first sixty years of the period under study. In the period 1570–99, two-thirds of all paid medical or nursing interventions were exclusively of a nursing character. Even the best-connected and wealthiest group of patients, status A individuals, with the greatest number of household servants, paid for nursing assistance more frequently than they paid for medical services. But in all groups, the use made of paid nurses tended to stasis or gradual decline until the

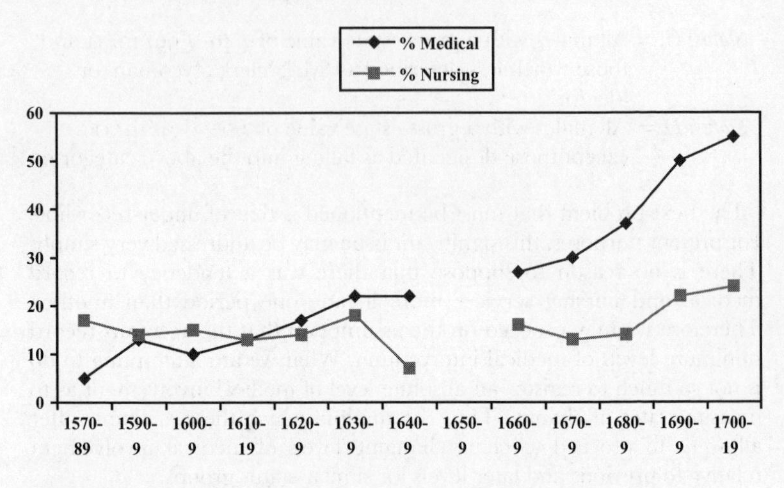

Figure 1 Percentage of all status A accounts indicating paid medical and nursing services

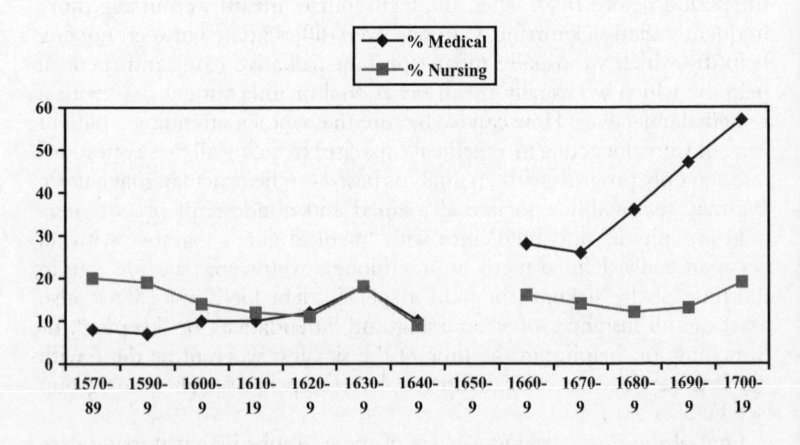

Figure 2 Percentage of all status B accounts indicating paid medical and nursing services

Civil War. In the 1640s a sharp dip in nursing services is noticeable. After the Interregnum an increase in nursing may be noted, first among the accounts of the lower status groups from the 1670s, and a decade later among the two higher status groups. Close examination of the accounts shows that this was nursing care in a slightly different guise: in the earlier

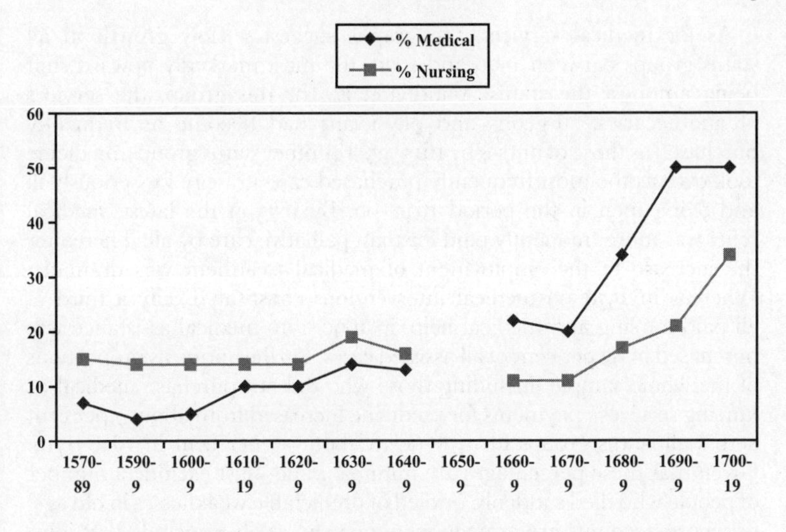

Figure 3 Percentage of all status C accounts indicating paid medical and nursing services

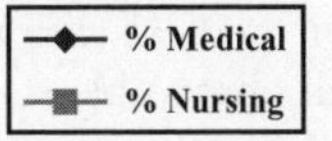

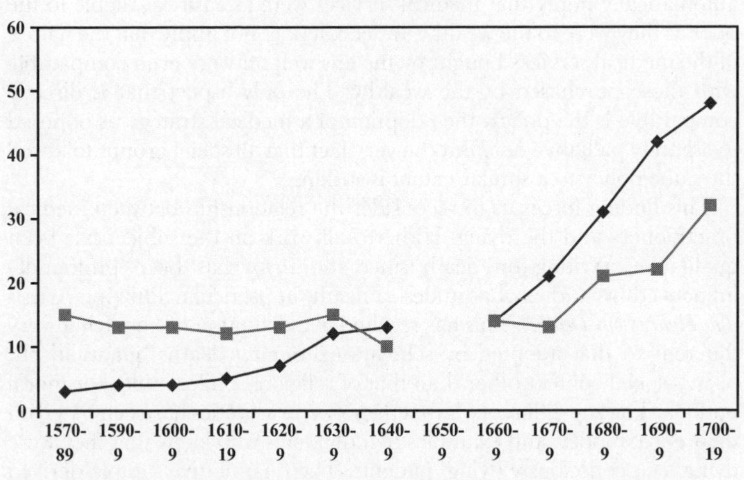

Figure 4 Percentage of all status D accounts indicating paid medical and nursing services

period most nursing care was conducted without recourse to medical practitioners. By 1700 nearly all payments for nursing services were made by people who also purchased medical help.

As for medical services, the graphs suggest a slow growth in all status groups between 1590 and 1630, the most markedly upward shift being amongst the status A individuals. For this group, the services of apothecaries, surgeons and physicians had become as frequently purchased as those of nurses by 1615–25. For other status groups, medicine took over as the most frequently purchased care strategy for seriously ill and dying men in the period 1640–60. By 1675 at the latest, medical relief was more frequently paid for than palliative care by all. Thereafter the increase in the employment of medical treatment was dramatic. Whereas in 1570–99 medical interventions constituted only a third of all paid nursing and medical help, in 1690–1719 medical assistance was purchased in 92 per cent of all assisted cases. Furthermore, as proportions of the whole sample (including those who did not purchase medical or nursing services), payments for medicine increased from about 7 per cent across all status groups in 1570–99 to about 53 per cent in 1690–1719. Given that these percentages are minima – and must exclude a number of people who died suddenly, or died of predictable weaknesses in old age, or whose accounts are ambiguous – one can safely conclude that after 1690 the great majority of non-destitute dying men who wanted medical assistance obtained it.

The above point – that medical care was the predominant form of assistance purchased by all observable status groups by 1675 – does not automatically imply that medical services were as easily available to the poor as they were to the wealthy. Indeed, it does not imply that the nature of the medical services bought by the less well-off were even comparable with those purchased by the wealthy. The only aspect that is directly comparable is the policy: the adoption of a medical strategy as opposed to a purely palliative one. But the very fact that all social groups followed the same policy to a similar extent is striking.

This finding forces us to reconsider the relationship between medical practitioners and the dying. Hitherto all work on the subject has been qualitative. Writing on death since the 1970s has been profoundly influenced by studies of attitudes to death, in particular Philippe Ariès's *The Hour of our Death*.[11] This has resulted in a definition of 'the dying' very different to that adopted by scholars examining deaths quantitatively, or in a social context other than that of religious, philosophical or moral outlook. The key difference is that the work on attitudes has been based on theoretical models and examples of individuals who knew that they were dying, i.e. 'consciously dying' patients. The quantitative sample derived from a series of probate documents is of an altogether different nature, for some individuals in that sample will have known or believed that they were dying, others will have suspected it, others will not have suspected it,

[11] Philippe Ariès, *The Hour of Our Death*, trans. Helen Weaver (Oxford, 1991).

and in between these will be a range of people who may have suspected their illnesses or injuries were serious but not fatal, and others who feared the worst. Furthermore, the 'consciously dying' sample is by definition closer in time to death than the sample of those who are in doubt, who might linger for weeks, months or even years. In short: the 'consciously dying' sample adopted by the followers of Ariès is much narrower than the death-based sample adopted here.

The above distinction is important, for almost all the work to date on the relationship between medical assistance and 'the dying' has been based on the consciously dying. It is fair to say that, as a result of this, we are almost totally ignorant of the relationship between medical assistance and the fatally ill and injured. Fewer therapeutic options are open to the consciously dying man, who has acknowledged to himself that he is beyond hope, or whose doctor has given up on him. His theoretical equivalent, the dying man who is the subject of preachers' and moralists' writings, who provides evidence for Ariès and others interested in attitudes to death, is similarly past all medical cure and always on the very verge of meeting his maker. The effect of this narrow definition from a medical point of view is illustrated by Lucinda Beier: 'Illness, not death, was the healer's province; healers generally withdrew when death seemed inevitable. The management of death was left to ministers, family friends and the sufferer.'[12] While this may be true in the context of the last hours of life, it was not necessarily so in the days, weeks or months beforehand. At what point may a fatally ill patient be termed 'dying'? From the point of view of the individual concerned, death is only the very last stage in a much longer process of sickness tending towards death. Death may be a clear-cut termination of life but dying is not a clear-cut process, except in hindsight, as it cannot be separated from serious illnesses and injuries which, to the best knowledge and experience of those involved, need not necessarily have ended in death.

Given the much broader range of dying people represented in the probate accounts, and given that these were people who actually died, not fictitious characters invented by moralists wishing to stress the virtues of a 'good death', we may picture the actual relationship between the dying and medical practitioners as one of great change in the period 1620–1700. Indeed, one has to say that by the end of the century it cannot be characterised as one of avoidance at all: precisely the opposite. This requires us to examine why: why did people start obtaining physic in greater quantities and with so much greater regularity, and refuse to commit themselves exclusively to the care of nurses?

[12] Lucinda McCray Beier, 'The Good Death', in *Death, Ritual, and Bereavement*, ed. Ralph Houlbrooke (1989), 53.

Let us begin with geography. A relatively even increase across all the status groups in East Kent, coupled with a trend in the seventeenth century increasingly to obtain medical remedies for the poor (as shown in parish accounts), suggests that there was a strong cultural movement in favour of obtaining medical assistance that affected society at all levels. However, it is entirely possible that each social group increased its consumption of its own particular type of medical services through a 'rural shift' of practices, as practitioners moved into rural areas, or as urban practitioners travelled more frequently to rural areas. If such a 'rural shift' occurred, one would expect to find a significant discrepancy between rates of increase in urban and rural parishes. To test this with regard to East Kent, the changes in the propensity to obtain medical assistance between the upper and lower status groups (including women)[13] have been tabulated, divided between urban areas (towns with which at least nine resident medical practitioners may be associated over the whole period) and 'rural' parishes which predominantly lie at least one mile from these towns.[14]

As Table 1 clearly shows, there were very dramatic increases across the board in East Kent. Although urban residents did not increase their take-up of medicine as much as their rural counterparts after *c.* 1625, they nevertheless experienced very significant increases. They also started at a higher initial level of medicalisation. These figures suggest geography was partly – but not wholly – a factor affecting medicalisation in East Kent. Although the rural low status groups more than trebled their use of medicine between *c.* 1625 and *c.* 1645, their urban contemporaries more than doubled theirs.

How representative is East Kent of other parts of southern England? Theoretically, we could check this by applying the same methodology to the next best surviving sets of accounts which, for the south of the country, include the diocese of Sarum (predominantly the counties of Wiltshire and Berkshire) and the consistory court of the archdeaconry of

[13] Women have been included in this sample as, below, the comparison is made between Kent and other dioceses. While in Kent one may fairly examine the sexes separately, there are many fewer accounts in the other dioceses, and urban/rural status-relevant examinations can only be sustained by grouping the sexes in Berkshire, West Sussex and Wiltshire.

[14] The towns here regarded as 'medical towns' are Canterbury, Maidstone, Dover, Faversham, Milton and Sittingbourne (as one), New Romney and Lydd (as one), Cranbrook, Deal, Sandwich, Ashford, Hythe, Tenterden, Wye and Elham. Lenham has been regarded as a 'medical town' for those parishes which are more than six miles from one of the other towns. This list is more or less consistent with the lists of towns provided by Lambarde (1570), quoted in J. Bower, 'Kent Towns, 1540–1640', in *Early Modern Kent 1540–1640*, ed. Michael Zell (Woodbridge, 2000), 141–76; and John Norden, *An Intended Guyde for English Travaillers*... (Edward All-de, 1625). Although excluding some small 'towns', such as Appledore, it actually probably exaggerates the importance of Lenham, Hythe, Wye and Elham as medical centres.

Table 1 *Increments in the use of medical services on behalf of men and women in urban and rural contexts in East Kent (increments to nearest 5%)*

Date	Urban status A and B men and women	Urban status C and D men and women	Rural status A and B men and women	Rural status C and D men and women
1570–99	12/119 (10%)	38/565 (7%)	20/249 (8%)	48/1385 (3%)
1600–49	125/562 (22%)	214/1,719 (12%)	146/1,118 (13%)	219/3,259 (7%)
1660–89	177/495 (36%)	192/701 (27%)	241/862 (28%)	242/1,130 (21%)
1690–1719	42/91 (46%)	33/69 (48%)	125/238 (53%)	41/96 (43%)
Increments				
From *c.* 1585 to *c.* 1625	+120%	+85%	+65%	+95%
From *c.* 1625 to *c.* 1675	+60%	+120%	+110%	+220%
From *c.* 1675 to *c.* 1705	+30%	+70%	+90%	+100%

Chichester (West Sussex).[15] However, there are two problems. First, there are no significant numbers of accounts for these other dioceses before 1590 or after 1690, and, second, even the most cursory examination shows that the much greater detail of the East Kent accounts makes these other counties – which far less regularly mention medical details – inappropriate for direct comparison. Nevertheless, we may still compare rates of change by comparing increments between *c.* 1625 and *c.* 1675. Subjecting all the available accounts in these counties to the same process as those for East Kent yields the results shown in Tables 2, 3 and 4.

It is the rural areas that stand out in Tables 1–4. All four counties show growth rates of 100 per cent or 110 per cent among the rural higher status groups, and Berkshire and West Sussex demonstrate low status rural increments of 170 per cent and 250 per cent respectively (comparable with 220 per cent in East Kent). Urban low status groups in Berkshire seem to

[15] The testamentary business of the archdeaconry of Chichester passed to the consistory court in the first decade of the sixteenth century.

Table 2 *Increment in the use of medical services on behalf of men and women in urban and rural contexts in West Sussex*

Date	Urban status A and B men and women	Urban status C and D men and women	Rural status A and B men and women	Rural status C and D men and women
1600–49	6/38 (16%)	9/86 (10%)	18/191 (9%)	13/344 (4%)
1660–89	10/31 (32%)	11/30 (37%)	32/161 (20%)	14/107 (13%)
Increment				
From *c.* 1625 to *c.* 1675	+100%	+250%	+110%	+250%

Table 3 *Increment in the use of medical services on behalf of men and women in urban and rural contexts in Berkshire*

Date	Urban status A and B men and women	Urban status C and D men and women	Rural status A and B men and women	Rural status C and D men and women
1600–49	4/50 (8%)	24/196 (12%)	11/158 (7%)	23/555 (4%)
1660–89	7/40 (17%)	3/51 (6%)	20/143 (14%)	17/154 (11%)
Increment				
From *c.* 1625 to *c.* 1675	+120%	−50%	+100%	+170%

display a decrease in their use of medicine, but this sample is small and hence less reliable. Only Wiltshire – the most westerly county – stands clearly outside the pattern established by the others, but even here, in all but the rural low status groups, there is a marked increase in the propensity to adopt a medical strategy. We may conclude that there seems to have been a significant and widespread adoption of paid medical assistance as a strategy to cope with situations ending in death in southern England, and that this largely transcended social and geographical boundaries, and by implication was not simply a function of transport to rural areas or practitioners being increasingly resident in rural areas (although both probably occurred).

At this point we must pause to consider a methodological explanation of these figures. As we are measuring increased *payments* for medicine (not just medical interventions), we might argue that the increase was in the frequency of payment, not medical assistance itself. Medicine assistance

Table 4 *Increment in the use of medical services on behalf of men and women in urban and rural contexts in Wiltshire*

Date	Urban status A and B men and women	Urban status C and D men and women	Rural status A and B men and women	Rural status C and D men and women
1600–49	1/23 (4%)	3/128 (2.3%)	5/70 (7%)	8/288 (2.7%)
1660–89	8/29 (28%)	7/60 (12%)	10/69 (14%)	2/73 (2.7%)
Increment				
From *c.* 1625 to *c.* 1675	+530%	+400%	+100%	0%

Note: Due to the difficulties in defining a 'town' in Wiltshire only places with a clear medical contingent have been used, and 'rural' in these cases relates only to the one- to six-mile hinterlands directly relating to these 'medical towns'.

might have been more freely given in the earlier decades. A model for such a system of free care might be built on the supposed widespread use of gentlewomen and clergymen, which Ronald Sawyer in particular postulated in his study of Napier.[16] However, this approach collapses on a basic point: if clergymen and gentlewomen were administering physic to the dying on a large scale, why did none of them charge for the (often expensive) medicines they would have needed to obtain in order to treat their patients? Such payments simply do not exist in the accounts. In fact there are only two possible instances of clergymen being paid in any way for medically assisting a dying man in the 13,500 East Kent accounts, and neither of these is certain. Furthermore, of the forty-four payments to female 'medical practitioners', two were probably for nothing more than fetching medicines, seven were for tending children, thirteen were for treating skin or other minor ailments and twenty-two were for 'surgery' or providing 'physic'. Only two women were paid specifically for offering medical advice. None of these payments were to gentlewomen: if any gentlewomen or clergymen helped the dying, they did so merely in a capacity in which they incurred no significant financial expense for which they required to be reimbursed. The bottom line is that a culture of paying (sometimes very large) sums of money to occupational practitioners with

[16] Ronald Sawyer, 'Patients, Healers and Disease in the SE Midlands, 1597–1634' (Ph.D. thesis, University of Wisconsin–Madison, 1985), especially 196. See also Doreen Nagy, *Popular Medicine in Seventeenth Century England* (Bowling Green, OH, 1988), 54–78, on the subject of gentlewomen practitioners.

a range of qualifications is fundamentally different to soliciting the help of well-meaning amateurs, whose access to expensive treatments is not evidenced, at least not in East Kent.

We may now move on to discuss the economic basis of the changes in medical assistance in more depth. In order for people to obtain physic so much more frequently, there must have been changes in supply or demand, or more probably both. On the supply side, there are several factors that we might consider. One which we may dismiss at the outset is that the numbers of practitioners in East Kent who assisted the dying increased. Detailed examination of wills, inventories, rolls of freedom, diocesan and archepiscopal licences, university degrees and College of Physicians' records, plus an analysis of payments to unlicensed and unofficial practitioners in the probate accounts, reveals that the number of occupationally defined medical practitioners in East Kent did not significantly alter, averaging 191 for the diocese in 1620–40 and 195 in 1670–1710.[17] Another supply-side factor we may rule out is that medical services became much cheaper: average payments in respect of 'physic' by all status groups more than doubled over the seventeenth century.[18] But one supply-side factor that cannot be dismissed is that of the changing character of medicine and, in particular, the tendency to regard treatment as the administration of medicines. There is no doubt that there was a very substantial increase in the volume of metal-based medical substances imported into England in the last decade of the sixteenth century and the first two decades of the seventeenth.[19] We might say that after *c.* 1600 more treatments were effected by the administration of such medical substances by Paracelsian practitioners, to the detriment of the influence of traditional Galenic theorists. However, we should not assume that thereafter medicines were prescribed remotely, saving the practitioner the time of seeing the dying patient. It is important to note that there was an increased tendency for practitioners to visit their dying patients in the seventeenth century. The language of the accounts is very varied with respect to attendance, but if one assumes that references to

[17] Ian Mortimer, 'Medical Assistance to the Dying in Provincial Southern England, *c.* 1570–1720' (Ph.D. thesis, University of Exeter, 2004), I, 157–8.

[18] Payments for 'physic' by status groups A and B increased from an average of 18.1s in 1570–1609 to 30.2s in 1610–49, to 31.5s in 1660–89 and 38.4s in 1690–1719. Average payments on behalf of status C and D individuals remained between 50 per cent and 55 per cent of these amounts.

[19] The value of imports of metal-based medicines increased eightfold between 1600 and 1620. See Margaret Pelling and Charles Webster, 'Medical Practitioners', in *Health, Medicine and Mortality in the Sixteenth Century*, ed. Charles Webster (Cambridge, 1979), 165–236, especially 178–9; R. S. Roberts, 'The Early History of the Import of Drugs into England', in *The Evolution of Pharmacy in Britain*, ed. F. N. L. Poynter (1965); and R. S. Roberts, 'The Personnel and Practice of Medicine in Tudor and Stuart England', *Medical History*, part 1: 6, 4 (1962), 363–82, especially 369–70; part 2: 8, 3 (1964), 217–34, especially 227.

Table 5 *Status-related descriptions of practitioners paid*

	1570–1649		1660–1719	
	A and B	C and D	A and B	C and D
Apothecaries	68 (14%)	81 (11%)	72 (8%)	41 (6%)
Doctors	43 (9%)	44 (6%)	256 (29%)	154 (22%)
Physicians	76 (16%)	83 (11%)	149 (17%)	120 (17%)
Surgeons	62 (13%)	91 (12%)	60 (7%)	42 (6%)
Other specified	4 (1%)	8 (1%)	1 (0.1%)	1 (0.1%)
Not specified, total	217 (46%)	448 (59%)	352 (40%)	334 (48%)
For medicines	13 (3%)	21 (3%)	20 (2%)	9 (1%)
For 'physic'	150 (32%)	283 (37%)	283 (32%)	266 (38%)
For 'physic and surgery'	7 (1%)	3 (0.4%)	2 (0.2%)	1 (0.1%)
For surgery (incl. bloodletting)	7 (1%)	30 (4%)	9 (1%)	14 (2%)
For 'advice' only	3 (0.6%)	0	2 (0.2%)	0
For other services	37 (8%)	111 (15%)	36 (4%)	44 (6%)
Totals	470	755	890	692

practitioners themselves administering medicines to, carrying out surgery on and 'tending' the dying indicate attendance, then combining these with specific references to visiting, one may determine minimum attendance figures. After 1660, practitioners visited a minimum of 55 per cent of status A and B patients, compared to 22 per cent in the period 1570–1649. Similarly, practitioners visited a minimum of 47 per cent of status C and D individuals who paid for medical care after 1660, compared to just 14 per cent in the earlier period. These figures suggest that dying patients (or their families) increasingly summoned practitioners to attend them. In the context of a static number of practitioners this is not so much an indicator of increased supply as of demand. With minimum attendance levels increasing by factors of 150 per cent in respect of the higher status patients, and 235 per cent in respect of the lower, there seems to be a fundamentally different attitude on the parts of both provider and consumer towards medical help.

This difference of attitude seems to be reflected in a changing terminology. When the final accounts were made up, normally a year or so after the death, it was the next of kin who provided the description or epithet for the medical practitioner that appeared in the final account. As Table 5 makes quite plain, after 1660 the most common epithet applied to medical practitioners was 'doctor'.

Furthermore, these figures must be seen in the perspective of the significant increases in medical assistance noted in Figures 1–4. At a time when all the status groups were doubling if not trebling their use of medical services, the proportion of practitioners employed who were described as 'doctor' also more than trebled. The practitioners themselves, of course, were not all doctors of medicine in the sense of holding medical degrees; they were predominantly diocesan licentiates in surgery and medicine. But their clients called them doctors, thereby associating them with the term previously reserved for the best-qualified and most exclusive practitioners.

In the context of the above economic considerations, it is difficult to see how supply factors alone can explain the fundamental changes in the adoption of medical strategies. The increased proportions of dying patients who were visited by their practitioners, together with the ever-increasing numbers of patients requiring medical assistance, cannot easily be squared with a relatively unchanging number of medical practitioners. In addition, the increased tendency to describe practitioners by an informal but high status title, 'doctor', suggests that attitudes to medicine in the face of death were becoming more respectful. Thus, while acknowledging that supply almost certainly was a factor in the increased use of medicine by the dying, most probably based on the increased use of chemical medicines and a greater willingness to attend the dying, we must enquire as to what factors related to demand might have supported the rise of the 'doctor' in connection with treating the dying.

In considering demand, we cannot treat medical help as merely another commodity. Fear of death was considerable, fear of pain hardly less considerable, and the cost of paying for the alleviation of fear and pain – not to mention death – was of relatively little importance in comparison to the end result. Indeed, this is the problem with approaching medical history from an economic point of view: the traditional market forces one considers are two-dimensional, and what is required here is a multi-dimensional approach. One needs to consider the fundamental attitudes towards death and healing as well as towards medicine, and, in particular, the perceived power of God to punish sinners with illness and, conversely, to save the penitent from death. As a number of writers have pointed out, in the late sixteenth and early seventeenth centuries there was a widespread trust in religious causes and cures.[20] With regard to the former,

[20] See, for example, David Harley, 'Spiritual Physic, Providence and English Medicine', in *Medicine and the Reformation*, ed. Ole Peter Grell and Andrew Cunningham (1993), 101–17; Andrew Wear, 'Puritan Perceptions of Illness in Seventeenth Century England', in *Patients and Practitioners: Lay Perceptions of Medicine in Pre-industrial Society*, ed. Roy Porter (Cambridge,

David Harley, Andrew Wear and Paul Slack have demonstrated strong links between providence and sickness, from 'sickness ... as a fatherly correction by God', to 'afflictions ... as tokens of God's fatherly love' to situations where 'God might suspend the action of medicine if he saw fit' and even that experiencing 'sickness ... can mean the person is not lost forever to hellfire but may ... gain salvation'.[21] All such constructions of divine will required the penitent man to seek a solution to his malady by religious means: 'Christ the Physician' was a not-uncommon analogy at the start of the seventeenth century. However, at the same time, the importation of Paracelsian ideas and the increase in the use and availability of chemical medicines provided an alternative to spiritual physic. In this context, the probate accounts almost certainly demonstrate that, as medical strategies became available, they were taken advantage of by the dying.

The above passage might be taken to indicate that, broadly speaking, the evidence of the probate accounts supports the traditional and widely held belief that the advent of scientific methods challenged and ultimately reduced religious faith. This is a superficial reading of the evidence: it would be hard to argue that religion declined in importance over the course of the seventeenth century, and even harder to argue that it had declined by 1650, by which date the increase in medical assistance was well underway. Furthermore, there is ample evidence that providence remained an essential component of medical understanding long after the period 1620–50, when the first dramatic increases in medical usage took place. Late seventeenth-century petitions for ecclesiastical licences to practise physic and surgery normally place a very heavy emphasis on the religious credentials of the practitioner, so that he might be seen as a suitable channel for God's healing power.[22] Roy Porter contrasted Ralph Josselin making his family's illnesses a providential issue with Pepys, who understood his illnesses in purely secular and medical terms.[23] Ralph Houlbrooke has similarly contrasted the attitudes of Bulstrode Whitelocke and Ralph Josselin to demonstrate that providential and medical attitudes co-existed throughout the seventeenth century. Houlbrooke in fact makes a convincing case that providence still had a part to play in attitudes to

1983), 55–100; Andrew Wear, 'Religious Beliefs and Medicine in Early Modern England', in *The Task of Healing*, ed. Hilary Marland and Margaret Pelling (Rotterdam, 1996), 146–69.

[21] These quotes all come from Harley, 'Spiritual Physic', 102, 107, except the last which is from Wear, 'Religious Beliefs', 152. For providence as a cause of suffering see Paul Slack, *The Impact of Plague in Tudor and Stuart England* (1985), 39–40.

[22] Ian Mortimer, 'Diocesan Licensing and Medical Practitioners in South-West England, 1660–1780', *Medical History*, 48 (2004), 64.

[23] Dorothy Porter and Roy Porter, *Patients Progress* (1989), 5.

early eighteenth-century illness, based on the diary of Richard Kay.[24] Thus there can be little doubt that what we are witnessing in the medicalisation of the dying in provincial southern England is not a conflict between religious and medical strategies but a situation in which the latter emerged from the shadow of the former. Indeed, religious views on death and illness probably encouraged a shift towards medical strategies. This is most clearly illustrated in a letter from Maria Thynne to her husband, dated 1608:

> Remember we are bound in conscience to maintain life as long as is possible, and though God's power can work miracles, yet we cannot build upon it that because He can, He will, for then He would not say He made herb[s] for the use of man.[25]

Herein lies our 'conflict' between perceptions of spiritual cure and medical relief. Within a spiritual context one could take medicines because they were provided by God for that purpose.

The implications of this argument are considerable. Our multi-dimensional approach to medical intervention allows us to see the increased importation of medical substances and the spread of Paracelsian ideas within a framework of expanding religious horizons. Medicines were not just an alternative to prayer, they were a supplement to prayer. The adoption of a medical strategy alongside a religious one increased the number of ways in which God's cure might be effected. This explains why medical – normally characterised as scientific – ideas and discoveries so quickly took hold within communities: in the eyes of the dying man a new therapy was not a challenge to God's power but a blessing. Repeated decades of such blessings, however, resulted in the focus shifting from God as the provider to the therapy itself. After 1690, when the majority of people tended to choose a medical strategy to cope with fatal illness and injury, the religious framework to medical cure had ceased to dominate attitudes to treatment in the face of death.

Another important implication of this argument lies in its relevance to the debate about individualism and death initiated by Clare Gittings in her study of probate accounts.[26] Gittings argues, on the basis of funeral behaviour by families and kin networks after death, especially at the funeral, that life and death became conceptually separated in the seventeenth century along the lines proposed by Ariès, and that the individual came to fear death as a personal affliction. Her argument has been questioned by Ralph Houlbrooke in the introduction to his *Death, Ritual and Bereavement.*[27] He suggests that the evidence she presents

[24] Ralph Houlbrooke, *Death, Religion and the Family in England 1480–1750* (Oxford, 1998), 74, 184–5.

[25] Quoted in *ibid.*, 18–19.

[26] Clare Gittings, *Death, Burial and the Individual in Early Modern England* (1984).

[27] *Death, Ritual, and Bereavement*, ed. Ralph Houlbrooke (1989).

about 'traditional group ties' dissolving and leaving a core of family-only mourners does not fit the far broader explanatory framework she provides. However, the data presented here suggest that the treatment of the dying (rather than the dead) would support her broad idea of emerging individualism in relation to death. Individuals' increased tendency to pursue medical strategies to cope with death strongly suggests that they were not exclusively relying on prayer, and, by implication, that individuals and families were taking responsibility for their own physical well-being in the face of death.

Mention of the word 'individualism' immediately draws attention to other work, and in particular Alan Macfarlane's work on the origins of English individualism.[28] A comparison of 'individualism' as expressed in the passage above and in that work is instructive. Despite Macfarlane's generic use of the word in his title, he is actually describing economic individualism and independence in contrast to collective existence within peasant society. It could be said that the above passages locate medical individualism for the seriously ill and dying in the seventeenth century. Macfarlane stated that 'individualism in economic and social life is much older than this [1500] in England'.[29] If Macfarlane's thesis is correct, and if the above passages are correct in relating increased consumption of medical services by the dying to an emerging individualism, we have an apparent inconsistency in timing. However, there is no reason why economic 'individualism' could not have arisen much earlier than mortality-related 'individualism', defined as a deliberate and physical act of self-preservation in the face of death. Indeed, such a comparison invites the generic term 'individualism' to be broken into many sorts of behaviour, a whole series of 'individualisms', each a shard breaking away from collective existence.

The passages above allow us to propose a new model for the medicalisation of serious illnesses and injuries resulting in death, and to explain how that medicalisation might have been fostered within the apparently non-scientific framework of religious orthodoxy. The essence of this change we may regard lying in the nature of the new medical ideas and substances that came into England in the last decade of the sixteenth century and the early decades of the seventeenth. Being a medical philosophy essentially composed of *things*, which could be regarded as substances provided by God, and which thus did not in themselves question that the origin of healing power lay with God (unlike, for example, magic), they provided an ancillary process through which the desperate and dying could seek relief. This approach provides a refinement of the theory proposed by Keith Thomas in the last

[28] Alan Macfarlane, *The Origins of English Individualism* (Oxford, 1978).
[29] *Ibid.*, 196.

chapter of *Religion and the Decline of Magic*.[30] Therein Thomas argued that magic weakened as people gained greater control over the environment, although he admitted that the explanation of how 'magical' systems of belief came to be seen as 'intellectually unsatisfactory' was far from clear, there being 'too many "rationalists" beforehand and too many believers afterwards'.[31] Control over the 'environment' (including the landscape of disease) may well have been a contributory factor, but the process by which one belief system gives way to another should not necessarily be seen in terms of conflict. The strength of belief in spiritual physic when medical strategies to life-threatening diseases and injuries were becoming universally popular suggests rather that a religious system might have given way naturally to a scientific one through a process of accommodating scientific changes within the existing religious framework, the 'rationalists' being a consequence of the widespread development of a relevant 'individualism'.

In conclusion, the seventeenth century witnessed a revolution in attitudes to medical assistance on behalf of the dying. Practitioners who served them were elevated from receiving mere occupational descriptors – 'physician' and 'surgeon' – to an epithet of learning and distinction: 'doctor'. Furthermore, these 'doctors' in a short while gained control of a market which had hitherto been dominated by that most mighty of physicians: God. They succeeded in persuading the seriously ill and dying that they offered a supplementary channel for divine healing power. In this they indeed triumphed. But it has to be remarked that their victory was due to a religious framework that proved broadly tolerant of medical development. It does not appear to have been a contest in which rationalism defeated religion, rather that religion encouraged individual choice and, with it, rationalism. In the course of this process, more medicines led to increased demand for medical services by empowering individuals to take responsibility for their own lives. Or at least it did so by encouraging people to believe they were taking action to facilitate divine healing. When trying to understand medical strategies in the face of imminent or likely death, one should not underestimate such beliefs.

[30] Keith Thomas, *Religion and the Decline of Magic* (1971).
[31] *Ibid.*, 647.

Transactions of the RHS 15 (2005), pp. 117–147
doi:10.1017/S0080440105000289 Printed in the United Kingdom

MODERNISATION AS SOCIAL EVOLUTION: THE GERMAN CASE, *c.* 1800–1880

By John Breuilly

READ 23 JANUARY 2004 AT THE GERMAN HISTORICAL INSTITUTE, LONDON

ABSTRACT. This essay outlines a theory of modernisation that is related to changes in the German lands. Modernisation is defined as societal transformation from corporate to functionally specialised institutions. The focus is upon institutions as modes of power (coercive, economic, cultural) and how these modernise through processes of social evolution. Specific types of change are considered for the periods 1800–15 (coercive-political power), 1815–48 (economic power), the revolutions of mid-century (cultural power) and the era of German unification (coercive-military power). A concluding section considers the main patterns of modernisation over the whole period and the kind of modern social order that had been achieved by 1880.

Introductory remarks

In less than a century the German lands became modern. In this essay I outline what I mean by that statement and propose a way of describing and analysing that change. I argue that modernisation should be understood as societal transformation. I criticise some approaches to modernisation. I propose treating modernisation as social evolution; the selection of some social practices in favour of others; a process which cumulatively and increasingly rapidly effects the transformation into a modern social order. I analyse a few examples to provide support for this argument.

Indices of societal transformation

Conventional indices of modernisation take the form of quantitative measures of political, social and economic change. Between 1780 and 1871 the number of states in the German lands reduced from hundreds to two. Figures 1–3 summarise population growth, urbanisation and labour force change.

One could add many more indices, e.g. on formal schooling, communication and transportation, elections, medical provision, the

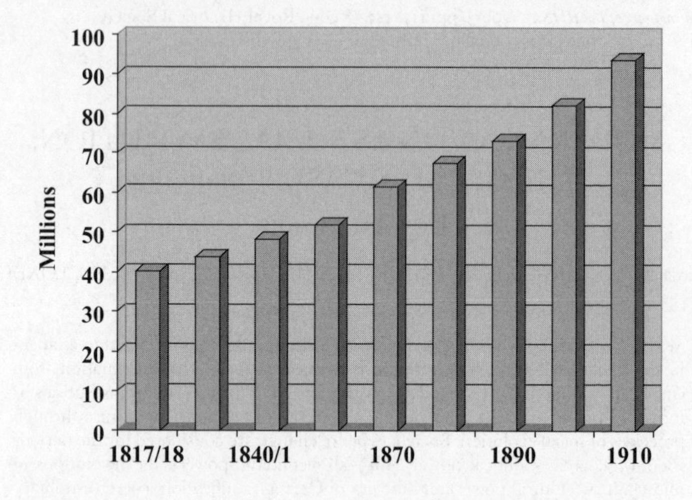

Figure 1 Population of the German lands (including Austria), 1817/18–1910

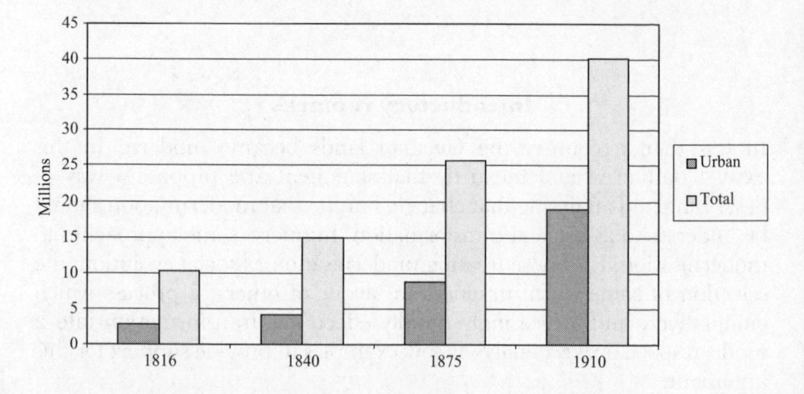

Figure 2 Urban growth and urbanisation in Prussia, 1816–1910

rise of new professions and research institutions, the industrialisation of warfare.[1] Why, however, should such specific and varied quantitative measures be regarded as indices of a broader, qualititative change called modernisation?

[1] For demography and labour force figures see *Sozialgeschichtliches Arbeitsbuch I*, ed. Wolfram Fischer *et al.* (Munich, 1982), 21, 52. For urbanisation see John Breuilly, 'Urbanisation and Social Transformation, 1800–1914, in *Germany: A New Social and Economic History*, III: *Since 1800*, ed. Sheilagh Ogilvie and Richard Overy (2003), 193.

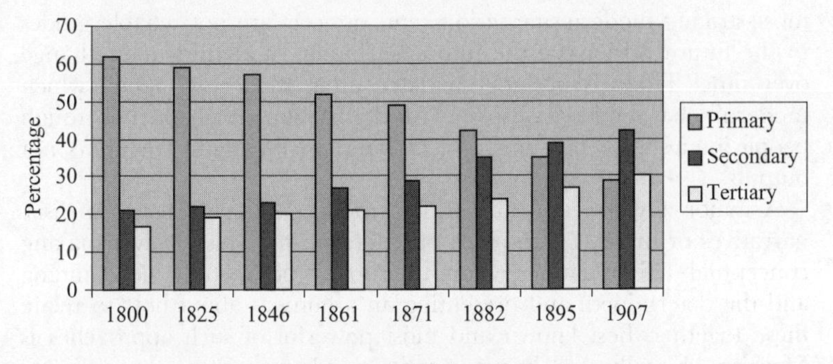

Figure 3 Distribution of the labour force, 1800–1907

I argue that modernisation is a *determinate transformation* rather than just one phase in an open-ended, long-term process of loosely related changes. Specific changes in economy or polity or culture are connected to one another. To demonstrate these connections requires a conceptual framework that engages with the transformation as a whole.

It is not enough to describe change in terms of lists, such as provided by these indices. Grand narratives connecting items on the list are better but still inadequate. A narrative requires a subject that is the bearer of the story told. That is possible with a genre such as biography, though even then one confronts problems concerning identity and boundaries. However, where large-scale, long-term change is involved there is no immediately identifiable subject. What do we mean, for example, when we use the word 'Germany' to designate the subject of a narrative history? Germany is usually taken to be some end-point, such as the German Second Empire or the Third Reich, and 'its' earlier history is the story of how this 'Germany' came about. This is not an illegitimate approach but it tells us nothing about that earlier 'Germany' which is both more and less than an anticipation of that later Germany. Furthermore, the 'Second Empire' or the 'Third Reich' are concepts, not some immediately apprehended subject. Grand narratives only work when, operating beneath their surface, are concepts which do the necessary interpretative work.[2]

Modernisation cannot be understood as a *project*, that is the successful and consciously intended work of modernisers. Long-run, large-scale transformation is the product of many interactions between agents with severe if variable limitations on their power and foresight. Even the

[2] This is the case, for example, with Thomas Nipperdey's narrative history of nineteenth-century Germany as I argued in an extensive review of the first volume, *Deutsche Geschichte 1800–1866: Bürgerwelt und starker Staat* (Munich, 1983), published in the *Bulletin of the German Historical Institute*, 16 (1984), 23–34.

most striking modernising visions and projects are not reliable guides to the future. Visions of the future, including modernist ones, change over time. There is nothing so dated as a 'modernist' vision which modernity has rendered obsolete.[3] Modernisation only happens through people intentionally pursuing projects but those intentions are inputs, not outputs.

A major advance upon describing modernisation in terms of lists, narratives or projects is the idea of determinism. This involves making conceptual differentiations within the subject (between the determining and the determined) and presenting an argument about how to relate these together. Best known and most powerful of such approaches is Marxism. Equally well known are its problems such as the difficulty of making the determining/determined distinction or, once made, of connecting what is distinguished, e.g. as economic base and non-economic superstructure. The point applies with even greater force to less clear or developed determinist approaches that focus on technology or culture or politics.

Given these difficulties and the crudity and ideological character of 'modernisation theory' developed in the 1960s, it is understandable if the dominant reaction of historians is to finesse or avoid the challenge of explaining the achievement of modernity. One finesse is to break down 'grand narrative' into 'special narratives' (political, economic, cultural, etc.). This only displaces the problem of identifying subjects for analysis to the level of special narratives and raises an additional problem of linking together the narratives. One can see this in the *Gesellschaftsgeschichte* project of Hans-Ulrich Wehler.[4] The Germany that Prussia unified in 1871 identifies the subject, and the narrative for the preceding period is an elaborate anticipation of this unification. Modernisation is treated as a project in which certain social types (industrialists, profit-seeking farmers, rational scientists, professional bureaucrats) prevail over other types (subsistence farmers, guildsmen, priests, courtiers). The ideal typical distinctions between politics, economics and culture provide the basis for the special narratives, though the connections are presented in explicitly Weberian and non-determinist terms. A fourth set of chapters on 'social inequality' functions as a device for linking together the special narratives. Wehler's work represents the most sustained and theoretically explicit

[3] For studies of changing conceptions of the (modern) future see Eric Dorn Brose, *The Politics of Technological Change in Prussia: Out of the Shadow of Antiquity, 1809–1848* (New Jersey, 1993); and Rudolf Boch, *Grenzenloses Wachstum? Das rheinische Wirtschaftsbürgertum und seine Industrialisierungsdebatte 1814–1857* (Göttingen, 1991).

[4] Hans-Ulrich Wehler, *Deutsche Gesellschaftsgeschichte*. So far four volumes have been published (all Munich): covering 1700–1815 (1987), 1815–45/9 (1987), 1849–1914 (1995), 1914–49 (2003) with a fifth volume planned.

engagement with the challenge of grasping modern German history as societal transformation but remains a very problematic achievement.[5]

The final response is evasion. Micro-history and the analysis of discourse have made valuable contributions to our historical understanding but they rest on an implicit understanding of a macro-historical and non-discursive context within which their own subjects make sense. If one does accept that there actually *was* a distinct societal transformation, that modernity *is* a distinct kind of social order unlike anything that preceded it, then one requires a definition of modernisation and concepts for analysing it.

Modernisation as a determinate societal transformation

I define modernisation as *a transformation in the societal division of labour from multi-functional to single-function institutions*. Modernisation is societal change in the direction of institutions with specialised functions and extensive societal reach.

Pre-modern multi-functional institutions vary greatly, making such terms as 'pre-modern' or 'traditional' vacuous. One requires concepts with more specific content. In the case of pre-modern central Europe I argue that the institutional order is best characterised as *corporate*. So my specific definition of modernisation in relation to the German lands is: *a transformation in the societal division of labour from corporate to single-function institutions*.

I use two ideal types: corporate and single-function institutions, and trace out the paths by which one moves from one to the other. I focus on the way these institutions function as modes of power, considering other features only when necessary to understand these institutions as modes of power. In developing the notion of modes of power I draw on Mann and Runciman.[6] Mann distinguishes four modes of power: political, military, economic and ideological. I largely follow him, except I argue that with the rise of the modern state political and military power are so closely integrated as to require common treatment. I adopt Gellner's term of coercion for this combined form of power.[7] I use the term 'cultural power' instead of 'ideological power'.[8] Figure 4 provides a crude representation

[5] I have developed these criticisms in an extensive reviews of the first two volumes of *Deutsche Gesellschaftsgeschichte* in *German History*, 9/2 (1991), 211–30.

[6] Michael Mann, *Sources of Social Power*, II: *The Rise of Classes and Nation-States, 1760–1914* (Cambridge, 1993); W. J. Runciman, *A Treatise on Social Theory*, II: *Substantive Social Theory* (Cambridge, 1989).

[7] Ernest Gellner, *Plough, Sword, Book* (1988), operates with the tripartite scheme of coercion, cognition and production. Runciman criticises Mann's two kinds of coercive power but uses the term political power to describe the single category.

[8] Runciman, like Mann, uses the term ideological. Gellner uses the more neutral term cognition but that seems too broad to me. I have fastened upon the term 'cultural' because

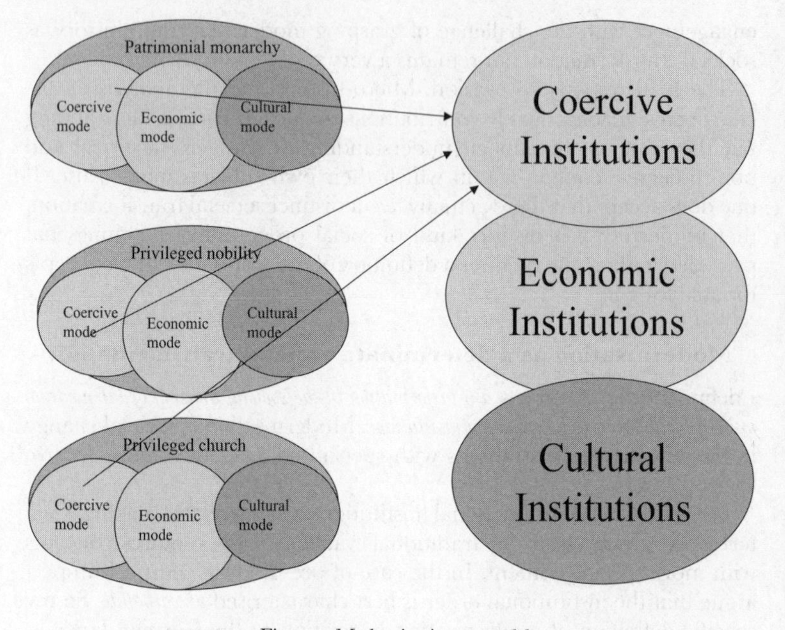

Figure 4 Modernisation: a model

of the transformation involved. The corporate institutions represent a selection; one could add others such as artisan and merchant guilds, privileged towns and city-states.

Modernisation thus defined involves a 'double transformation' of functional concentration and specialisation. This is why modernisation is simultaneously associated with an increase of both individual freedom and institutional power. The state becomes *more* powerful as a set of coercive institutions into which political and military power is concentrated, reaching across all society; it also becomes *less* powerful as these institutions are deprived of significant economic and cultural powers which in turn are concentrated into other institutions with wide societal reach. One of the great problems that modernity confronts concerns the tensions created by this double transformation.

My definition and focus is institutional. (I understand institutions to include all patterned forms of interaction in which people play

it can be understood in modern society in terms of specific institutions and spheres of life (although some theorists extend it to cover all forms of life), unlike cognition, but does not carry associations of indoctrination, class rule or false consciousness which the term ideology has come to acquire. However, there is no fully satisfactory term available.

determinate roles, i.e. not just formal organisations but also labour markets, elections, citizenship and religious worship.) One advantage of this focus is that historical evidence relating to the actions of large groups is tied closely to institutions because many sources are produced either by the institutions themselves or as testimony from observers of those institutions. A second advantage is that institutions, being shaped by the values and interests of their members, can be treated as quasi-agents. One difficulty with a focus on class or occupation as a set of social positions within a structure is that of moving from the objectively defined set to the values and interests embodied in social action. Conversely, a difficulty with a focus on culture as subjectively affirmed values, meanings and interests is that of connecting these to collective social action. (More concisely: classes – or other similarly defined collectivities – do not 'act' or 'speak', so how can actors be understood in class or other collective terms?) Institutions that are made up of people, usually from specific social positions and sharing certain values, meanings and interests, enable the historian to make such connections.

So far what I have presented is simply the juxtaposition of two ideal types and the logic of how one moves from one to the other. Logic does not explain historical change. One could as easily place the 'modern' ideal type before the 'corporate' one. ('De-modernisation' is not just logically possible but sometimes happens.) To turn this into an instrument of historical explanation I introduce the notion of social evolution. I understand the exercise of power within a particular institution to be a 'social practice'. There is constant competition between different social practices (within and between institutions) as well as modifications to such practices. Some practices fare better in that competition than others; through a process of selection some practices replace others as the principal modes of power. Using modernisation as a way of explaining rather than simply describing change involves asking why modern social practices displace corporate ones. I further argue that such displacement in one area has dynamic effects in other areas, forcing either further change or reversal of the original change. This helps account for the rapid and expanding nature of modernisation.

Putting the ideas to work

Historians reading thus far could reasonably ask why this essay appears in an historical journal and not a periodical concerned with abstract social theory. As an historian I have found it necessary to think theoretically in the ways described but the justification for so doing is to understand specific historical change.

I begin by relating the 'corporate' ideal type to late eighteenth-century Germany, detailing the pressures that were already undermining this societal division of labour. I then focus on changes in the coercive-political mode of power in the Napoleonic period, the economic mode of power in the decades after 1815, the cultural mode of power during the revolutions of the mid-century and the coercive-military mode of power in the era of the wars of national unification. Finally I present Germany in *c.* 1880 as 'modern' societal order of a specific kind and draw some brief conclusions about the major patterns of modernisation.

The unravelling of corporate institutions

The societal division of labour in mid-eighteenth-century central Europe, including the German lands, can be described as corporate. Such a model would be inappropriate for Britain, the Netherlands or North America where competitive commerce, individualised property rights and parliamentary politics, amongst other practices, prevailed. It would make little sense in the Romanov empire that lacked an elaborate range of semi-autonomous corporations. It would not work in such non-European settings such as Mughal India, the Ottoman Empire and Manchu China. Furthermore, the corporate model varies in form and character across central Europe, as contrasting patterns of land tenure make clear. I am not presenting a general theory of modernisation but a specific theory tailored to the conditions of the German lands.

Many scholars would dispute the validity even of this narrowly focused corporate model. One could argue that it represents an idealised mode of thinking, comparing the 'good old times' when guild masters, noble landowners, patrimonial monarchs and privileged church establishments worked harmoniously together to sustain a stable order in which all knew their place. There never was such a time; even when corporations were powerful and effective they were riven with personal conflicts (masters against journeymen, courtiers against ministers), intra-institutional conflict (guilds against one another, churches in doctrinal conflict) and inter-institutional conflict (monarchs encroaching on noble power, city oligarchs attacking guilds). They were also engaged in constant efforts to repress alternative social practices (rural craftsmen against urban guilds, free churches against church establishments).

One could further argue that the last two kinds of conflict had already undermined the corporate model. The expansion of monarchical power involved the destruction of other corporations. Free thinking and free labour (the latter associated with demographic growth that produced an underclass with no 'place' in the corporate order) was pressing towards a different kind of social order, the kind we associate with the Enlightenment and political economy. The rapid changes that followed the French revolution of 1789 were only possible given this earlier hollowing out of the corporate order.[9]

However, one should not exaggerate these pressures. Church establishments still wielded much corporate power. Peasant emancipation had barely begun and privileged claims, whether directly over labour services or over payments in kind or money made in lieu of such services, dominated the agrarian economy. A monarch's own patrimony remained a major part of his revenue. Even if some textile and metal manufacturing for distant markets had escaped corporate controls, much production for local markets remained under guild control. The battles that would be fought over the next century on issues such as expropriation of church property, abolition of guilds and peasant emancipation provide indications of the continued significance of the corporate order.

The French revolution included a cultural assault upon this order. Yet, so tenacious was the hold of that corporate world even upon its critics, that they often simply transferred corporate values into a non-corporate setting. The stress upon the 'honour' of the citizen that dominated revolutionary rhetoric in the 1790s represents an attempt to preserve the prestige of corporate honour (the honour of the nobleman, of guilded labour) and attach it to new social practices while 'dishonouring' the older social practices.[10]

However, my concern is not with France but with the German lands. I take up the analysis at the point where Napoleon's domination and reorganisation of the German lands has been seen as a crucial step towards modernisation.

Napoleonic Germany and political modernisation[11]

By 1810 Napoleon had completely reorganised the state system of the German lands. Figure 5 represents the territorial dimension of this reorganisation.

France annexed various German lands such as the left-bank of the Rhine (organised into four French departments) and the Hanseatic towns. Within the Confederation of the Rhine (*Rheinbund*) it established new states under direct French rule (principally the 'model states' of the Kingdom

[9] For the eighteenth-century background see Wehler, *Deutsche Gesellschaftsgeschichte*, I; and more specifically on demographic growth and 'free' labour, see Jürgen Kocka, *Weder Stand noch Klasse. Unterschichten um 1800* (Bonn, 1990).

[10] Gail Bossenga, 'Status, Corps and Monarchy: Roots of Modern Citizenship in the Old Regime', in *Tocqueville and Beyond: Essays on the Old Regime in Honor of David D. Bien*, ed. Robert M. Schwartz and Robert A. Schneider (Newark, 2003), 127–54.

[11] For a fuller version of the arguments of this section see John Breuilly, 'Napoleonic Germany and State-Formation', in *Collaboration and Resistance in Napoleonic Europe: State-Formation in an Age of Upheaval, c. 1800–1815*, ed. Michael Rowe (Basingstoke, 2003), 121–52. I refer the reader to the notes to that essay for further secondary literature.

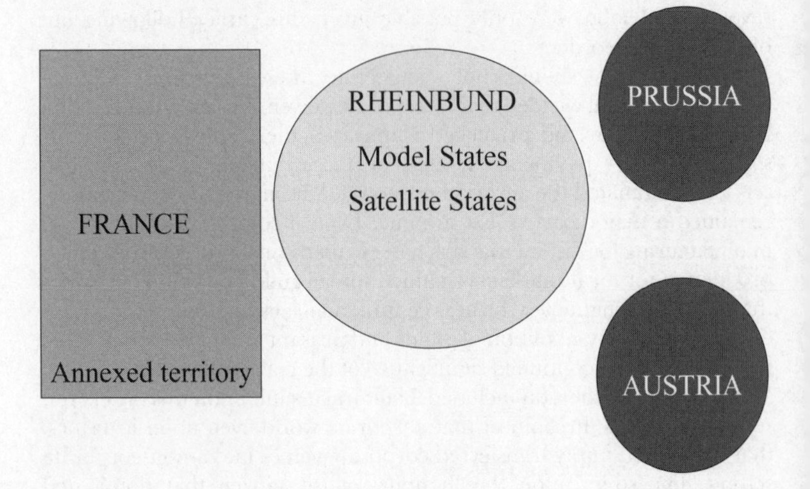

Figure 5 Napoleon's empire – the German lands

of Westphalia and the Grand Duchy of Berg) as well as making extensive territorial changes to lands ruled by established German princes. Prussia and Austria remained outside the Confederation but within the French zone of influence, bound by treaties (such as the military alliance that required Prussia to furnish troops for the invasion of Russia in 1812) and dynastic ties (the marriage of Napoleon to the daughter of the Austrian emperor).

There is a well-founded interpretation of the Prussian response to Napoleon as modernisation, drawing upon research into such subjects as guild reform, peasant emancipation, financial, constitutional, bureaucratic and military reform. This research developed, in a sociological and theoretical way, an older historiography that already discerned in Napoleonic Prussia the instrument for the later unification of Germany.

Research of the 1970s and 1980s into the 'third Germany' was also concerned with modernisation. Fehrenbach analysed resistance to the French Civil Code, seen as a modern legal framework, and how the code was diluted or turned to other purposes.[12] Berding showed how modernising political and economic reforms in model states were undermined by military exploitation and the creation of an imperial

[12] Elizabeth Fehrenbach, 'Der Kampf um die Einführung des Code Napoléon in den Rheinbundstaaten', in *Politische Umbruch und gesellschaftliche Bewegung*, ed. Hans-Werner Hahn and Jürgen Müller (Munich, 1997), 49–72.

nobility.[13] Ullmann analysed the modernisation of state debt.[14] Wunder described the formation of modern state bureaucracies.[15] This research shifted the concern with modernisation from Prussia to the medium-sized states and introduced new themes such as constitutionalism and representation.

Finally, there was a general, if unspoken, assumption that Austrian Germany, after the stalling of the Josephine reform movement in the late eighteenth century, failed to participate in this modernisation drive.

Much of this research is ongoing, for example on the impact of secularisation of church lands and powers. To this one must add work placing Napoleonic Germany within a European perspective, relating it to innovative research elsewhere. However, the idea of modernisation is less central in much of that non-German research. Insofar as there is a concern with modernisation there are three points of agreement.

First, modernisation was was a 'top-down' process, focused on political and military reform. Even apparently 'societal' reforms such as peasant emancipation or abolition of guilds were motivated by political projects such as raising tax revenue, reducing state expenditure and evoking citizen loyalty.

Second, modernisation was an intentional project. The use of adjectives like defensive and offensive imply this for Prussia while the main focus of 'third Germany' research has been on rulers and their key officials as deliberate modernisers, seeking to continue an older absolutist project and to emulate Napoleon.

Third, the brevity of the Napoleonic period means that reform is only significant if it continues into the post-Napoleonic period.

I seek instead to shift the focus from modernisation as project to modernisation as process and to see this process in terms of how more modern social practices were selected (or not) for success.

One can start by noting differences between reform projects in various regions. Take the issue of abolishing privileged inequality, a crucial feature of a corporate society. There were three different methods: through civil law, constitutional law and societal reform. Models for all three were available from the German Enlightenment and absolutist reform traditions and, more importantly, the French example. Austria introduced in 1811 a civil code that attacked privilege and made no attempt at constitutional innovation. Subjects were made equal not by conferring

[13] Hermut Berding, *Napoleonische Herrschafts- und Gesellschaftspolitik im Königreich Westfalen 1807–1813* (Göttingen, 1973).

[14] Hans-Peter Ullmann, *Staatschulden und Reformpolitik: die Entstehung moderner öffentlicher Schulden in Bayern und Baden, 1780–1820* (Göttingen, 1986).

[15] Bernd Wunder, *Privilegierung und Disziplinierung: die Entstehung des Berufsbeamtentums in Bayern und Württemberg (1780–1825)* (Munich and Vienna, 1978). Wunder has published a further study of the Baden bureaucracy and a general history of German bureaucracy.

citizenship or representational rights but in the private sphere of society. Bavaria enacted a constitution with the focus on equality before the state, not representation in the state. Prussia experimented with devices for political representation and consultation but did not seek to enact a constitution, only trying this in one limited sphere with an urban government ordinance. Prussia did not introduce a civil code formally abolishing privilege; instead it enacted a series of societal reforms such as peasant emancipation and abolition of guilds.

In all these cases there were people with competing reform projects as well as those resisting such projects. The difficult task is not to narrate stories of 'success' but to explain the underlying selection process involved. One can start with failure rather than success. The most obvious case is where a project encounters resistance that leads to abandonment. The attempt made by the chancellor, Karl August von Hardenberg, at a sweeping centralisation of state power with his *Polizei Edikt* of 1812 failed in the face of opposition from nobles defending their local privileges, including policing powers. Selection here is a function of entrenched power.

More difficult to understand is why an appropriate policy failed even to become significant. Here one must identify crucial background conditions that shape selection. I enumerate three: territorial change, degree of external autonomy and degree of internal autonomy.

Napoleon changed state boundaries radically and often. There was only one short period of relative stability, between 1807 and 1812, and in this period urgent but different problems were posed by the kind of territorial changes made.

Crudely one can distinguish between states which expanded, those which remained static and those which contracted. The more important *Rheinbund* states were created by means of expansion; Austria and Prussia both lost territory.

Expansion came about in two basic ways: the addition of peripheral territories to a state 'core' or the amalgamation of a number of small territories. The most extreme example of the first was the annexation of left-bank Rhine territories to France; the most extreme example of the second was Nassau. Bavaria was a weaker example of core plus periphery, Baden a weaker example of amalgamation. Pure amalgamation tended to 'pure' state despotism as the new ruler could not draw upon the traditions and interests of a core territory but at the same time confronted fragmented and weak elites in the various parts of the new state that could not put up much resistance to centralising and rationalising measures. A strong core provided the basis for extending its political practices to the periphery. In both cases the stress of state reform was on integration and creating legitimacy for the new state.

Contraction increased rather than diluted the power of political practices in the core territory: the crownlands of Austria, Brandenburg and East Prussia. Secure in that core, the government did not face a problem of integration. Any reform programme had other concerns.

We can see what these might be by turning to the degree of external autonomy. The *Rheinbund* focus on integration and legitimacy of the new state was intensified by the fact that these states had virtually no external autonomy. Furthermore, their reform programme was constantly at threat from France. Indeed, Napoleon's interventions in such forms as seizing land to endow an imperial nobility or requisitioning men, money and materials for his military projects, undercut the internal reform programme. In turn it exposed tensions, if not contradictions, between different aspects of his own imperial project, neatly summarised by Napoleon himself: 'Either we must bring the governments of our neighbours into line with ours, or we must align our political system more with theirs. There will always exist a state of war between the old monarchies and a new republic.'[16]

What one faces here is 'incoherent empire' in the sense that different modes of power – culturally through exporting participatory notions of the revolution, militarily through brute requisition, economically through co-opting local elites, politically by creating an imperial nobility – worked against each other.[17]

Austria and Prussia had more autonomy. Austria, as the greater power, had the most, so much so that it could go to war once more in 1809, with disastrous consequences. Even after that Austria sought to stabilise its relationship with France by drawing Napoleon back to traditional political practices: notably, marriage to the daughter of the Austrian emperor. It was not a coincidence that this return to old regime practices as an alternative either to military resistance or emulatory reforms was associated with the appointment of Metternich as Austrian chancellor in 1810.

Prussia had no capacity for such negotiation or leverage, a rump state located precariously between France and Russia. However, it possessed more autonomy than *Rheinbund* states in internal matters. With territorial contraction state integration was not a problem. The first purpose of reforms was to recover from the devastating effects of 1806. Reforms focused on trying to settle deserted agricultural land, increase state revenue (to pay off the indemnity imposed by Napoleon) and streamline government. Recovery was not about restoration of pre-1806 power; only a small minority harboured such fantasises. The main tension was between the reform programme and the elite power of the core territory, above all the landed nobility. As Koselleck argued powerfully, schemes of representation, necessary to gain elite consent to borrowing and other

[16] Quoted in Andreas Schulz, *Herrschaft durch Verwaltung. Die Rheinbundreformen in Hessen-Darmstadt unter Napoleon (1803–1815)* (Stuttgart, 1991), 67.

[17] I take the term from the title of Michael Mann's book *Incoherent Empire* (2003).

measures, foundered on the realistic fear of reformers that representative institutions would block the most necessary reforms.[18] Success was only possible in urban government because urban elites were too weak to pose such a threat.

These considerations take us to the third major condition for selection of reforms: the availability of elites that could act as vehicles for reforms. Creating a regime of free landed property would only produce radical, modernising change if there was a class of people – a bourgeoisie well-endowed with capital and seeing commercial possibilities or a prosperous peasantry seeking secure property rights – that could buy up the land made available. This was not the case in war-devastated Prussia. So peasant emancipation worked mainly to the benefit of the nobility. When Bavaria could not find purchasers for the church lands it secularised, it continued to run these lands as the church had done. However, in the left-bank regions annexed to France there was a wealthy class of merchants who seized the opportunities provided by French law and institutions. Elsewhere Fehrenbach has shown that attempts to introduce the Code Napoleon foundered on the absence of such a monied bourgeoisie as well as of a professional class of lawyers able to operate the code.[19]

The degree and type of territorial change, the amount of autonomy and the structure of available elites explain why some reforms were never attempted, although they were 'thinkable', why other reforms were blocked or distorted, and why in some cases there was success. The account starts with intentional projects but explanation focuses on the conditions that mean that one rather than another project is selected for success.

There remains the question of whether such reforms as did result constituted modernisation. To answer this one must go beyond 1815 because a longer time perspective is necessary.

In making such an evaluation the first thing is to note that it is *function, not form* which matters. Obtaining efficiency in central government by means of rationalisation is *not* to be equated with modernisation. If the central government simply seizes the assets of other institutions but continues to use them in the same way as before, albeit more intensively ('rationally'), this could block modernisation. Wunder, for example, interprets the construction of a 'modern' bureaucracy in Bavaria as a sign of modernisation. Yet what actually occurred was the formation of a new corporate elite, complete with uniforms and strict rules about internal hierarchy and security of office.[20]

[18] Reinhard Koselleck, *Preußen zwischen Reform und Revolution: Allgemeines Landrecht, Verwaltung und sozialen Bewegung von 1791 bis 1848*, 3rd edn (Stuttgart, 1981).

[19] Elizabeth Fehrenbach, *Traditionale Gesellschaft und revolutionäres Recht: die Einführung des Code Napoléon in den Rheinbundstaaten*, 2nd edn (Göttingen, 1978).

[20] Wunder, *Privilegierung.*

Furthermore, many such reforms did not extend beyond the centre. If we consider the state not as central government, but as the sum total of politically coercive institutions and practices operating over a given territory, for most subjects nothing significant changed. Government officials rather than monks might collect dues from peasants but it was the continuity of the exactions that mattered to peasants.

By contrast many Prussian reforms were genuinely modernising. The Prussian state was less successful than some *Rheinbund* states in centralising power and establishing a powerful state bureaucracy. However, it was more successful in taking coercive powers away from corporations such as guilds. It also undermined the hereditary caste power of noble manorial owners, facilitating the rapid turnover of estates in the deflationary period of the early 1820s.

However, it was vital that conditions continued to favour selection of modern social practices after 1815. Retrenchment – above all the running down of large armies – undid many military and associated reforms. Yet retrenchment also continued the undermining of corporate power begun in Napoleonic Prussia. It was beyond the power of the state to lead an offensive to restore powerful guilds or restrictive noble privilege, even if it had wished to do so. Weaker corporate power made easier the abolition of internal tariff barriers, the integration of enclaves separating Prussia's post-1815 western provinces from the rest of the state, the move to a general customs union project and later the enforcement of freedom of movement across the whole state. As such policies were institutionalised, so a new class of officials were socialised into an ideology of economic liberalism which reflected and justified such policies.

Where guild or land tenure reform was carried out for fiscal or economic purposes, this had unintended consequences for such matters as local government and peasant/privileged landowner relations. Rural craftsmen or peasant proprietors with economic freedom became dissatisfied with owners of noble estates maintaining exclusive powers over local judicial and government offices.[21] Thus a dynamic was built into the modernising process. For the period after 1815 I will pick up on one aspect of this: economic regionalisation.

Economic regionalisation, 1815–48

The period after 1815 is frequently presented in negative terms. The term 'Restoration' looks back to the pre-1815 period; that of 'Vormärz' (meaning before March 1848) looks forward to the 1848 revolution.

[21] Prussia instituted an interesting practice whereby owners of what had been noble estates acquired the privileges of nobility associated with those estates, even if not personally of noble title. The *form* of nobility is preserved but the *function* is quite different, related to the commercial pursuit of land and farming.

Metternich, the Austrian chancellor, is the archetypal figure for the period, associated with opposition to progressive movements associated with nationalism, liberalism and democracy.

At the economic level this period can appear as uneventful. The rural–urban distribution remained constant; factory manufacturing a marginal feature of total production. Yet this conceals significant changes. Most important were sharp increases in agrarian productivity and output of manufactured articles such as clothing, shoes and metal goods produced domestically or in small workshops located both in town and countryside.[22] In considering these changes as modernisation of economic power, I focus on regionalisation. Regionalisation provides a measure of functional specialisation and helps explain modernisation in the agricultural and proto-industrial sectors.

It is not easy to formulate a concept of region that is both conceptually satisfactory (exemplifying specialised economic activity on a territorial basis) and operational (linked to good data). States, the best unit for data collection, do not correspond to significant economic regions. (For example, the two western provinces of Prussia cannot be included in an economic region with the other six provinces.) The dynamics of regional interaction extend beyond the German lands, rendering a 'national' perspective on economic development misleading.[23] As complementary economic exchange becomes more significant, the characteristics of exchanging regions diverge. If region A comes to specialise in manufactured goods which it exchanges for food with region B, as the two regions become more closely bound to each other, so will agriculture decline in A and manufacture in B. Conversely, similar patterns of development (especially if they suggest regional self-sufficiency) indicate a lack of intensive interaction. One has to look for other indices, either directly, such as trade statistics, or indirectly, such as significant correlations in price movements across exchanging regions. The best indications of significant regional specialisation and interaction are furnished by a combination of complementary structures, converging price movements and increased trade. In the optimal case one would expect to find product specialisation (a measure of complementarity), convergence of price movements (a measure of inter-regional dependence) and specialised trade flows (direct evidence of exchange).

[22] I will call these forms of manufacturing, insofar as they are specialised, fully commercial and oriented to supra-regional markets, 'proto-industry' although this term is much debated and often used to refer to only one aspect of such production, namely decentralised, rural and domestic manufacture organised by merchant capital.

[23] For a pioneering approach to European economic history in regional terms, see Sydney Pollard, *Peaceful Conquest: The Industrialisation of Europe, 1760–1970* (Oxford, 1981; repr. 2000).

Table 1 *German agricultural production and labour productivity, 1800–50*

Year	Plant production	Animal production	Total product	Labour productivity
1800/10	100	100	100	100
1811/20	108	98	103	104
1821/5	129	107	122	116
1826/30	136	117	130	120
1831/5	153	150	152	139
1836/40	168	164	167	144
1841/5	182	185	183	150
1846/50	192	202	198	165

Central to regionalisation was a growth in agrarian productivity. Without such growth it would not have been possible to release economic resources for non-food production without catastrophic falls in living standards.[24] One basic index of German agricultural production suggests it doubled between 1800 and 1850 (1800/10 = 100).[25] Labour productivity was somewhat less as the agrarian labour force increased over this period.

This growth can be related to the ways in which peasant emancipation, carried through in most German lands between 1820 and 1845, created free-standing units of production, whether large holdings or peasant farms. There remained corporate features in some areas, such as manorial policing and judicial powers, as well as continued legal discrimination against farm servants. But this corporate combination of coercive and economic power mattered less when the owner of noble estates confronted either independent peasants or exercised power over his workers as an employer of wage-earners than it had when there had been common lands, and peasants had to provide dues or services.

The second key component, in addition to individualised property rights over consolidated blocks of land, was the ability to specialise in response to supra-regional markets. Dumke has proposed a triangular trade flow model that helps us understand this process (Figure 6).[26]

One can note three points from this. (1) One side of the triangle – the western to eastern German side – is hypothetical as we lack statistical data. Nevertheless, it is a reasonable hypothesis given what we can establish

[24] A fuller argument would need to consider other factors such as overseas trade.

[25] Wehler, *Deutsche Gesellschaftsgeschichte*, II, 43, 45. Labour productivity is measured by per capita weight of corn production.

[26] Rolf Dumke, *German Economic Unification in the 19th Century: The Political Economy of the Zollverein* (Munich, 1994).

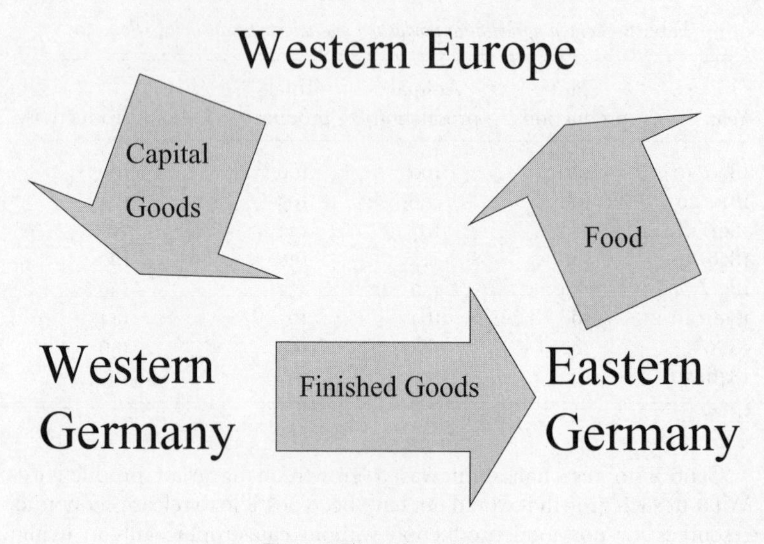

Figure 6 Triangular trade flow

about the other two sides of the triangle.[27] (2) The pattern suggests that economic regionalisation is unrelated to 'national' boundaries. (3) The pattern involves divergence between increasingly interacting economic regions. If anything there is 'de-industrialisation' (or rather a decline in commercial manufacturing) in some eastern regions, a shift towards light industry and the manufacture of consumer articles in the western regions, while Britain in particular is able to run down its agrarian sector and rapidly build up its capital goods industries as well as coal exports. The potential for this regionalisation had long existed; the end of general warfare in 1815 enabled its rapid realisation.

The pattern makes sense of German tariff policy, especially that of Prussia. There is a presumption in favour of low tariffs to bolster agricultural exports and enable the income thus earnt to be used to buy goods as cheaply as possible from western regions. Such a policy initially has no 'national' meaning. The inclusion of non-Prussian territories into a customs union not only promoted east–west trade flows but further increased tariff revenue by reducing the ratio between the circumference and area of the tariff zone.

Later Prussian tariff policy, especially during the first decades of the existence of the German Customs Union (*Zollverein*, established 1834)

[27] The main objection is that this 'side' might actually be more complex, creating something like a quadrilateral or pentangle.

may have impeded 'national' economic development because of key exclusions such as Hannover. It may also have had negative growth impacts with some high and effectively enforced tariffs that interfered with the dynamic of the non-national triangular trade flow. In particular, given an inelastic demand for 'colonial' goods which, along with tariffs on foodstuffs, provided some 75 per cent of *Zollverein* revenue, a high tariff on such goods depressed demand for domestic manufactures and reduced the pressure towards more specialised manufacturing. One of the contributions made by Dumke and other economic historians has been to show how complex are the relationships between tariff policy, trade and growth, the need to consider unintended consequences, and to question the view of the *Zollverein* as a national and/or modernising institution, especially in the first decade or so of its existence.

The fastest export growth was in agricultural goods and less technically advanced manufacturing (e.g. finished metal goods, high-class textiles). When one arrives at what some historians have identified as the first 'take-off' period, the 1840s, associated with sharp increases in railway building, this was an import-hungry, export-poor sector. The savings accrued through agricultural and proto-industrial production (whether made available privately or through state taxation or borrowing) and based on a non-national pattern of regional specialisation was a key resource for this industrialisation spurt.

By the 1840s one can distinguish what Herrigel has termed two kinds of modern industrial order: a flexible rural and artisanal consumer goods sector, especially strong in parts of western and southern Germany but with enclaves elsewhere such as Silesia, and a more heavily capitalised and centralised sector, starting in technologically innovative parts of light industry such as cotton spinning but increasingly located in railways and closely related fields of coal, iron and steel manufacturing.[28] These were concentrated regionally, especially on major coalfields such as the Ruhr but also in a few growing urban complexes, above all Berlin. However, it should be stressed that these heavy and urban industrial developments only become significant in the 1840s and many historians see them as having a major macro-economic impact only from the mid- to late 1850s.

What makes both of Herrigel's orders 'modern' is that firms operate as self-standing economic units, free of guild controls, with capitalist employers (whether putting-out merchants, small businessmen or large industrialists) able to hire and fire wage-labour at will. For such entrepreneurs the *Zollverein* was most valued as providing a predictable environment in relation to distant markets. Given, however, that we lack statistics for internal *Zollverein* trade patterns, it is difficult to measure

[28] Gary Herrigel, *Industrial Constructions: The Sources of German Industrial Power* (Cambridge, 1996).

regional integration in that direct way. However, we do know that there were convergences in price movements across regions. For example, Prussian grain prices through the *Vormärz* period increasingly come to move in step with grain prices in other parts of Europe.[29]

The development of these two modern industrial orders, as well as the growth of export-oriented agriculture based on individualised and consolidated land holdings, can be contrasted with two kinds of backward or fragile manufacturing orders – non-traditional rural industry and pauperised handicrafts – as well as with areas of non-commercial agriculture. These regions were in danger of being marginalised in the process of economic modernisation.

Shifts in migration patterns help select the modern production regions for increased significance while marginalising the backward regions. There was still not much long-distance and one-way movement (and much of that took the form of emigration, especially to the USA) but there was a lot of shorter-distance, back and forth migration, as well as significant longer-distance migration in sectors of skilled labour. It is in the context of this economic regionalisation and labour migration that one needs to understand the Prussian decision in December 1842 to dismantle the poor relief system that tied it to claimants born in the parish.

Research such as that of Herrigel on different production orders and Sabel and Zeitlin on alternative patterns of manufacturing to that of the factory point up the limitations of seeing 'modern' economic development in terms of centralised, large-scale, highly capitalised and technologically innovative manufacture.[30] Decentralised, less heavily capitalised forms of production possessed clear advantages where, for example, there were volatile economic cycles, especially if it was also possible to obtain economy of scale advantages through cooperative arrangements on specific production or marketing functions, as for example in the Solingen cutlery industry, decentralised but a world leader.[31]

This approach to economic modernisation also enables us to contextualise changing conceptions of modernity. Some time ago there was an interesting debate over opposing kinds of liberalism presented as a 'pre-industrial' *Mittelstand* set of values and an 'industrial' vision framed in terms of modern class divisions.[32] Yet the contrast is better

[29] Helge Berger and Mark Spoerer, 'Economic Crises and European Revolutions of 1848', *Journal of Economic History*, 61 (2001), 293–326.

[30] See *World of Possibilities: Flexibility and Mass Production in Western Industrialisation*, ed. Charles Sabel and Jonathan Zeitlin (Cambridge, 1997).

[31] Rudolf Boch, 'The Rise and Decline of Flexible Production: The Cutlery Industry of Solingen since the Eighteenth Century', in *World of Possibilities*, ed. Sabel and Zeitlin, 153–87.

[32] Lothar Gall, 'Liberalismus und "Bürgerliche Gesellschaft". Zu Charakter und Entwicklung der liberalen Bewegung in Deutschland', *Historische Zeitschrift*, 220 (1975), 324–56; Wolfgang Mommsen, 'Der deutsche Liberalismus zwischen "klassenloser

analysed in terms of *two* conceptions of modernity. Interesting recent work on Schulze-Delitzsch, the Prussian liberal who advocated cooperation amongst craftsmen, supports this view.[33] Both of these modernist views in turn can be contrasted with a wholly non-modern *mittelständisch* ideology that took radical political forms.[34]

We can also see that the state functioned as an agency for economic modernisation primarily by undermining corporate power rather than itself taking on planning or production functions. This is the most important continuity in Prussian policy before and after 1815: the attack on guilds, promotion of individualised land holdings, clearing away of tariff barriers and dismantling of local poor relief.

Economic regionalisation itself undermined corporate power. Corporate power tends to be localised.[35] The growth of inter-regional trade places economic resources beyond local control. It is the specialised economic agent who can quickly respond to changing supra-regional markets, such as the putting-out merchant, who increases in importance while the corporate economic agent with substantial local and unspecialised power is marginalised.

A fuller account would need to link these economic changes to other changes such as the rise of powerful liberal ideologies and the increased vulnerability of governments to 'public opinion' on key economic matters. However, I think by now one can see the way the argument can make such connections.

Cultural power and the 1848 revolutions

I can only sketch some arguments about the modernisation of cultural power. The most important institutions of cultural power were the Christian churches. At elite levels, especially amongst state official, professional and commercial groups, Enlightenment values had undermined Christian beliefs and practices. In the German lands there was less evangelical enthusiasm – both in the established and free churches – than one finds in nineteenth-century England. Equally, there was little of the

Bürgergesellschaft" und "organisiertem Kapitalismus"', *Geschichte und Gesellschaft*, 4 (1978), 77–90. For a more recent and English-language consideration see Dieter Langewiesche, *Liberalism in Germany* (Basingstoke, 2000).

[33] Ruth Aldenhoff, *Schulze-Delitzsch. Ein Beitrag zur Geschichte des Liberalismus zwischen Revolution und Reichsgründung* (Bonn, 1984).

[34] See Paul Nolte, 'Bürgerideal, Gemeinde und Republik. "Klassischer Republikanismus" im frühen deutschen Liberalismus', *Historische Zeitschrift*, 254 (1992), 609–56.

[35] I find illuminating the analogy of a network. A network carrying many different kinds of messages can only carry those messages a short distance; a network which specialises in carrying just one type of message sends much 'thinner' information but can do this over much greater distances.

fierce popular anti-clericalism or even de-Christianisation reported for the growing industrial towns of provincial England or Paris and Lyon.[36]

Economic and political change narrowed the sphere of operation of churches. During the Napoleonic period much Catholic church property was taken over by the state and new agreements concluded between governments and the Papacy. Catholic church secular power was further reduced by the refusal of the Allies at the Congress of Vienna to restore the ecclesiastical states swept aside by Napoleon. The Catholic clergy were becoming a state salaried class like their Protestant counterparts, though the church retained much authority over recruitment, training and discipline. In the major Protestant state, Prussia, the union of Calvinist and Lutheran branches into a single church establishment – a work of faith for Frederick William III – unified organisationally but at the sacrifice of enthusiasm.

In Catholic areas the more narrowly focused church could become a vehicle for religious enthusiasm and revival, especially where Catholics were in a minority, deprived of the privileges of church establishment. The priesthood no longer reflected a broader social hierarchy with parish priests of peasant origin and scions of the Catholic German aristocracy dominating high offices. Instead it was becoming both vocation and career. To exercise power one needed to reach the emotions of men and, increasingly, of women. The Trier Pilgrimage of 1844 offers a good example of this.[37] The decision to exhibit what was claimed to be a part of Christ's clothing up to the time of his crucifixion was linked to political tensions with the Prussian state. The impetus came from local enthusiastic clergy as well as lay initiatives, involved emotional appeals of a kind which broke with Enlightenment traditions, deployed print media and had state wide and even national repercussions.

Yet this narrowing of focus also meant that such religious enthusiasm did not necessarily make the Catholic church influential in other, 'non-religious' spheres of life.[38] There was a distinct patchiness to church influence, especially in more urban, commercial and Protestant areas. This was connected with the growth of new cultural institutions and values. Some were directly associated with economic regionalisation.

[36] A good recent collection of essays in English dealing with secularisation and religious revival in nineteenth-century Europe, including Germany, see *Culture Wars: Secular–Catholic Conflict in Nineteenth-Century Europe*, ed. Christopher Clark and Wolfram Kaiser (Cambridge, 2003).

[37] Wolfgang Schieder, 'Kirche und Revolution. Sozialgeschichtliche Aspeke der trierer Wallfahrt von 1844', *Archiv für Sozialgeschichte*, 14 (1974), 419–54; Rudolf Lill, 'Kirche und Revolution. Zu den Anfängen der katholischen Bewegung im Jahrzehnt vor 1848', *Archiv für Sozialgeschichte*, 18 (1978), 565–75.

[38] In elections in 1848 Trier electors returned a radical, not a political Catholic, to the German National Assembly.

It was necessary for merchants to have frequent, detailed and reliable information about supra-local, even supra-national markets. This was not just a matter of hard data such as prices and shipping movements but of informed assessments about political stability in likely markets or the prospects for a mining or railway construction enterprise. Entrepreneurs published intelligence sheets designed to meet these demands.[39]

The notion of 'opinion' became prominent. The creation of information about dealings across extensive distances escaped governmental control. Indeed, many officials recognised the necessity as well as inevitability of such autonomous information exchange. Not only information but people moved around more, and as they did so they formed new relationships which carried knowledge and values. For example, the traditional practice of artisan roving was expanding and transforming as a way of skilled labour markets responding to geographically enlarged opportunities and economic cycles. Institutional props for such mobile labour included support funds for tramping artisans and hostels that expanded their operations and powers. Such networks not only distributed funds and functioned as labour exchanges but acted as conduits through which radical artisans could ferry pamphlets and songs preaching ideas of egalitarian Christianity or republican credos derived from Paris or Swiss cantons.[40]

At elite level the most important values associated with modernisation were liberal. Liberalism, like all powerful ideologies, reflects intellectually the social changes it advocates. The specialisation of function that is at the heart of modernisation was expressed ideologically in the classificatory system of liberalism with its stress on a limited and specialised state, itself structured around divisions between executive, legislative and judicial powers; the growing recognition of the free market as the most efficient way of allocating economic resources, if not yet as an engine of growth; and the idea that opinion was a matter of free choice and thought which in turn could shape social development.

At the narrowly political area, there were particular problems about legitimating German states. In many places the state was new; introduced though the transformations of the Napoleonic period and/or the decisions taken at Vienna in 1814–15. With the exception of the Hohenzollerns, the other monarchies were nineteenth-century creations, even if linked to earlier dynastic lineages. The Austrian Imperial title was also new,

[39] Rachid Láoufir, 'Wirtschaftskommunikation im Prozess der Industrialisierung in Preussen 1815–1848: Strukturen, Akteure, Institutionenwandel' (Ph.D. thesis, Berlin and Paris, 2002).

[40] John Breuilly, 'Artisan Economy, Ideology and Politics: The Artisan Contribution to the Mid-nineteenth Century European Labour Movement', in *idem*, *Labour and Liberalism in Nineteenth-Century Europe* (Manchester, 1992), 76–114.

created in 1804 in anticipation of the loss (which followed in 1806) of the Holy Roman Imperial title. Even in Prussia, the Hohenzollerns were new and unwelcome rulers in the Catholic Rhineland, parts of Westphalia, northern Saxony and the Grand Duchy of Posen. On what 'traditions' could such monarchies ground their claim to rule? Especially at elite level, the way was open for other arguments about the legitimacy of political authority, arguments that were not primarily Christian or monarchical.

It is against this erosion of traditional cultural power that one needs to set the outbreak of revolution in 1848. What is remarkable about 1848 is that it was not preceded by a political or military crisis of the kind that normally goes before revolution.[41] There had been a severe economic crisis in the mid-1840s but with the good harvests of 1847 the worst seemed to be passing. Yet between late February and late March 1848 governments toppled rapidly from France, through the German and Italian states into the Habsburg Empire. The very absence of crisis suggests a basic weakness of legitimacy.

Siemann has argued cogently that the German revolutions of 1848 should be linked to a crisis of modernisation.[42] Sperber has fleshed out such an argument in relation to the Rhineland.[43] The modernisation of craft manufacture and agriculture connects to effective peasant and artisan actions in those revolutionary years. In the case of the peasantry it ensured the rapid completion of the emancipation process. The most enduring element of the artisanal response led not to a reversal of modernising trends but rather to more effective skilled labour and small employer organisations, pressing for support for cooperatives and education.

Here I select one aspect of cultural power: the construction of a new, tougher kind of conservatism that began to address precisely the weaknesses underlying the collapse of authority in early 1848.

Liberals assumed ministerial positions by default in early 1848. Political and military power remained in the hands of established authorities: armies retired to barracks, taxes continued to be collected in an orderly manner. Liberals were well aware of their weaknesses and worried about radical threats. Their principal strategy was to come to an understanding with established authority, ideally organised through constitutional monarchy set within a liberalising economic and cultural order. However, liberals felt too weak to press hard for such an understanding. Their own

[41] John Breuilly, 'The Revolutions of 1848', in *Revolutions and the Revolutionary Tradition in the West 1560–1991*, ed. David Parker (2000), 109–31.

[42] Wolfram Siemann, *The German Revolution of 1848–49* (Basingstoke, 1998).

[43] Jonathan Sperber, *Rhineland Radicals: The Democratic Movement and the Revolution of 1848–1849* (New Jersey, 1991).

divisions and fragmentation as well as fear of and principled opposition to democratic pressures provided others with opportunities.

Until the revolution conservatism had presented itself as a principled and inveterate opponent of modernity. Insofar as vested interests were accommodating to change, for example, turning noble estates into capitalist enterprises, they did so without expressing this in terms of values. Practical conservatism was incoherent or silent. Under the threat of revolution this changed.

Church and state institutions agreed on the need to re-establish order and hierarchy. This was a general pattern in Europe following 1848–9.[44] The Prussian state settled its dispute with the Catholic church. Governments allied with church establishments in crushing free churches. The burgeoning primary school population, an effect of home–work separation and urban growth, now stimulated the entrenchment of Christian authority in the schools. This involved clashes with the growing class of school teachers, giving rise to a typical tension of modernity between a secular occupation seeking professional status and autonomy and churches trying to extend their specialised cultural power into new school institutions. The state apparatus itself divided and shifted in this conflict. Following 1848 state policy was largely allied to the churches.

Established authority could also play upon the fears unleashed by the revolution. Family and private property were presented as social goods that could only be adequately protected by strong monarchy and Christian values. This was a message that went down well with peasants who had finally secured control of their landholdings or amongst the growing class of shareholders in railway and other companies. The possibility that conservative values could take populist form was a novel one in 1848. Radicals like Karl Marx struggled intellectually to come to terms with new political phenomena such as the mass appeal of Louis Napoleon in France.[45]

Conservatives could utilise the new media of periodicals and newspapers and lithographs as effectively as their opponents. The Catholic church took the lead in forming popular associations, often with welfare and cultural functions designed to provide support for displaced migrants, the victims of cyclical labour markets.[46]

Bismarck's rise to power began with the formulation of this kind of conservatism. Before 1848 he was an eccentric squire making wild threats

[44] Jonathan Sperber, 'Churches, the Faithful, and the Politics of Religion in the Revolution of 1848', in *Europe in 1848: Revolution and Reform*, ed. Dieter Dowe *et al.* (New York and Oxford, 2001), 708–28.

[45] One can observe this in Marx's shifts of argument from *The Communist Manifesto* (1848) to *Class Struggles in France 1848–1850* (1850) to *The 18th Brumaire of Louis Napoleon* (1852).

[46] Jonathan Sperber, *Popular Catholicism in Nineteenth Century Germany* (New Jersey, 1984).

about repression. After 1848 he shifted towards a harsh realism which rooted conservatism in the appeal to interest. His conservatism was the politics of rhetoric, an electoral and publicist politics, and it gave him a degree of detachment and autonomy from more traditional, principled forms of conservatism.[47] Liberal and radical politicians also adjusted to the new, specialised world of politics with its constitutionalism, manifestoes, election meetings and speechmaking. The liberalism of the 1850s prided itself on *Realpolitik*, a phrase coined by a Prussian liberal, August von Rochau. The socialism of the 1860s appealed to labour interests and the notion of class rather than a classless idealism. The revolutions of 1848–9 had accelerated the modernisation of cultural power.

The modernisation of coercive-military power

Military modernisation can persuasively be presented as an intentional project. Armies are 'designed' and there is an obvious site of selection on the battlefield. In this particular case there is even one prime candidate as designer: Helmut von Moltke. However, it is still necessary to identify unacknowledged conditions and deeper levels of analysis than battlefield success. The conditions have been emphasised in much of the historiography.[48] Less attention has been paid to such questions as why Prussia's opponents did not pursue modernising military reforms as thoroughly or effectively as Prussia.

The most obvious conditions were technological innovations such as railways, the telegraph and breech-loading rifles that could be rapidly mass produced. It was crucial that these technological possibilities coincided with a period of unprecedentedly fast economic growth in Prussia that removed public finance obstacles to increased military expenditure. There was a constitutional crisis when Wilhelm pressed ahead with military expansion and renewal but opposition was on political rather than financial grounds and existing tax revenue plus borrowing enabled Bismarck to get through the crisis period.

These policies need to be placed within broader and narrower contexts. The broader one is the development of a set of Prusso-German institutions, above all in the German Customs Union and network of voluntary associations with the greatest density in north and central Germany, especially in urban and Protestant regions. The specialised politics of constitutional rule and the increasing importance of political ideologies, especially national liberalism, marginalised particularist politics and meant that by the early 1860s there was already an intense

[47] Lothar Gall, *Bismarck: The White Revolutionary*, I: *1815–1871* (1986).

[48] There is a good English-language literature. I have found especially valuable Arden Bucholz, *Moltke and the German Wars, 1864–1871* (2001). Some of the points made here can be found in my book *Austria, Prussia and Germany 1806–1871* (2002), especially chs. 6 and 8.

anticipation of national unity, even if no consensus on how and in what form that would arrive.[49]

More narrowly there was the good fortune that Prussia avoided major warfare until 1866 while its principal opponents, Austria and France, fought against each other in 1859. At the same time military mobilisations in 1850 and 1859, and the limited Austro-Prussian war against Denmark in 1864, enabled new military methods to be tried out and brought Moltke to a position of command in the army.

Why did Prussia's opponents so signally fail to respond to its military modernisation programme? Prussia, before 1871, did not face the problem of 'overstretch' but was able to focus its efforts on expanding its sphere of influence in northern and central Germany.[50] By contrast, Austria had to be ready to use military power against Russia (during the Crimean War Austria mobilised its army in support of a policy of armed neutrality directed against Russia), to maintain an armed presence in northern Italy both before and after the war of 1859, to share German defence duties with Prussia on the Rhine, to act with Prussia against Denmark and finally to prepare for war with Prussia. France also had a range of military commitments: on the Rhine against Prussia, against Russia in the Crimea, against Austria in north Italy, in the Mediterranean and its north African empire and in Mexico. Finally, Austria and France fought a war against each other in 1859. It was difficult to find the breathing space for military reform and also there were so many prospective wars for which to prepare that it was difficult to focus on a particular type of warfare.

In the case of Austria military setbacks (above all in 1859) intensified the financial crisis of the state. Not only was there a rapid reduction in military expenditure between 1859 and 1866 but this in turn made it impossible to contemplate innovations such as re-equipping the infantry with breech-loading rifles or embarking on expensive railway construction for military use. This financial context conditioned military planners to find 'traditional' policies persuasive. In the case of France, the 1859 victory induced complacency while the parliamentarisation of the regime in the later 1860s reduced chances for expensive innovation. Louis Napoleon lacked the authority to override public opinion in the way that Wilhelm was able to during the constitutional crisis.

The issue is not an either/or choice: modernisation or its refusal. Rather it is about the degree and pace of innovation, about the merits

[49] See *Germany's Two Unifications: Anticipations, Experiences, Responses*, ed. John Breuilly and Ronald Speirs (Basingstoke, 2004), which contain a number of essays dealing with the anticipations of the first unification.

[50] The notion of 'imperial overstretch' is used in Paul Kennedy, *The Rise and Fall of the Great Powers: Economic Change and Military Conflict from 1500 to 2000* (1988).

of which there can also be legitimate debates. The whole point about innovation is that one cannot be sure how it will turn out. There are debates within the field of military history that suggest that Prussian successes in 1866 and 1870–1 were not due to a modernisation programme but rather to some combination of luck, the incompetence of opponents and the chance of battle.[51]

Nevertheless, I would argue strongly for the key role of 'modernity' in the victories of 1864 (e.g. the artillery bombardment of Dybbol), 1866 (the superior speed of Prussian troop movement, the impact of rifle fire) and 1870–1 (again the speed of movement, the use of artillery). This modernity has to be understood primarily in terms of societal transformation and only secondarily in terms of particular technologies. First, there was the attachment of the army to society through the universal obligation of all young men to conscription. At the same time this army became more functionally specialised through the extension of the length of service and with the growing professionalisation of the officer corps. The army was no longer a privileged corporation but a specialised institution acting on behalf of an impersonal state and society. The institution of conscription was unique to Prussia and only effectively realised in the 1860s.

More specifically, the Prussian army was only able to innovate rapidly in the 1860s on the basis of advances in primary schooling which created the type of 'generic', standard culture which Gellner has stressed lies at the heart of modern national culture.[52] The Prussian army had higher literacy rates at non-commissioned and rank-and-file levels than its Habsburg or French counterparts as well as operating with less linguistic diversity. That made possible the use of training manuals and other forms of printed instruction which enabled rapid retraining in new weaponry, one problem which Austrian officers had used to justify not adopting the breech-loading rifle. Internally the Prussian army became more specialised, above all with development of planning functions in the General Staff. These specialisations increased the societal reach of the army, not just through conscription but in terms of mobilisation. Moltke virtually invented operational warfare as a large-scale form of military action between strategic planning and battlefield manoeuvre. The specialised organisation and the rational time–space coordination such warfare entailed can be seen in the planned contraction by the Prussian General Staff of the military theatre from over 40,000 square miles on 6 June 1866 to just 4 square miles (the battlefield at Königgrätz)

[51] For battlefield detail see now the two studies by Geoffrey Wawro: *The Austro-Prussian War: Austria's War with Prussia and Italy in 1866* (Cambridge, 1996) and *The Franco-Prussian War: The German Conquest of France in 1870–1871* (Cambridge, 2003).

[52] Ernest Gellner, *Nations and Nationalism* (Oxford, 1983).

by the afternoon of 3 July. Nothing like this had ever happened before; 'modern' warfare had arrived.[53]

Finally, this modernised form of warfare received its specifically modern ideological celebration. In the space of less than a year, in 1866–7, the national liberal movement shifted from hostility towards militarism, condemned as an internal instrument of authoritarian monarchy, to eulogising the new army of the nation which used science and reason to wage successful war against foreign enemies. The militarist stereotypes were quickly projected on to the enemy instead.[54]

Modernisation is a dynamic process. The very success of the Prussians bred emulation. The French modernised their rifles after 1866 but did not sufficiently adjust to issues of rapid mobilisation and use of artillery. By the mid-1870s specialised planning staffs had been extended to all military establishments. For a brief moment, however, in the 1860s, conditions in Prussia had favoured the more intensive selection of modern forms of military power, making a crucial contribution to the formation of the Prussian-led German state in 1871.

Concluding remarks

I have approached modernisation in the German lands as a transformation of the modes of power from corporate to functionally specialised forms. For each of four periods covering the period from Napoleon to unification I have focused on the modernisation of one of these four modes of power. That entailed radical selectivity. There is actually constant interaction between changes in the different modes of power and a full account would have to trace those out for each of these periods. In this essay I have only been able to sketch out some ways such an argument works.

I am sceptical of sweeping claims about German modernisation in response to Napoleon, especially when such claims focus on deliberate political rationalisation projects. These confuse rationality as a value system linked to the Enlightenment and/or as an instrumental attitude favouring more efficient organisational methods with modernisation as a societal transformation towards functional specialisation. The truly modernising trends of the Napoleonic and immediate post-Napoleonic period were less to do with state bureaucracy and centralisation and more to do with the ways in which the state, especially in Prussia, withdrew from corporate, non-political functions and contributed to the destruction of other corporations. The shift to more familiar patterns of modernisation

[53] I follow Bucholz, *Moltke.*

[54] Frank Becker, *Bilder von Krieg und Nation. Die Einigungskriege in der bürgerlichen Öffentlichkeit Deutschlands 1864–1913* (Munich, 2001).

associated with factory production, urbanisation, railway growth, military technology, long-distance migration, constitutional and electoral politics and interventionist bureaucray only became really significant after 1850. It built on an earlier but different kind of modernisation. It is important to connect the two and to see them as stages in one societal transformation.

Societal transformation is not the transformation of 'a society'. It is not a transition from one quasi-organic condition to another. To continue with analogies taken from biological evolution, such transformation is instead about the marginalisation, even extinction, of some social practices while other practices become increasingly central. What makes cultural evolution different from and more complex than biological evolution is that intentionality, learning and adaptation are part of the process.[55] Nevertheless, they are only parts. Competing social practices are, given the situations in which they are located, in principle equally rational. The uncertainty and rapidity of modernisation, once the dynamic of functional specialisation was at work, makes it impossible to know which social practices will succeed in particular competitions. Furthermore, modern social practices bring with them their own internal conflicts and high costs. Modernisation cannot be understood as the successful realisation of modern projects but rather as a selection process in which more functionally specialised social practices come to prevail for specific reasons which in turn need analysing.

Such functional specialisation creates new problems of coordinating different kinds of social practice. Large-scale and specialised military power, for example, presented coordination problems for the other modes of power. How were politicians to prevent the military machine developing its own logic? How were economic and technological processes to be coordinated with military projects? How was an increasingly technical and autonomous set of military institutions to command cultural prestige and support within the population? It is in this context that one has to understand the modernising function of the national idea. The national idea provided a coordinating set of values across these specialised spheres. Yet understandably this idea itself had diverse meanings for those holding political, military, economic and cultural power and in turn was given conflicting meanings by social groups subject to these various forms of power.[56]

These are general features of the emergent modern social order by the later nineteenth century: free markets, bureaucratic and representative state institutions, specialised and technologically innovating military forces, specialised churches, voluntary associations and educational

[55] See W. G. Runciman, 'Culture Does Evolve', *History and Theory*, 44 (Feb. 2005), 1–13.

[56] For a recent consideration of the various forms of the national idea see Stefan Berger, *Inventing the Nation: Germany* (2004).

institutions, and the elaboration of a set of values which represented state and society in national terms. What was specific about the German form of this order was the rapidity of change and that the political framework was created by means of collapsing multiple state sovereignties into one, by means of short, limited wars. The result was a sharp separation between liberal values that were entrenched in powerful cultural and economic institutions that had taken shape in the first 'de-corporating' phase of modernisation and conservative-authoritarian values, moulded in reaction to revolution and then embedded in the political and military institutions that conducted the unification process. This created a specifically German form of modernity and its characteristic tensions are central to understanding the subsequent history of Germany.[57] The purpose of this essay was to sketch out an argument about how that problematic modernity was achieved. How it was then handled is another matter.

[57] This problematic is central to the debates about the German *Sonderweg* or special path which have been central to post-1870 historiography.

Transactions of the RHS 15 (2005), pp. 149–174
doi:10.1017/S0080440105000320 Printed in the United Kingdom

THE ENVIRONMENTAL HISTORY OF THE RUSSIAN STEPPES: VASILII DOKUCHAEV AND THE HARVEST FAILURE OF 1891*

By David Moon

READ 22 OCTOBER 2004 AT THE UNIVERSITY OF THE WEST OF ENGLAND

ABSTRACT. This article examines aspects of the environmental history of the Russian steppes in the long term and in a comparative framework by focusing on the work of the prominent Russian scientist Vasilii Dokuchaev in response to the drought and harvest failure that afflicted large parts of the steppes in 1891. Dokuchaev analysed the causes of the disaster in the long-term context of natural and human-induced changes in the environment. He drew up a plan to address the environmental constraints on agriculture in the region, and led a scientific expedition to examine the feasibility of putting parts of his plan into practice.

In 1891 large parts of the steppe region of southern and south-eastern Russia were hit by a serious drought, which caused the harvest to fail across a wide area, and contributed to a famine that lasted long into 1892. The commercial attache in the British embassy in St Petersburg, E. F. G. Law, conveyed the scale of the disaster with his estimate that the Imperial Russian government had 'to find the means of supplying a deficit of food to 35,500,000 people in sixteen provinces'. His report was not positive about the ability of the Imperial Russian government and population to alleviate the consequences of the harvest failure, nor about the prospects for Russian agriculture in the medium term.[1] The subject of this essay is not the famine or the attempts by the government and society to alleviate

* This paper is dedicated to the memory of Aleksei Enverovich Karimov (1966–2004) who provided much help and advice for this research project. The author would like to acknowledge the assistance of the Leverhulme Trust, which funded a six-month reseach visit to Rostov-on-Don and Stavropol' (in the steppe region of Russia) in the spring and summer of 2003, and the British Academy and the University of Strathclyde in Glasgow, which funded shorter visits to St Petersburg and Helsinki. He would also like to extend his gratitude to the staffs of the universities, archives, libraries and nature reserves where research was carried out. Neil Edmunds, T. C. Smout and Richard Stites kindly commented on part or all of previous drafts. The author remains solely responsible for any errors.

[1] *Russia. Report on Russian Agriculture and the Failure of the Harvest in 1891* (UK) Foreign Office, 1892, Miscellaneous Series No. 254, Reports on Subjects of General and Commercial Interest (1892), quotation, 21.

the human suffering.[2] Rather, the aim is to analyse the response to the drought and harvest failure by Russian scientists, in particular the prominent soil scientist Vasilii Dokuchaev in the long-term context of the environmental history of the Russian steppes. The unfolding catastrophe prompted Russian scientists to investigate its causes and to propose ways of dealing with the recurring problem of droughts and crop failures on the steppes. The most comprehensive study was carried out by Dokuchaev. He examined the causes of the drought and harvest failure in a book entitled *Our Steppes: Past and Present*, which was published in the spring of 1892.[3] He considered the evolution of the steppe environment over the millennia since the end of the last ice age, and the more recent impact of human activity on what he termed 'virgin nature'. Dokuchaev believed that this human impact was partly responsible for the harvest failure. At the end of the book, he presented a detailed plan of measures to prevent such future disasters by seeking to reverse the impact of human action and to 'improve' nature. The government sponsored Dokuchaev to lead a major scientific expedition to the steppes to carry out research into the viability of putting some of the measures into practice. The environmental history of the Russian steppes has broader significance. The steppes were one of several grassland regions around the globe, for example the prairies of north America, that came under the plough from the eighteenth or nineteenth centuries and experienced similar environmental problems. Scientists in all these regions examined and debated what was taking place.

I

The steppe region[4] of the south and south-east of the territory of the European part of the Russian Empire (contemporary European Russia and Ukraine) is part of the immense Eurasian steppes that extend from the Hungarian plain in the west to Mongolia and northern China in the east.

[2] For works in English on the famine, see R. G. Robbins, *Famine in Russia, 1891–1892: The Imperial Government Responds to a Crisis* (New York and London, 1975); J. Y. Simms, 'The Crop Failure of 1891: Soil Exhaustion, Technological Backwardness, and Russia's "Agrarian Crisis"', *Slavic Review*, 41 (1982), 236–50; *idem*, 'The Economic Impact of the Russian Famine of 1891–92', *Slavonic and East European Review*, 51 (1982), 63–74; S. G. Wheatcroft, 'The 1891–92 Famine in Russia: Towards a More Detailed Analysis of its Scale and Demographic Significance', in *Economy and Society in Russia and the Soviet Union, 1860–1930*, ed. L. Edmondson and P. Waldron (Basingstoke and London, 1992), 44–64.

[3] V. V. Dokuchaev, 'Nashi Stepi prezhde i teper'', in *Sochineniya* (9 vols., Moscow and Leningrad, 1949–61), VI, 13–102 (first published in book form as V. V. Dokuchaev, *Nashi Stepi prezhde i teper'* (Spb, 1892)).

[4] On the wide variety of regions and their significance, see D. Saunders, 'Regional Diversity in the Later Russian Empire', *Transactions of the Royal Historical Society*, sixth series, 10 (2000), 143–63.

In Russia, between the steppes and the forest zone to the north, is a belt of transitional forest-steppe, where areas of open land are interspersed with woodland. In the south, however:

> up to the shores of the Black Sea, over a vast area is stretched a treeless, lightly rolling plain, here scored by deep gullies, there smooth and level for hundreds of versts,[5] [formerly] covered in the main by a herbaceous steppe vegetation, or in some parts also by steppe shrubs . . . The real high steppes are so bereft of woody vegetation that their horizon, sometimes for many hundred versts, is not broken by a single tree. Only in the deep ravines and along the valleys of the rivers [e.g. the Dnepr, Don and Volga] intersecting the steppes, where the conditions of moisture are more favourable, thick growths of shrubs find shelter and clumps of trees lift their heads. The steppe, [where it is] as yet untouched by the plough, strikes the observer with the wealth and beauty of its flora, the rapid changeability of its colouring at different seasons of the year and the abundance of animal life.

This was how the Russian Department of Agriculture (of the Ministry of State Domains) described the steppes in a volume prepared for the World's Columbian Exposition in Chicago in 1893. The description carried on:

> During the last few decades tillage has greatly altered the steppe region. The untouched virgin steppes with their peculiar vegetation and life in the majority of places have vanished yielding room to endless fields of wheat and other kinds of grain. The virgin steppe is preserved only here and there in unfrequented spots, where the population is thinner and where the plough has not yet broken up all the land possible.

Readers were referred for more detailed information to an English translation of Professor Dokuchaev's book on the Russian steppes that had been prepared specially for the exposition. The translation of Dokuchaev's book had an additional chapter on 'The Study of the Soil', in particular the celebrated, prodigiously fertile, black earth (*chernozem*), that covered the largest part of the steppes.[6]

The steppes were not ancient Russian or Slavonic lands. Nor had arable farming been the main activity of the inhabitants for most of their recorded history. Most of the region had come under Russian control since only the mid-sixteenth century, and the treeless steppes to the south were settled and cultivated by a predominantly Slavonic population from only the eighteenth century. The first written description of the region to the north of the Black Sea is from a very long time before the Russian

[5] 1 versta = 0.66 of a mile or 1.06 km.

[6] *The Industries of Russia*, III: *Agriculture and Forestry*, ed. John Martin Crawford (Spb, 1893), xxii–xxiii (originally published as *Sel'skoe i lesnoe khozyaistvo Rossii* (Spb, 1893)); V. V. Dokuchaev, *The Russian Steppes. Study of the Soil in Russia, its Past and Present*, ed. John Martin Crawford (Spb, 1893). For descriptions of the steppe environment preserved in scientific nature reserves (*zapovedniki*) in contemporary Russia, Ukraine and Moldova, see *Zapovedniki evropeiskoi chasti RSFSR*, II, ed. M. N. Stroganova (Moscow, 1989); *Zapovedniki Ukrainy i Moldavii*, ed. E. E. Syroechkovskii (Moscow, 1987).

conquest and settlement, however, when it was on the fringes of the world of the Ancient Greeks, and belonged to Herodotus.[7] Writing in the middle of the fifth century BCE, Herodotus described the land he knew as Scythia as a 'level plain with good deep soil', which was watered by numerous rivers, for example the Tanais (the Don),[8] and which was 'treeless', with the exception of an area he called Hylaea, which was probably located near the mouth of the river Dnepr in contemporary Ukraine.[9] The most notable features of the climate, for this native of Asia Minor, were the long, hard winters and violent thunderstorms in the summer. A Soviet historian of climate wryly noted that Herodotus exaggerated the length of the winters and, like other travellers from the Mediterranean world, tended to note the cold winters rather than the hot summers on the steppes.[10] Herodotus's Scythia was inhabited partly by settled agricultural tribes, who grew grain and other crops, and partly by nomadic peoples, who lived off their livestock and knew 'nothing of agriculture'. Settled agriculture had spread to parts of the west of the Eurasian steppes long before the 'father of history' described the region. For several millennia, however, from around 3,000 BCE to the latter part of the second millennium CE, the steppes were inhabited largely by nomadic pastoralists. The nomads grazed their flocks of sheep and goats and herds of cattle, horses and camels on the rich grasslands that flourished on the 'good deep soil'. Over these millennia, a succession of nomadic peoples, including the Scythians, Huns and Mongols, invaded from the east. In the thirteenth century, the Mongols under Chinghiz Khan and his sons and grandsons conquered the entire Eurasian steppes and surrounding territories, including much of contemporary Russia and Ukraine. Under pressure from the regular invasions and raids by nomadic pastoralists, settled agricultural peoples moved north and north-west from the steppes

[7] Herodotus, *The Histories*, trans. Aubrey de Selincourt, further rev. edn (2003), IV, 17–23, 28–9, 46–58.

[8] The identification of Herodotus's 'Tanais' has been the subject of debate. A. P. Medvedev, 'K voprosu ob identifkatsii reki Tanais po dannym Ptolemeya', in *Istoricheskaya geografiya chernozemnogo tsentra Rossii (dooktyabrskii period)*, ed. V. P. Zagorovskii (Voronezh, 1989), 132–49.

[9] Herodotus's description of the steppes as 'treeless' and attempts to locate 'Hylaea' played an important role in a long-running debate over whether the steppes had once been forested. See, for example: I. Palimpsestov, *Stepi yuga Rossii byli-li iskoni vekov stepami i vozmozhno-li oblesit' ikh?*, rev. edn (Odessa, 1890), 128–54; V. Taliev, 'Bednyi Gerodot i drugie "svetil'niki" v rukakh pochvenno-botanicheskoi geografii', *Estestvoznanie i geografiya*, 8 (1905), 28–43. See also D. Moon, 'Were the Steppes ever Forested? Science, Economic Development, and Identity in the Russian Empire in the 19th Century', in *Dealing with Diversity: 2nd International Conference of the European Society for Environmental History: Proceedings*, ed. L. Jelecek *et al.* (Prague, 2003), 206–9.

[10] I. E. Buchinskii, *O klimate proshlogo Russkoi ravniny* (Leningrad, 1957), 44–6.

into what became northern Ukraine and central Russia, where the forests afforded them some protection.[11]

Over time, states based on settled farming on the periphery of the steppes built up advantages over nomadic empires. In particular, agrarian states developed the ability to support larger populations and centralised administrations that could mobilise their resources, principally land and people, to maintain powerful armed forces. The tide turned in favour of the agrarian state based on Moscow in the 1550s. Tsar Ivan the Terrible defeated two of the successor states of the Mongol Empire, the Khanates of Kazan' and Astrakhan', on the middle and lower Volga. This proved to be the start of the Russian conquest of the steppes, which was spearheaded by bands of cossacks. By the end of the eighteenth century, the Russian Empire had extended its southern borders to the northern shores of the Black and Caspian seas and into the foothills of the Caucasus mountains. In the process, the steppes were opened to settlement by large and growing numbers of peasant farmers (mostly Russians and Ukrainians but also some Germans), who moved south and east out of the forests and on to the fertile plains. In time, peasant farmers displaced the nomads and replaced their extensive pastoral economy with settled agriculture.[12] Peasant settlement of the open steppes in the south and south-east took off in the mid-eighteenth century. In 1719, the total peasant population of the region was a little over 50,000. Less than two centuries later, at the time of the 1897 census, there were nearly 5 million peasants on the open steppes. In addition, there were almost 2.4 million cossacks in the region, many of whom, since the late eighteenth century, engaged in arable farming.[13]

The main attractions for the peasants who moved on to the steppes were the prospects of greater freedom, away from the oppression and exploitation of life in the central regions, and of relative prosperity from

[11] D. Christian, *A History of Russia, Central Asia and Mongolia*, I: *Inner Eurasia from Prehistory to the Mongol Empire* (Oxford, 1998), 77–80, 85; M. Zvelebil and P. Dolukhanov, 'The Transition to Farming in Eastern and Northern Europe', *Journal of World Prehistory*, 5 (1991), 248–62.

[12] See D. Christian, 'Inner Eurasia as a Unit of World History', *Journal of World History*, 5 (1994), 173–211; M. Khodarkovsky, *Russia's Steppe Frontier: The Making of a Colonial Empire, 1500–1800* (Bloomington and Indianapolis, IN, 2002); W. H. McNeill, *Europe's Steppe Frontier, 1500–1800* (Chicago, 1964); D. Moon, 'Peasant Migration and the Settlement of Russia's Frontiers 1550–1897', *Historical Journal*, 30 (1997), 859–93; W. Sunderland, *Taming the Wild Field: Colonization and Empire on the Russian Steppe* (Ithaca, NY, 2004).

[13] Data from V. M. Kabuzan, *Izmeneniya v razmeshchenii naseleniya Rossii v XVIII-pervoi polovine XIX v. (Po materialam revizii)* (Moscow, 1971), 59–175 (figures for males have been doubled); *Obshchii svod po imperii rezul'tatov razrabotki dannykh pervoi vseobshchei perepisi naseleniya, proizvedennoi 28 Yanvarya 1897 goda*, ed. N. A. Troinitskii (2 vols., Spb, 1905), I, 165–71. On the settlement of southern Ukraine, see E. I. Druzhinina, *Severnoe Prichernomor'e v 1775–1800 gg.* (Moscow, 1959); *idem*, *Yuzhnaya Ukraina v 1800–1825 gg.* (Moscow, 1970); *idem*, *Yuzhnaya Ukraina v period krizisa feodalizma 1825–1860 gg.* (Moscow, 1981). See also R. P. Bartlett, *Human Capital: The Settlement of Foreigners in Russia, 1762–1804* (Cambridge, 1979). On cossacks, see S. O'Rourke, *Warriors and Peasants: The Don Cossacks in Late Imperial Russia* (New York, 2000).

cultivating the rich, black earth.[14] The fertility of the black earth of the steppes was noted by the predominantly German scientists who took part in expeditions organised by the Russian Academy of Sciences in the late 1760s. Samuel Georg Gmelin described the steppes as a land which the 'Providential Creator had endowed with fertility' and where there were great prospects for the development of agriculture.[15] Peter Pallas, who returned to the steppes in 1790s, waxed lyrically about the productivity of the virgin land around Taganrog (on the Sea of Azov). He may have been exaggerating, however, when he wrote that the land: 'is so fertile that in a recently tilled soil, wheat may be sown without manure during four or five successive years; its crops frequently are from twenty to thirty fold and in good seasons, even thirty-eight grains are obtained from one'.[16] Another of the Academy's German scientists, Johann Anton Gueldenstaedt, made the more sober but still high estimate of grain yields of 1:10 on the Don steppes in the early 1770s.[17] The expeditions organised by the Academy of Sciences in the late eighteenth century were the start of serious scientific study of the steppes, and were precursors to Dokuchaev's expeditions over a century later. In the decades after Pallas and his colleagues explored the steppes, the Russian government sought to promote the agricultural development of the steppes. In 1828 it supported the foundation of the Imperial Society for Agriculture of Southern Russia in Odessa, in southern Ukraine, with the aim of improving all branches of agriculture, including growing crops, that were appropriate to the steppe environment.[18] Russian officials, for example Konstantin Veselovskii – a senior figure in the Ministry of State Domains in the mid-nineteenth century – expressed optimism for the prospects of the settlement and cultivation of this fertile land. He specifically argued that the climate of the steppes was better suited to arable farming – the main occupation

[14] See D. Moon, *The Russian Peasantry 1600–1930: The World the Peasants Made* (London and New York, 1999), 254–62.

[15] Samuel Georg Gmelin, *Puteshestvie po Rossii dlya issledovaniya trekh tsarstv estestva* (2 vols., St Petersburg, 1771–7), I, 269–70. On the expeditions, see V. F. Gnucheva, *Materialy dlya istorii ekspeditsii akademii nauk v XVIII i XX vekakh* (Moscow and Leningrad, 1940), 97–108, 126.

[16] Peter Simon Pallas, *Travels through the Southern Provinces of the Russian Empire, in the Years 1793 and 1794*, trans. from the German (2 vols., London, 1802), I, 498–9.

[17] I. Ya. Gil'denshtedt, 'Dnevnik puteshestviya v Yuzhnuyu Rossiyu akademika S. Peterburgskoi Akademii Nauk Gil'denshtedta v 1773–1774 g.', *Zapiski Imperatorskogo Odesskogo obshchestva istorii i drevnosti*, 11 (1879), 180–228. Grain yields approaching or exceeding 1:10 were sometimes attained in good years on the steppes, especially on land only recently ploughed up, in the late nineteenth and early twentieth centuries. For high yields in the Don region, see *Gosudarstvennyi arkhiv Rostovskoi oblasti* [hereafter *GARO*], f.46, op.1, d.3222, l.50 ob (1894), d.3440, l.109 (1909).

[18] M. P. Borovskii, *Istoricheskii obzor pyatidesyatiletnei deyatel'nosti Imperatorskogo Obshchestva Sel'skogo Khozyaistva Yuzhnoi Rossii s 1828 po 1878 god* (Odessa, 1878), 5.

of the peasant settlers – than raising livestock, which had sustained the steppe nomads for millennia.[19]

The settlement of the steppes by Slavonic farmers, expeditions by scientists and government-sponsored development were followed by the incorporation of images of the steppe landscape into Russian (and Ukrainian) culture. An important evocation of the steppes in literature was that of Nicholas Gogol' in his novella *Taras Bul'ba* about a cossack band in sixteenth-century Ukraine. The novella contained descriptions of the treeless steppe as a 'green and gold ocean' with tall grasses that could conceal mounted cossacks up to their caps. For Gogol', moreover, the steppe was 'beautiful'.[20] Gogol' was describing the unploughed steppe around his home at Dikan'ka, in Poltava province, and in doing so made it famous. Dokuchaev visited Dikan'ka during one of his expeditions to Poltava province in 1888.[21] Anton Chekhov, another native of the steppes (from Taganrog), captured the space, distance, heat, dust and monotony, but also the familiarity, of a long journey across steppes in his short story of 1888.[22] The story was reputed to be a favourite of Dokuchaev's,[23] who made many such journeys. The nineteenth century witnessed the development of Russian landscape painting. Artists such as Arkhip Kuindzhi (who was from Mariupol', not far from Taganrog) painted striking landscapes of the steppes, capturing the light and the skies as well as the land, that complemented the more traditional, and some may say more 'Russian', forest landscapes.[24] Christopher Ely has recently argued that over the nineteenth century, many Russian writers and artists consciously constructed a landscape that incorporated forest and steppe (and rivers and mountains) as beautiful and, above all, as a national space that was 'Russian'.[25] The argument can be extended to late-nineteenth-century Russian music. In his symphonic poem 'In the

[19] K. S. Veselovskii, 'Prostranstvo i stepen' naselennosti Evropeiskoi Rossii', in *Sbornik Statisticheskikh Svedenii o Rossii*, I (Spb, 1851), 28–9; *idem*, *O Klimate Rossii* (Spb 1857), 49–52. See also D. Mun [Moon], 'Predstavleniya o vozdeistvii khlebopashestva na prirodu stepei yugo-vostoka Evropeiskoi chasti Rossii, 1850–1900', *Izvestiya Vysshikh Uchebnykh Zavedenii. Severo-Kavkazskii region. Yubileinyi vypusk* (2002), 30–8.

[20] N. V. Gogol', *Taras Bul'ba*, ed. E. I. Prokhorov and N. L. Stepanov (Moscow, 1963), 16–18. See also C. Ely, *This Meagre Nature: Landscape and National Identity in Imperial Russia* (DeKalb, IL, 2002), 91–4.

[21] I. Krupenikov and L. Krupenikov, *Puteshestviya i ekspeditsii V. V. Dokuchaeva* (Moscow, 1949), 74.

[22] Anton Chekhov, 'The Steppe', in Anton Chekhov, *The Steppe and Other Stories, 1887–1891*, trans. R. Wilks, introduction by D. Rayfield (2001), 3–101.

[23] S. V. Zonn, *Vasilii Vasil'evich Dokuchaev, 1846–1903* (Moscow, 1991), 146.

[24] *Russian Landscape*, ed. D. Jackson and Patty Wageman (2003). [Catalogue to 'Russian Landscape in the Age of Tolstoy' at the National Gallery, London, 23 June – 12 September 2004.]

[25] Ely, *This Meagre Nature*.

Steppes of Central Asia' and opera 'Prince Igor' (which tells the story of a campaign against the nomadic Polovtsians in today's Ukraine in the twelfth century), Alexander Borodin skillfully interwove Russian and 'oriental' themes to symbolise the 'unification' of the diverse lands of the empire.[26]

Russia's rulers, bands of cossacks, waves of peasant migrants, expeditions of scientists, government officials and, latterly, writers, artists and composers thus constructed images of the steppes as a land of fertile soil, opportunity, prosperity, freedom, beauty and Russianness. These images were only one side of the coin. The massive influx of settlers and the development of arable farming had a massive impact on the environment. It has been estimated that the proportion of the total land area of the region that had been ploughed up and thus converted to arable land increased from 6 per cent in 1725 to 31 per cent in 1887. This was at the expense of pasture and meadowland, woodland, which fell by almost half, and virgin steppe.[27] The area of land that was being ploughed up, moreover, was increasing rapidly on the eve of the disaster of 1891–2. By the early 1890s, in most provinces of the steppe region, arable land approached or exceeded half the total land area. In southern Ukraine and the Don Cossack region, the area of woodland had been reduced to only around 2 per cent of the total area.[28] In good years, as has already been indicated, the settlers reaped bumper harvests from the fertile land. Right from the early stages of the settlement and cultivation of the steppes, however, they also experienced periodic bad harvests that were usually caused by droughts. Gmelin reported that the harvest on the lower Don in 1769 was not profitable due to the 'excessive aridity'.[29] Over the nineteenth century, there were serious drought-induced harvest failures on parts of the steppes in 1822, 1832–3, 1840, the late 1840s, 1875, 1885 and 1891.[30] The dilemma for farmers was, and still is, that the fertile soil of the steppes does not always receive sufficient rainfall

[26] S. Diani, *Borodin*, trans. Robert Lord (1963), 226–8, 278–9; R. W. Oldani, 'Borodin, Aleksandr Porfir'yevich', in *The New Grove Dictionary of Music and Musicians,* 2nd edn (London and New York, 2001), III, 913–14.

[27] Mun, 'Predstavleniya', 31; M. A. Tsvetkov, *Izmenenie lesistosti evropeiskoi Rossii: s kontsa XVII stoletiia po 1914 god* (Moscow, 1957), 111, 115, 117.

[28] *Sel'skoe i lesnoe khozyaistvo Rossii,* map 2 (facing 54), map 3 (facing 56). See also A. Fortunatov, 'O svyazi khlebnykh tsen i urozhaev s nekotorymi izmeneniyami v russkom zemledelii', in *Vliyanie urozhaev i khlebnykh tsen na nekotorye storony russkogo narodnogo khozyaistva,* ed. A. I. Chuprov and A. S. Posnikov, I (Spb, 1897), 268; V. K. Yatsunskii, 'Izmeneniya v razmeshchenie zemledeliya v evropeiskoi Rossii s kontsa XVIII v. do Pervoi Mirovoi Voiny', in *Voprosy istorii sel'skogo khozyaistva krest'yanstva i revolyutsionnogo dvizheniya v Rossii,* ed. *idem* (Moscow, 1961), 113–48.

[29] Gmelin, *Puteshestvie*, I, 241.

[30] See A. Kahan, 'Natural Calamities and their Effect on the Food Supply in Russia,' *Jahrbuecher fuer Geschichte Osteuropas*, 16 (1968), 353–77; 'Neurozhai na Rusi', *Trudy Imperatorskogo*

to support the cultivation of cereals and fodder grasses. The unreliable rainfall and other climatic fluctuations have condemned the steppes to periodic disasters such as that of 1891–2.

II

From the perspective of environmental history, one of the most important points about the peopling and ploughing up of the Russian steppes is that the settlers moved from one type of environment to another. Thus, they encountered unfamiliar natural conditions, introduced ways of life that differed substantially from those of the previous inhabitants and in the process had a significant impact on the environment.[31] Peasant migrants moved to the drier, fertile, grasslands of the steppes from the wetter, less fertile, forested lands of central Russia and northern Ukraine. As they displaced the nomads, much of the land they cultivated was pasture land, which in many cases had never seen a plough before, and they sowed cereal crops in place of wild grasses. It was the impact of the settlement and ploughing up of the grasslands that was at the heart of Dokuchaev's study of the steppes. Thus, the agricultural settlement of the Russian steppes provides a valuable case study of the environmental consequences of human migration. Indeed, as the prominent environmental historian John McNeill recently pointed out: 'the sweep of Russian frontier expansion' is 'cry[ing] out . . . for the attention of environmental historians'.[32]

Environmental history is almost by definition global in its approach and perspective. The environmental history of the Russian steppes cannot be considered in isolation, but as part of the wider history of the interaction between humans and grasslands in temperate lands throughout the world. Dokuchaev was one of the pioneers of such a perspective in his work on environmental zones. He explicitly linked the zones of Russia with similar zones around the northern hemisphere. The Russian steppes were thus part of the 'black-earth steppes of Hungary, Russia, Asia and America' that had once all been a 'sea' of steppe grasses. The steppes of Eurasia and the prairies of north America are also similar to the pampas of southern America, the veldt of southern Africa and grasslands in Australia and New Zealand. From the eighteenth and especially the nineteenth centuries, semi-arid grasslands all around the world were being settled and ploughed up by farmers from Europe to supply the growing worldwide market for

---

Vol'nogo Ekonomicheskogo Obshchestva, 2, 5 (1891), 145–77; L. Vesin, 'Neurozhai v Rossii i ikh glavnye prichiny', *Severnyi vestnik*, 1 (1892), 85–123, no. 2 (1892), 41–75.

[31] For discussion of these issues on a broader canvas, see A. J. Crosby, *Ecological Imperialism: The Biological Expansion of Europe, 900–1900* (Cambridge, 1986); J. F. Richards, *The Unending Frontier: An Environmental History of the Early Modern World* (Berkeley, CA, 2003).

[32] J. R. McNeill, 'Observations on the Nature and Culture of Environmental History', *History and Theory*, 40 (2003), 30, 41–2.

grain. In all these regions, farmers from environments with fairly heavy soils and adequate rainfall encountered the problem of growing crops in environments with fertile soils, but lower and unreliable rainfall. In 'good' years, the farmers reaped bumper harvests and prospered; in years of drought, the land yielded little or nothing in return for their labour. Everywhere, moreover, removing the previous vegetation and ploughing up the land seemed to lead to the erosion of the fertile soil that had attracted the settlers in the first place.[33]

In the worst years, farmers watched in horror as the wind blew away the rich soil in dust storms that obliterated the sun and their hopes for the future:

> The dry autumn . . . , the snowless winter and, finally, the dry spring turned the top layer of . . . earth partly into a dry dust, [and] partly into a fine-grained, crumbly, powder, which, with the onset of strong storms in April, lost their hold, and were raised up in whole clouds, concealing the sun's rays and turning day into night. Witnesses unanimously testified that the phenomenon had such a dreadful and frightening character that everyone expected 'the end of the world'.

The source continues that it was impossible to go outdoors, trains were halted by drifts of earth blocking the tracks, crops were killed by the blows of the dust and seeds that were just starting to germinate were blown from one place to another and perished. Huge areas were left without any vegetation at all; there were not even any weeds left after the dust storms had wreaked their havock. This image could have come from John Steinbeck's graphic depiction in *The Grapes of Wrath* of the dust bowl on the southern plains of the USA in the 1930s. It is actually a description of the dust storms on the southern steppes of Russia in the spring of 1892 by P. Zemyatchenskii, who was one of the scientists on Dokuchaev's expedition.[34] Another of the scientists on the expedition, N. Adamov, noted that a century earlier, in the 1790s, Pallas had described how the scorching summer winds raised clouds of dust on the steppes. This was before the wholesale ploughing up of the steppes and removal of so much

[33] See J. McNeill, *Something New under the Sun: An Environmental History of the Twentieth Century* (London, 2000), 38–43, 212–16, 276–81; D. Worster, *Dust Bowl: The Southern Plains in the 1930s* (New York, 1979); A. G. Zarrili, 'Capitalism, Ecology, and Agrarian Expansion in the Pampean Region, 1890–1950', *Environmental History*, 6 (2001), 561–83.

[34] P. Zemyatchenskii, 'Velikoanadol'skii uchastok', *Trudy Ekspeditsii, snaryazhennoi Lesnym Departmentom, pod rukovodstvom professora Dokuchaeva, Nauchnii otdel*, 1, 3 (1894), 15, 17. For further descriptions of the dust storms on the steppes in the early 1890s, complete with 'before and after' illustrations, see N. Adamov, 'Meteorologicheskie nablyudeniya 1892–1894 godov', *Trudy Ekspeditsii, snaryazhennoi Lesnym Departmentom, pod rukovodstvom professora Dokuchaeva, Nauchnii otdel*, 3, 1 (1898), 235–43. For a measured analysis, see G. Vysotskii, 'Materialy po izucheniyu chernykh bur v stepyakh Rossii', *Trudy Ekspeditsii, snaryazhennoi Lesnym Departmentom, pod rukovodstvom professora Dokuchaeva, Sbornyi otdel*, 1 (1894), 1–16. For an account of sand storms on the steppes of the north Caucasus, see *Gosudarstvennyi Arkhiv Stavropol'skgogo Kraya*, f.101, op.4, d.894, 19 Sept. 1880–5.

of the natural vegetation. Adamov was careful to point out that the effect of the wind on the steppes was far greater in the 1890s than the 1790s as a result of the changes made to the environment in the intervening century.[35] Other scholars have not been so measured in their analyses. Descriptions of dust storms on southern plains of the USA in 1830 (not 1930), prompted the historian James Malin to call the argument 'that the dust storms of the 1930s were *caused* by "the plow that broke the Plains"' a 'brazen falsehood'.[36] Malin's assertion has, of course, been disputed, by Donald Worster amongst others.[37] The problem for environmental scientists and historians is to distinguish between phenomena that occur independently of human actions, and those that are caused or exacerbated by the changes made by people. Such debates continue among environmental scientists to the present day.[38]

III

In Russia, over the course of the nineteenth century, an increasing number of landowners, scientists, government officials and other educated people made a connection between the changes the settlers had made to the land, especially but not solely the destruction of the small areas of woodland on the steppes, and the droughts, which seemed to be recurring more frequently and with ever more disastrous consequences. Such views were often expressed in the wake of serious droughts, such as that of 1832–3,[39] and built up momentum over the following decades. With increasing vigour, it was asserted and reasserted in the specialist and more general periodical press that, as a result of deforestation and other human activity, the climate was becoming drier, droughts more frequent and the drying influence of the hot winds from Asia (the *sukhovei*) more marked as the woods that that had sheltered the land were destroyed.[40] In the autumn

[35] Adamov, 'Meteorologicheskie nablyudeniya 1892–1894', 235.

[36] J. C. Malin, 'The Grassland of North America: Its Occupance and the Challenge of Continuous Reappraisals', in *Man's Role in Changing the Face of the Earth*, ed. William L. Thomas (2 vols., Chicago, 1956), II, 355–6.

[37] Worster, *Dust Bowl*, 205–6.

[38] See, for example, W. B. Meyer, *Human Impact on the Earth* (Cambridge, 1996), 201–15.

[39] See 'Rassuzhdenie o neobkhodimosti okhraneniya vladel'cheskikh lesov ot istrebleniya i o pol'ze pravil'nogo lesnogo khozyaistva', *Lesnoi zhurnal*, pt 1, bk 1 (1833), 51–103; Breitenbakh, 'O pol'ze lesov v prirode', *Lesnoi zhurnal*, pt 1, bk 3 (1835), 383–91; 'O vliyanii lesov i istrebleniya onykh na klimat', *Lesnoi zhurnal*, pt 1, bk 3 (1837), 427–42. On the drought and harvest failure of 1832–3, see D. Moon, *Russian Peasants and Tsarist Legislation on the Eve of Reform, 1825–1855* (Basingstoke and London, 1992), 41–4; J. R. Staples, *Cross-Cultural Encounters on the Ukrainian Steppe: Settling the Molochna Basis, 1783–1861* (Toronto, 2003), 87–92.

[40] For a few examples, see I. Palimpsestov, 'Peremenilsya li klimat yuga Rossii?', in *Sbornik statei o sel'skom khozyaistve yuga Rossii, izvlechennikh iz Zapisok Imperatorskogo Obshchestva sel'skogo khozyaistva yuzhnoi Rossii s 1830 po 1868 god*, ed. *idem* (Odessa, 1868), 1–35; [Valuev], *Doklad vysochaishe uchrezhdennoi komissii dlya issledovaniya nyneshnego polozheniya sel'skogo khozyaistva i sel'skoi*

of 1891, as the full extent of the catastrophe was becoming apparent, the agricultural specialist Nicholas Vereshchagin put words to the anxiety felt by many when he linked the 'harmful influence of the hot, Asiatic winds' with the devastating Mongol invasion of the thirteenth century.[41] The hot, dry winds from Asia were the new Mongols. And such concerns were picked up by writers and artists, most famously by Chekhov in his play 'Uncle Vanya', completed in 1896. The character Dr Astrov makes an impassioned speech about the need to preserve the forests: 'Forests keep disappearing, rivers dry up, wild life's become extinct, the climate's ruined and the land grows poorer and uglier every day.'[42] Some scientists, however, were more wary about making such direct, causal links between deforestation and climate change. In a debate in the Free Economic Society in late 1891, the meteorologist Alexander Voeikov noted that the available data did not seem to show a decline in the total level of precipitation. Dokuchaev, in his book *Our Steppes: Past and Present*, doubted that the climate was becoming drier, and also pointed to the lack of adequate information to support the argument that the climate was changing. Both scientists called for more funds to support research.[43]

As the disaster of 1891–2 unfolded, Russians tried to find out what had caused it and what could be done to prevent repetitions. There was general agreement that the main cause was abnormal meteorological conditions. Future Minister of Agriculture Aleksei Ermolov gave a detailed account of the conditions that preceded the harvest failure in

---

proizvoditel'nosti v Rossii (Spb, 1873), 7, 41; V. Vasil'chikov, 'Chernozem i ego budushchnost'', *Otechestvennye zapiski*, 2 (Feb. 1876), 2nd pagn, 167–82; D. L. Ivanov, 'Vliyanie Russkoi kolonizatsii na prirodu Stavropol'skogo kraya', *Izvestiya Imperatorskogo Russkogo Geograficheskogo Obshchestva*, 22, 3 (1886), 225–54; P. L. Korf, 'Po povodu neurozhaya nyneshnego goda', *Trudy Imperatorskogo Vol'nogo Ekonomicheskogo Obshchestva*, 2, 6 (1891), 203–21; V. Solov'ev, 'Narodnaya beda i obshchestvennaya pomosh',' *Vestnik Evropy*, 10 (Oct. 1891), 781. See also O'Rourke, *Warriors and Peasants*, 50–5, 76–8. Russians were influenced by north American and western European scientists. See Georg Marsh, *Chelovek i priroda, ili o vliyanii cheloveka na izmenenie fiziko-geografiskikh uslovii prirody*, trans. from English by N. A. Nevedomskii (Spb, 1866); Bekkeral' [Becquerel], 'Vliyanie istrebleniya lesov na klimat', [review], *Zhurnal Ministerstva Gosudarstvennykh Imushchestv*, 52, 4 (1854), 54–68.

[41] N. V. Vereshchagin, 'Po povodu neurozhaya tekushchego goda', *Trudy Imperatorskogo Vol'nogo Ekonomicheskogo Obshchestva*, 2, 5 (1891), 183. (He was the brother of the war artist Vasilii Vereshchagin, who had a growing distaste for the 'Orient'. D. Schimmelpenninck van der Oye, *Toward the Rising Sun: Russian Ideologies of Empire and the Path to War with Japan* (DeKalb, IL, 2001), 207–8.)

[42] Anton Chekhov, *Five Plays*, trans. and with an Introduction by Ronald Hingley (Oxford, 1977), 127–8. See also J. Costlow, 'Imaginations of Destruction: The "Forest Question" in Nineteenth-Century Russian Culture', *Russian Review*, 62 (2003), 91–118.

[43] 'Besedy v I Otdelenii Imperatorskogo Vol'nogo Ekonomicheskogo Obshchestva po voprosu o prichinakh neurozhaya 1891 goda i merakh protiv povtoreniya podobykh urozhaev v budushchem', *Trudy Imperatorskogo Vol'nogo Ekonomicheskogo Obshchestva*, 1 (1892), 110, 121–2, 124. See also A. Voeikov, 'Po voprosu lesnoi meteorologii', *Meteorologicheskii vestnik*, 2 (1892), 51–60; Dokuchaev, *Sochineniya*, VI, 88–9.

a book published in early 1892. The unusual weather began in 1890. The first half of the summer was very wet. The rain was so heavy that many rivers burst their banks in early June. The weather changed sharply, however, in the second half of the month. There followed a 'tropical' heatwave, drought and scorching hot winds from the south-east. As a result, the harvest in 1890 was adversely affected, and in many places the sowing of the winter crops was delayed until late September or early October. Winter began early. There were hard frosts in late October and early November. When the snow came, it was accompanied by strong winds that blew it around in snow storms and, crucially, denuded the fields of the snow cover needed to protect the winter crops. In the spring of 1891, consequently, there was little water in the rivers and no floods that usually irrigated the meadows. Nevertheless, the fields absorbed sufficient moisture from what melting snow there was to allow the spring crops to be sown as usual, and the winter crops began to recover. The turn for the better was short-lived, however. In late April and May, the weather swung from cold snaps and hard frosts to heat waves and droughts and then back again. The young crops could not survive such conditions: the arable fields remained bare, and meadows were scorched and yellow. Moreover, trees dried up and died in dozens and even weeds shrivelled and died. The drought continued for much of the summer. The worst affected was the area around Tsaritsyn (later Stalingrad) on the lower Volga, where there was no rain for ninety-six days: over three months. Large parts of the steppes received no rain for two months. The effects of the drought were exacerbated by the return of the scorching winds from the east, that dried out the parched topsoil even more, and then blew it around in dust storms similar to those described earlier. The land was drying out not just on the surface, but also underneath. Ground water levels fell; ponds, springs and wells dried up; rivers were lower than usual.

And the harvest failed. In the seventeen provinces of the south and south-east worst affected, the harvest was down by 45.4 per cent compared with average harvests in 1883–7. The most badly hit provinces were Orenburg, in the east of the steppe region, where the shortfall was 73 per cent, and Voronezh, on the boundary of the open steppe and forest-steppe, where it was 69 per cent down. The disaster hit roughly one third of European Russia. The steppes of southern Ukraine, part of the Don and the North Caucasus, however, escaped the drought and had good harvests in 1891. They were not enough to compensate. In the fifty provinces of European Russia as a whole, the total grain harvest was 26 per cent below the average for the years 1883–7.[44] Although conditions in the atmosphere were held largely responsible for the disaster, the role

[44] [A. S. Ermolov], *Neurozhai i narodnoe bedstvie* (Spb, 1892), 3–34. (The book was published anonymously, but the author was recognised as A. S. Ermolov. *Novyi Entsiklopedicheskii Slovar'*, ed. F. A. Brokgauz and I. A. Efron (Spb, n.d.), XVII, 514–15.) See also M. N. Raevskii,

of other factors, such as agricultural practices, the system of communal land tenure and indeed the wider social and economic system were also discussed. And, scientists agonised over whether human impact on the meteorological environment was also to blame.[45]

At the same time, many schemes were put forward to seek to deal with the environmental constraints on arable farming on the steppes, and so avert future disasters. One of the most comprehensive was that of Ermolov, which he published in early 1892.[46] Ermolov's plan, together with others put forward, built on previous plans and experience. The most widely proposed solutions were conservation of existing woodland, tree planting and artificial irrigation. While deforestation was believed by many to have a detrimental impact on the climate, making it drier and more extreme, conservation and planting more trees was thought to have the opposite effect. Many specialists added that trees sheltered the land from the hot, dry winds from Asia, and assisted in moisture retention in the soil.[47] Early tree-planting schemes on the steppes met with mixed success, as the saplings struggled to overcome droughts, the salty subsoil and pests.[48] By the latter part of the century, however, much experience had been accumulated in steppe forestry. An important centre of research was the Velikii Anadol'skii plantation, which had been founded in 1843 on the open steppes of Ekaterinoslav province near the Sea of Azov.[49]

The second main solution proposed to deal with the shortage of moisture on the steppes was artificial irrigation. Many books and pamphlets advocating irrigation were produced. Most involved damming gulleys and ravines to store water from rain and melted snow, which was then to be released to irrigate the fields. It proved much harder to put the

'Neurozhai 1891 goda v svyazi s obshchei kharakteristikoi nashei khlebnoi proizvoditel'nosti a takzhe vyvoza khlebov zagranitsu za pred"idushchie gody', *Izvestiya Imperatorskogo Russkogo Geograficheskogo Obshchestva*, 28, 1 (1892), 1–29; N. Kravtsov, 'Po povodu neurozhaev v 1891 i 1892 godakh', *Sel'skoe khozyaistvo i lesovodstvo* (Apr. 1893), 1st pagn, 317–35.

[45] See 'Besedy v I Otdelenii Imperatorskogo Vol'nogo Ekonomicheskogo Obshchestva'.

[46] [Ermolov], *Neurozhai*, 34–78. See also P. Barakov, *O vozmozhnykh merakh bor'by s zasukhami* (Odessa, 1892); P. A. Kostychev, *O bor'be s zasukhoi v chernozemnoi oblasti postredstvom obrabotki polei i nakopleniya na nikh snega* (Spb, 1893).

[47] See P[alimpsestov], 'Lesovodstvo. Nechto v rode "Vvedeniya" v uroki lesovodstva dlya Novorossiiskogo kraya', *Zapiski Imperatorskogo Obshchestva Sel'skogo Khozyaistva Yuzhnoi Rossii*, 1 (Jan. 1852), 15–80; Vasil'chikov, 'Chernozem i ego budushchnost''; Ya. Veinberg, *Les: znachenie ego v prirode i mery k ego sokhraneniyu* (Moscow, 1884). For a dissenting view, see P. A. Kostychev, 'Sposobstvuet le razvedenie lesov unichtozheniyu zasukh?', *Otechestvennye zapiski*, 3 (1876), 2nd pagn, 1–33.

[48] *GARO*, f.301, op.14, d.7, 1849–52; d.10, 1850; d.22, 1852–60.

[49] N. G. Rachinskii, 'O stepnom drevovozrashchenii v Novorossiiskom krae po povodu preobrazovaniya Veliko-Anadolskogo lesnichestva', *Zapiski Imperatorskogo Obshchestva Sel'skogo Khozyaistva Yuzhnoi Rossii* (1865), 426–38; G. N. Vysotskii, 'Stepnoe lesorazvedenie', in *Polnaya entsiklopediya russkgo sel'skogo khozyaistva i soprikasayushchikhsya s nimi nauk* (11 vols., Spb, 1900–9), IX, 443–99.

schemes into practice. Some private landowners built irrigation schemes, but they were usually restricted to providing water for people, cattle, vegetables and orchards.[50] In the 1880s, in the wake of serious droughts and harvest failures in Samara province on the Volga, the Ministry of State Domains put Lieutenant-General I. I. Zhilinskii in charge of an expedition to investigate irrigating the steppes. Supplying water for the use of livestock and humans, and irrigating low-lying meadows proved much easier and cheaper than irrigating arable fields.[51] Nevertheless, a programme of public works to irrigate the steppe region was planned on the eve of the disaster and put into operation under General Annenkov in 1892. Dokuchaev was one of the technical advisors. The programme was not a great success, however, and Annenkov was charged with misuse of the funds allocated to him.[52]

Dokuchaev's work in the aftermath of disaster of 1891–2, including his plan to address the environmental constraints on arable farming on the steppes, thus did not come out of the blue but, as he readily acknowledged, was part of a larger body of theoretical and practical work by his contemporaries and predecessors.[53]

IV

Vasilii Dokuchaev is one of the major figures in nineteenth-century Russian, and world, science; he is on a par with the chemist Dmitrii Mendeleev, who drew up the periodic table of elements. Educated in the natural sciences at St Petersburg University, Dokuchaev went on to conduct pioneering work in geomorphology, geology and, above all, soil science. He devoted a great deal of time and energy to organising and leading scientific expeditions, and was committed to applying science to the problems experienced by agriculture in late nineteenth-century Russia.[54] His early work, in the 1870s, concerned the formation of ravines

[50] A. Bode, 'O dobyvanii vody v stepnykh mestakh yuzhnoi i yugo-vostochnoi chasti Evropeiskoi Rossii', *Zhurnal Ministerstva Gosudarstvennikh Imushchestv*, 9 (1843), 4th pagn, 141–5; *GARO*, f.46, op.1, d.780 (1866–9); S. Kizenkov, 'Oroshenie', in *Polnaya entsiklopediya russkogo sel'skogo khozyaistva*, VI, 414–68.

[51] I. I. Zhilinkskii, *Ocherk rabot ekspeditsii po orosheniyu na yuge Rossii i Kavkaze* (Spb, 1892); *idem*, *Zemledel'cheskie gidravlicheskie raboty* (Spb, 1893), 21–39. See also M. N. Gersevanov, 'Ob obvodnenii yuzhnoi stepnoi polosy Rossii', *Zapiski imperatorskogo russkogo tekhnicheskogo obshchestva* (Jan. 1891), 1st pagn, 1–30.

[52] *Stenograficheskii otchet o soveshchaniiakh pri [Imperatorskom Moskovskom] Obshchestve [Sel'skogo Khoziaistva], s 18-go po 22-e Dekabria 1892 goda, po obshchestvennym rabotam po obvodeniiu iugo-vostochnoi chasti Rossii, proizvennym v 1892 g. rasporiazheniem Zaveduiushchego Obshchestvennymi rabotami Generala M. N. Annenkova*, ed. A. P. Perepelkin (Moscow, 1893); Robbins, *Famine*, 110–12.

[53] Dokuchaev, *Socheniniya*, VI, 105.

[54] On his career, see L. A. Chebotareva, 'Vasilii Vasil'evich Dokuchaev (1846–1903). Biograficheskii ocherk', in Dokuchaev, *Sochineniya*, IX, 49–152; G. V. Dobrovol'skii,

and river valleys. He challenged catastrophist theories, and emphasised the role of erosion caused by flowing water over the long term.[55] In the mid-1870s he turned his attention to the study of soil, in particular the black earth of the steppes. The drought of 1875 prompted the Free Economic Society to fund Dokuchaev to carry out a detailed study of the black earth in the major agricultural regions of Russia. In 1883, he published his major work, *The Russian Black Earth*, in which he presented a detailed analysis of the geographical distribution of the black earth, its fertility and a comprehensive theory for its origins.[56] On the basis of this work, between 1882 and 1894, he led teams of scientists in expeditions to evaluate the soil and natural resources of Nizhnii Novgorod province, in the north of the black earth region, and Poltava province, in the heart of the black earth region in Ukraine.[57]

Dokuchaev's work in Poltava province provided much of the material for his book *Our Steppes: Past and Present*.[58] It was in this book that Dokuchaev put forward his explanation for the long-term, natural and human-induced causes of the drought and harvest failure of 1891–2, and presented his plan to address the problems. At the heart of the book is the question of moisture, which was crucial to the success of agriculture on the steppes, and the lack of which in 1891 had caused the disaster. The book took the form of a series of chapters on different aspects of the environment of the steppes (geology, hydrology, soil, flora, fauna, climate). Most chapters described the natural processes involved in the evolution of the steppe environment since the end of the last ice age. He also described the later human impact on that environment. He allowed little or no role for human activity in the formation of the steppe environment, which, therefore, for Dokuchaev was a 'virgin' (*devstvennyi*) or natural environment. Human impact came towards the end of Dokuchaev's story. In examining the effects of human actions, he paid particular attention to the felling of much of the small amount of natural woodland in river valleys and other specific parts of the region, to the removal of much of the original vegetation, in particular the steppe grasses, and the destruction of the structure of the black earth by wholesale ploughing. (Ploughing, but not grazing, destroys the structure of the soil.) Dokuchaev, who had

'Vsya zhizn' v nauke i bor'be', in V. V. Dokuchaev, *Dorozhe zolota russkii chernozem*, ed. G. V. Dobrovol'skii (Moscow, 1994), 5–44; Krupenikov and Krupenikov, *Puteshestviya*.

[55] V. V. Dokuchaev, 'Ovragi i ikh zhachenie', in Dokuchaev, *Sochineniya*, I, 103–11 (1st published in *Trudy Vol'nogo Ekonomicheskogo Obshchestva*, 3, 2 (1877), 167–78); *idem*, 'Sposoby obrazovaniya rechnykh dolin Evropeiskoi Rossii', in *Sochineniya*, I, 113–273, esp. 153–73 (1st published in *Trudy S.-Peterburgskogo obshchestva estestvoisp*, 9 (1878), 1–222).

[56] Dokuchaev, *Sochineniya*, III (1st published as *Russkii chernozem: Otchet Imperatorskomu Vol'nomu Ekonomicheskogo Obshchestva* (Spb 1883)).

[57] Krupenikov and Krupenikov, *Puteshestviya*, 31–82.

[58] Dokuchaev, 'Nashi Stepi'.

visited the home of the late writer Gogol' at Dikan'ka in Poltava province in 1888, bemoaned the disappearance of the 'virgin steppe' that the writer had lauded and made famous.[59]

The loss of the natural vegetation of the steppes and ploughing up the black earth had all led, he argued, to very serious consequences. Virgin soils and land covered by virgin steppe grasses, together with the larger areas of woodland that had previously existed, were, he argued, better able to absorb and retain moisture from melted snow and rain. Ploughed soil and cultivated or mown land, on the contrary, were more liable to lose moisture through evaporation and run-off. Ploughing and cultivation, moreover, exacerbated soil erosion and gulleying. These, in turn, further increased the drainage of water – along the enlarged gulleys and into the rivers – that would otherwise have been retained and absorbed into the land. The consequence of all these, he maintained, was that ground water levels were falling and the steppes were gradually drying out. This drying out of the land made crops more vulnerable to the periodic droughts that afflicted the steppes. He pointed to evidence that 'virgin' (*tselinnii*) land was better able to support vegetation, including fodder grasses, even in 'extraordinarily dry years' when artificial meadows or land that had been previously ploughed and left fallow for a few years, yielded no hay. For Dokuchaev, therefore, the crop failure of 1891 was explained by the drying out of the land.[60] Dokuchaev thus presented his interpretation of the history of the evolution of the natural environment of the steppes and the impact of human activity. And it was the latter, which in his view had upset 'virgin' nature, to which he attributed the harvest failure of 1891.

Dokuchaev's conclusions were supported by the work of a colleague and close friend, A. A. Izmailovskii, who was involved in a research project investigating the 'drying out of the steppe'. In the 1880s and 1890s Izmailovskii conducted field work in Kherson and southern Poltava provinces, in Ukraine. Like Dokuchaev, Izmailovskii argued that the alleged drying out of the steppe was due to the removal of the 'virgin' vegetation and ploughing up the land. The two scientists became acquainted during Dokuchaev's expedition to Poltava province in the 1880s, and were influenced by each other's work.[61] Thus, Dokuchaev and Izmailovskii dissented from the view of many of their contemporaries that the disaster of 1891 was a result of climate change, in particular the allegedly increasing frequency in droughts, that was in turn claimed to be

[59] Krupenikov and Krupenikov, *Puteshestviya*, 74, 77. Dokuchaev, *Sochineniya*, VI, 58.

[60] Dokuchaev, *Sochineniya*, VI, esp. 57–61, 87–9.

[61] A. A. Izmail'skii, 'Kak vysokhla nasha step'. Issledovaniya otnositel'no vlazhnosti pochvy i podpochvy', *Sel'skoe khozyaistvo i lesovodstvo: Zhurnal Ministerstva Gosudarstvennikh Imushchestv*, pt 173 (Aug. 1893), 2nd pagn, 267–89, pt 174 (Sept. 1893), 2nd pagn, 1–27. For their correspondence, see 'Iz perepiski s A. A. Izmailovskim (1888–1900)', in Dokuchaev, *Sochineniya*, VIII, 243–325.

a consequence of deforestation (see above). The two scientists maintained that it was the land, not the climate, that was changing and becoming drier.

V

Having outlined his interpretation of the long-term causes of the harvest failure of 1891, Dokuchaev went on to propose a series of measures to overcome the problems which were undermining agriculture in the steppe region which we can call 'The Dokuchaev Plan':

I. Regulation of rivers – narrow and straighten courses of the major rivers, reduce spring floods, stop rivers silting up, reinforce banks with trees to stop sand etc. getting into rivers, remove sand bars; and dam smaller rivers and upper reaches of larger rivers to regulate flow and retain water in reservoirs.
II. Regulation of ravines and gulleys – reinforce steep slopes with trees, ban ploughing on steep slopes and, where appropriate, dam them to create ponds to hold rain and melt water.
III. Regulation of the use of water on the open steppes and watersheds – dig ponds on watersheds to hold melt and rain water and reinforce the banks with trees; elsewhere on the open steppes, plant hedges and build long, low dykes to help retain snow, melt and rain water; and plant trees on sandy soil, hillocks and other areas unsuitable for ploughing to act as wind breaks; dig wells to tap the replenished ground water for irrigation.
IV. Work out norms for relative areas of arable land, meadows, forest and water in conformity with local climate, ground and soil conditions as well as local agriculture.
V. Establish ways to cultivate the soil in order to make best use of the moisture, and work out the best varieties of crops to grow with regard to local soil and climatic conditions.[62]

Dokuchaev recognised that points IV and V could not be implemented immediately and would require much more preparatory work, but stated that the first three were fully attainable and were matters of utmost urgency in the interests of the state.[63] He further recognised that the successful implementation of his plan required science, technology, state

[62] The plan was published towards the end of Dokuchaev, 'Nashi stepi', and again in the introduction to the works of the scientific expedition that was set up to research the plan. Dokuchaev, *Sochineniya*, VI, 87–96, 112–18. For earlier proposals by others to regulate rivers, see *GARO*, f.46, op.1, d.590, 1857; I. Bentkovskii, 'Reka Kuma i neobkhodimost' uluchshit' ee ekonomicheskoe znachenie', *Stavropol'skie gubernskie vedomosti*, chast' neoffitsial'naya, 27–8 (1882).

[63] Dokuchaev, *Sochineniya*, VI, 90–2.

expenditure, and also good will, enlightened outlook and love of the land on the part of the landowners.[64] On the surface, Dokuchaev's plan seems broadly similar to other such plans proposed in and before 1892. Where it differs, however, is in his approach. His solutions were based on his interpretation of the long-term environmental history of the steppes, and sought to undo what he saw as the effects of human activity by working with natural processes in order to 'improve' the steppes for agriculture. According to one recent scientist, Dokuchaev's plan was, in present-day terminology, 'profoundly ecological' as well as 'talented propaganda'. Dokuchaev, moreover, was 'thirsting for action'.[65] Another difference between Dokuchaev's plan and others was that he received backing to put some of it into action.

VI

Dokuchaev tried, without success, to seek funding from the Free Economic Society, which had supported his study of the black earth.[66] Support was soon forthcoming from official sources. This is clear evidence for the grave concern that the drought and harvest failure had caused in official circles. The impetus for action seems to have come first from the provincial authorities in the steppe region. On 30 October 1891, the governor of Samara province reported to the minister of internal affairs on the seriousness of the drought and crop failure in his province. He identified irrigation and forestation as ways to avert such disasters in the future, and urged the minister to take steps to compel village communities and landowners, including the state and imperial family, to carry them out. He also called on the government to make the necessary technology and finance available in the form of loans. At a meeting of the Committee of Ministers in December 1891, the tsar himself noted the seriousness of the proposal. The committee referred the matter to the Ministry of State Domains, where it was passed to the Forestry Department of the Ministry. On 20 January 1892, the Department recommended finding out the following: how far and in what direction forestation of the steppes could influence crops, and the proportion of forest to steppe that would be necessary for a noticeable influence; how best to distribute new forests

[64] *Ibid.*, 102.

[65] I. A. Krupenikov, 'Ekspeditsii V. V. Dokuchaeva', *Pochvovedenie*, 2 (1996), 145.

[66] 'Zhurnal Obshchego Sobraniya Imperatorskogo Vol'nogo Ekonomicheskogo Obshchestva 19 May 1892', *Trudy Imperatorskogo Vol'nogo Ekonomicheskogo Obshchestva*, 1 (1893), 2nd pagn, 2; 'Otchet sekretarya o deistviyakh Imperatorskogo V. Ek. Obshchestva za 1892 g.', *Trudy Imperatorskogo Vol'nogo Ekonomicheskogo Obshchestva*, 3 (1893), 3rd pagn, 5. The Society did take a keen interest in the disaster, organising a temporary bureau to investigate the crop failure and holding a series of discussions that addressed the key issues.

on the steppe to achieve the desired goal; if any experiments would be needed to plan them, and, crucially, how much it would all cost.[67]

In the spring of 1892, the Forestry Department invited Dokuchaev to a special meeting to discuss 'the development of forestation work with the aim of regulating the management of water resources on the steppes'. The meeting decided to carry out those parts of Dokuchaev's plan that involved planting trees in ravines, on the open steppe, around reservoirs, along rivers and on sandy areas. In order to carry out such work, field research stations were to be established on three plots of state land. A total of 21,300 roubles was to be assigned to cover the salaries and expenses of the head of the expedition, his assistants and other specialists, and the cost of hired labour, equipment and analysis of samples of soil and water. Dokuchaev was invited to lead the expedition.[68] On 22 May the Minister of State Domains, M. N. Ostrovskii, approved the creation of the 'Special Expedition for testing and costing various methods and approaches for management of forestry and water resources on the steppes of Russia under the leadership of Professor Dokuchaev' attached to the ministry's Forestry Department.[69]

Dokuchaev put together a team of scientists to carry out the work. He appointed colleagues he had worked with on previous expeditions, for example N. M. Sibirtsev, and younger scientists who went on to greater importance, such as the forestry specialist G. N. Vysotskii and the botanist G. I. Tanfil'ev. He then reconnoitred and set up the three field research stations of around 5,000 hectares. He consulted Izmailovskii, and carefully selected sites which contained various combinations of typical features of the environment of the steppes. Dokuchaev chose plots, moreover, that were situated on watersheds, i.e. far from large rivers, in places with little water that regularly suffered from drought, strong winds and other 'unfavourable features of steppe nature'. The plots of land he selected were as follows: Starobel'skii (Derkulinskii) in eastern Khar'kov province, on the watershed between the Donets and Don rivers, which was an example of exposed, open steppe; Khrenovskoi in Voronezh province, between the Don and Volga river systems, which included areas of steppe as well as natural coniferous and broad-leaved woodland and was

[67] *Rossiiskii Gosudarstvennyi Istoricheskii Arkhiv*, f.1387, op.28, 1892, d.1023, ll.1–6. The Ministry had also received requests for action from local *zemstva*. Dokuchaev, *Sochineniya*, VI, 105–6. The Appanage Dept, which was responsible for the estates of the imperial family, also carried out anti-drought measures and experiments in 1891–2. *Meropriyatiya udel'nogo vedomstva v bor'be s zasukhami i drugimi klimaticheskimi vliyaniyami, prepyatstvuyushchimi khozyaistvu v yugo-vostochnykh stepnykh imeniyakh* (Spb, 1893).

[68] Dokuchaev, 'Osobaya ekspeditsiya, snaryazhennaya lesnym departamentom, pod rukovodstvom professora Dokuchaeva', in *Sochineniya*, VI, 105–8, 118–19.

[69] Dokuchaev, 'Osobaya ekspeditsiya', 118; Chebotareva, 'Vasilii Vasil'evich Dokuchaev', 105–10.

thus an example of forest-steppe; and Veliko-Anadol'skii in Ekaterinoslav province, between the Donets and Dnepr rivers, which contained the famous forestry plantation on the open steppe.[70] The research stations contained agricultural land, forestry plantations and what Dokuchaev believed to be examples of the 'virgin' environment of the steppes, of which only small areas were left on account of wholesale ploughing. These examples were vital for Dokuchaev, because it was the 'undisturbed', virgin environment that he maintained was better able to retain moisture in the soil and support vegetation even in years with low rainfall (see above).

Dokuchaev's teams of scientists carried out detailed research into the relief, hydrology, soil and geology, meteorological conditions and flora and fauna of these samples of 'virgin' nature. Dokuchaev believed that the various component parts of the natural environment of the steppes were all linked together. Bore holes were dug, meteorological stations set up and detailed data on the weather collected, samples of soil and ground water were collected and sent for chemical analysis, painstaking fieldwork and lists of species of plants and animals were made. The botanist Tanfil'ev wrote a very detailed account of the 'limits of forests in southern Russia', on the basis of Dokuchaev's technique of determining past vegetation from analysis of the organic content of the soil. Tanfil'ev followed Dokuchaev in concluding that, with the exception of river valleys and a few other exceptional areas, the steppes had never been forested.[71] The results of all this work were published in a number of volumes over the next few years.[72] The data gathered were essential for assessing the impact of the experiments that the expedition was to carry out. Thus, the samples of 'virgin' nature were to serve as 'baselines', or controls, for scientific research into ways of overcoming the environmental constraints on agriculture on the steppes. Furthermore, the 'virgin' environment could provide models on which the scientists could draw to achieve this by seeking to emulate the natural conditions on cultivated land.[73]

[70] Dokuchaev, 'Osobaya ekspeditsiya', 118–22. For correspondence with Izmailovskii, see *Sochineniya*, VIII, 306–12

[71] G. Tanfil'ev, 'Predely lesov na yuge Rossii', *Trudy ekspeditsii, snaryazhennoi Lesnym Departamentom, pod rukovodstvom professora Dokuchaeva, Nauchnyi otdel*, II, Geobotanicheskie i fenologicheskie issledovaniya i nablyudeniya, part 1 (1894). See also V. V. Dokuchaev, 'Metody issledovaniya voprosa, byli li lesa v yuzhnoi stepnoi Rossii', in Dokuchaev, *Sochineniya*, I, 336–68.

[72] *Trudy Ekspeditsii, snaryazhennoi Lesnym Departmentom, pod rukovodstvom professora Dokuchaeva, Nauchnii otdel*, 4 vols. (1894–8).

[73] Dokuchaev, 'Osobaya ekspeditsiya', 122–5. For more detail on Dokuchaev's ideas for his 'field research stations', see V. V. Dokuchaev, 'K voprosu ob organizatsii opytnykh (polevykh) stantsii v Rossii', in *Sochineniya*, VII, 165–8; *idem*, 'Chislo, mesto, osnovy i zadachi sel'skokhozyaistvennykh opytnykh stantsii', in *ibid.*, 169–76; *idem*, 'Mesto, chislo, zadachi i

The team of scientists then went to on to carry out a wide range of experiments into ways of addressing the environmental constraints on agriculture in the steppe regions. They investigated which types of trees would grow best in different types of soil and other aspects of the steppe environment by drawing on the experience of existing plantations, in particular Velikii Anadol'skii, as well as planting different species themselves and monitoring the results. They discovered that oak and birch followed by apple and pear trees grew best. Further experiments were carried out into different methods of planting trees. In 1893–5, Dokuchaev and his team planted around 100 hectares of trees to form shelterbelts to protect the exposed steppe of the Starobel'skii field research station from the drying influence of the wind. More trees were planted on the sides of ravines and gulleys to reinforce them and prevent further soil erosion. Tree planting was used as a way preventing dust storms, such as those in the spring of 1892 described earlier. In addition, experiments were carried out into ways of retaining, and if possible increasing, the available moisture in the soil that was so badly needed by farmers on the steppes. To this end, dams were built across ravines and gulleys so that they could serve as reservoirs. Ponds were dug for the same purpose. And trees were planted around the reservoirs and ponds to reinforce the sides and create shade to reduce evaporation. To investigate a further way of increasing the available moisture belts of trees were planted to retain snow that would otherwise have blown away and to reduce the run-off of rain water. They then monitored ground water levels, to ascertain whether they were increasing as a result of more water seeping into the land rather than drain away through gulleys and rivers. Wells were then dug to extract water from underground. The scientists also experimented with irrigation schemes, but their research stations contained few areas with the appropriate conditions for irrigating arable fields. Attempts to regulate the course of rivers came up against the interests of private landowners across whose land the rivers flowed.

Further experiments were carried out to ascertain the agricultural methods and crops that were most appropriate to the environmental conditions of the steppes. In particular, they were seeking to find those that would make the best use of the available moisture. Dokuchaev was particularly interested in working out the most appropriate balance between different types of land use: woodland, water, meadows, arable land, etc. He suggested that it would be advantageous to expand the area of land devoted to meadows, i.e. land with cultivated fodder grasses, that were closest to the wild steppe grasses that Dokuchaev believed to be the natural vegetation of the steppes. The implication of this, of course, was

---

osnovy reorganizatsii nashikh sel'skokhozyaistvennykh shkol i tak nazyvaemykh opytnykh stantsii', in *ibid.*, 177–81.

that raising livestock – the main occupation of the steppe nomads who had lived in the region for millennia – was more appropriate to the steppe environment than growing crops, which the more recent peasant settlers were relying on to sustain themselves.

The results of all these experiments were carefully monitored. The scientists compared the results with the control environments, and compared the different experiments. For example, they compared the harvests in fields protected by shelterbelts with those which were left open to wind, and in fields near to ponds and reservoirs with those that were further away from surface water. Some of the results, for example on the exposed steppe in Starobel'skii, suggested that Dokuchaev and his team had indeed found ways of 'improving nature' and making agriculture more viable on the steppes.[74] Thus, Dokuchaev seems to have attained some success in his approach of investigating the natural conditions over a long period of time, and then using them as guides to work out appropriate ways to work the land in ways that would provide a basis for agriculture to flourish with less risk from the periodic droughts and causing less damage to the environment. This approach reflected Dokuchaev's deep respect for nature. He was a pioneer, therefore, of what today would be termed 'sustainable development'.[75]

Dokuchaev's ambitious plan was not, however, carried out in its entirety. In part this was a result of the enormous financial outlay that it would have entailed. Dokuchaev, moreover, had other matters to deal with in the 1890s as his expertise was much in demand. In the summer of 1892 the Ministry of National Education appointed him to reorganise the Novo-Aleksandriiskii Institute for Agriculture and Forestry in Lublin province in Russian Poland. He resigned as the leader of the expedition to the steppes in 1897, partly as a result of health problems, from which he never fully recovered. Dokuchaev died prematurely in 1903.[76] The work of the scientists whom Dokuchaev appointed to work on the expedition carried on, however, and some went on to have prominent careers.[77]

[74] Dokuchaev, 'Osobaya ekspeditsiya', 145–60; *idem*, 'Soobshcheniya o lektsiyakh V. V. Dokuchaeva "Ob osnovakh sel'skogo khozyaistva"', in *Sochineniya*, VII, 216–26; *Trudy Ekspeditsii, snaryazhennoi Lesnym Departmentom, pod rukovodstvom professora Dokuchaeva, Otdel prakticheskikh rabot*, 3 vols. (1894–8). See also Krupenikov and Krupenikov, *Puteshestviya*, 85–99; E. S. Pavlov, 'Zashchitnoe lesorazvedenie v rabotakh ekspeditsii V. V. Dokuchaeva', in *Tezisy dokladov*, ed. V. K. Savost'yanov, I, 35–7.

[75] See J. D. Oldfield and D. J. B. Shaw, 'Revisiting Sustainable Development: Russian Cultural and Scientific Traditions and the Concept of Sustainable Development', unpublished paper presented to BASEES annual conference, Apr. 2002.

[76] Chebotareva, 'Vasilii Vasil'evich Dokuchaev', 105, 109–17, 149–50; Krupenikov and Krupenikov, *Puteshestviya*, 96, 101.

[77] For a list of works published by the scientists involved in expedition on related topics down to 1906, see 'Perechen' rabot po lesnomu opytnomu delu, opublikovannykh v Trudakh Ekspeditsii, snaryazhennoi Lesnym Departamentom, pod rukovodstvom

VII

How much of Dokuchaev's work on the environment of the steppes has stood the test of time and the rapid progress made by environmental sciences since the 1890s? He is still revered among scientists in Russia.[78] With regard to the ideas expressed in his book *Our Steppes: Past and Present*, subsequent research has tended to support his scepticism about a connection between deforestation and precipitation, and his emphasis on soil moisture and ground water. Scientists still dispute the impact of clearing woodland and ploughing the soil on water flows and run-off, however, which were so crucial to Dokuchaev's argument.[79] Where he was almost certainly wrong was in considering the environment of the areas of unploughed steppe he encountered in the late nineteenth century to be a natural or 'virgin' environment and, by extension, his belief that human impact on the steppes had occurred to a significant extent only in the recent past. Studies of fossil pollen in the steppe region have shown that, between around 7,000 and 5,000 years ago, long before Herodotus's visit and description of the treeless steppes, there had been much more extensive tree cover on the steppes, far to the south of the more recent southern boundary of the forest-steppe. Recent studies have also shown that human impact, for example the use of fire to clear woodland for pasture and arable farming, together with natural climate change, led to the creation of the more recent, largely treeless, steppes.[80] Paradoxically, Dokuchaev's plan, greatly distorted, became the basis for massive intervention in the environment in the late 1940s and early 1950s as the 'Stalin Plan for the Transformation of Nature' that

professora Dokuchaeva i v Trudakh Opytnykh Lesnichestv', in *Trudy po lesnomu opytnomu delu v Rossii. Otchet po lesnomu opytnomu delu za 1906 god* (Spb, 1907), 59–63; 'Perechen' rabot po lesnomu opytnomu delu, opublikovannykh v raznykh izdaniyakh', in *Trudy po lesnomu opytnomu delu v Rossii. Otchet po lesnomu opytnomu delu za 1907 god* (Spb, 1908), 162–5. See also S. V. Zonn and A. N. Eroshkina, 'Ucheniki i posledovateli V. V. Dokuchaeva', *Pochvovedenie*, 2 (1996), 124–38.

[78] For example, a special scienfitic conference was held in 1992 to mark the centenary of his plan. *Tezisy dokladov*, ed. V. K. Savost'yanov, and a special issue of the major Russian soil science journal *Pochvovedenie* was dedicated to Dokuchaev in 1996 on the 150th anniversary of his birth.

[79] Meyer, *Human Impact on the Earth*, 5, 63, 118, 201–6.

[80] See M. I. Neishtadt, *Istoriya lesov i paleogeografiya SSSR v golotsene* (Moscow, 1957); *Zapovedniki*, ed. Stroganova, 26–7; P. E. Tarasov *et al.*, 'Present-day and Mid-Holocene Biomes Reconstructed from Pollen and Plant Macrofossil Data from the Former Soviet Union and Mongolia', *Journal of Biogeography*, 25 (1998), 1029–53; C. V. Kremenetski, O. A. Chichagova and I. N. Shishlina, 'Palaeoecological Evidence for Holocene Vegetation, Climate and Landuse Change in the Low Don Basin and Kalmuk Area, Southern Russia', *Vegetation History and Archaeobotany*, 8 (1999), 233–46.

envisaged planting massive shelterbelts across the steppes and vast dams and irrigation schemes.[81]

More in keeping with the spirit of Dokuchaev's work was his role as one of the pioneers of strict, scientific nature reserves (*zapovedniki*), where 'models of nature' (*etalony*) are preserved under inviolable management to exclude human activity other than carefully controlled scientific research. In the wake of his field research stations, a network of such nature reserves was established throughout Russia and the Soviet Union, and continues to exist at the present time.[82] A new nature reserve on the steppes was established in the south-east of Rostov region in 1996.[83] More recent ideas about the role of humans in the creation of environments previously thought to be completely 'natural' have led to newer, scientific rationales for the reserves.[84]

Dokuchaev was right, of course, to emphasise the impact of arable farming on the environment of the steppes. The area of land in the steppe region ploughed up for cultivating crops expanded considerably in the twentieth century as a result of Soviet agricultural policy. Even parts of the steppe nature reserves that had never been ploughed were ploughed up for cultivation and thus lost to science.[85] Khrushchev's virgin land campaign of the 1950s is best known for the ploughing up of former nomadic pasture land in Kazakhstan, but underutilised and marginal land in the steppes of the European part of the Soviet Union was also ploughed up, and shared the consequences of erosion and dust storms in the early 1960s.[86] The far greater use of chemical fertilisers in recent decades has also had a profound impact on the land. A new study of the black earth of the steppe region was conducted by scientists to mark the

[81] V. A. Kovda, *Velikii plan preobrazovaniya prirody* (Moscow, 1952). On the link with Dokuchaev's work, see I. V. Tyurin, 'Ot redaktsii', in Dokuchaev, *Sochineniya*, VI (1951), 6–12; Zonn and Eroshkina, 'Ucheniki i posledovateli V. V. Dokuchaeva', 130. See also P. Josephson, *Industrialized Nature: Brute Force Technology and the Transformation of the Natural World* (Washington, DC, 2002), 27–40.

[82] V. E. Boreiko, 'Starobel'skii stepnoi zapovednyi uchastok, vydelennyi V. V. Dokuchaevym, – sushchestvyet!', *Stepnoi Byulleten'*, 2 (1998) (www.ecoclub.nsu.ru/books/Step-2/step2-20.htm, accessed 19 Apr. 2003); F. Shtilmark, *The History of Russian Zapovedniks, 1895–1995*, trans. G. H. Harper (Edinburgh, 2003), 10–13; I. Vorob'ev, 'Idei Dokuchaeva i territorial'naya okhrana stepei', *Stepnoi Byulleten'*, 15 (2004) (www.ecolab.nsu.ru/books/Step-15/02.htm, accessed 13 Oct. 2004). See also D. R. Weiner, *Models of Nature: Ecology, Conservation and Cultural Revolution in Soviet Russia*, 2nd edn (Pittsburgh, PA, 2000); *idem*, *A Little Corner of Freedom: Russian Nature Protection from Stalin to Gorbachev* (Berkeley, CA, 1999).

[83] V. A. Minoranskii and A. V. Chekin, *Gosudarstvennyi stepnoi zapovednik 'Rostovskii'* (Rostov-on-Don, 2003). The present author visited the reserve with a party of botanists from the Rostov-on-Don botanical gardens in the summer of 2003.

[84] See Weiner, *A Little Corner of Freedom*, 374–401.

[85] *Ibid.*, 93–103, 130.

[86] M. McCauley, *Khrushchev and the Development of Soviet Agriculture: The Virgin Land Programme 1953–1964* (New York, 1976).

hundredth anniversary of the publication of Dokuchaev's book on the black earth in 1983. The study showed that the levels of organic matter in the black earth, which gave it its legendary fertility, had fallen sharply, and the old problems of erosion and shortages of moisture remained. A new plan to combat these problems by rational usage was proposed.[87] A more recent study, however, indicates that the problems have not been addressed and erosion remains a serious problem.[88] The latest of the long succession of periodic droughts that have punctuated the environmental history of the Russian steppes hit the Don and the North Caucasus in the spring 2003 and caused a serious shortfall in the harvest in some areas. This latest steppe drought and harvest failure was witnessed by the present author who spent the spring and summer of 2003 on a research visit to the steppes.

[87] *Russkii chernozem: 100 let posle Dokuchaeva*, ed. V. A. Kovda and E. M. Samoilova (Moscow, 1983).

[88] Anatoly Greshnevikov, *Ukhodit pochva iz-pod nog* (Moscow and Rybinsk, 2002).

Transactions of the RHS 15 (2005), pp. 175–195
doi:10.1017/S0080440105000307 Printed in the United Kingdom

A 'SINISTER AND RETROGRESSIVE' PROPOSAL: IRISH WOMEN'S OPPOSITION TO THE 1937 DRAFT CONSTITUTION

By Maria Luddy

READ 26 MARCH 2004 AT ROYAL HOLLOWAY, UNIVERSITY OF LONDON

ABSTRACT. This article explores the campaign waged by Irish women against the draft constitution of 1937. A number of articles within the constitution were deemed by women activists to threaten both their rights as citizens and as workers. A campaign, organised principally by the Women Graduates' Association, the Joint Committee of Women's Societies and Social Workers, together with the Irish Women Workers' Union, sought to amend or delete the offending articles. The campaign ran for two months and in that period, feminists, the press, parliamentarians, the Catholic Church and republicans all engaged in the debate about women's position in Irish society.

Irish women, throughout the nineteenth and twentieth centuries, have been politically engaged in nationalist, unionist, social, economic and feminist organisations. In the twentieth century they played an active role in the fight for Irish independence through their involvement in the Easter Rising of 1916, the War of Independence 1919–21 and the Civil War 1922–3. Equal citizenship had been guaranteed to Irish men and women under the Proclamation of 1916. Irish women won the right, with their British counterparts, to the parliamentary franchise in 1918. Active lobbying, particularly by women, saw all Irish citizens over the age of twenty-one enfranchised under the Irish Free State Constitution enacted in June 1922. It would thus appear that Irish women were well placed to benefit from the roles they had played in the fight for Irish independence. However, women did not retain a high profile in the political affairs of the country and from the foundation of the Free State women's political, economic and social rights were gradually eroded. The implementation of restrictive legislation in the economic and political spheres found echoes in the social sphere. For instance, the 1927 Juries Act made it very difficult for women to sit on juries. The 1929 Censorship of Publications Bill prohibited the advertisement of contraceptives. Other legislation had repercussions also on how women could live their lives in Ireland. There was a marriage bar in place and women were subjected to lower salary and pension rates to men.[1] Mary Kettle, who had consistently fought for the rights of women in the early twentieth century was to note with regard to the marriage bar in the civil service that 'women, from their entry until they reach the ages of 45 or 50 are looked on as if they were loitering with intent to commit a felony – the felony in this case being marriage'.[2] Women campaigned actively against much of the legislation that attempted to restrict their rights as citizens or workers.

It was not only Irish society which saw women, whether married or single, primarily in terms of their reproductive capacities and responsibilities to home and children. Most of western society had difficulty seeing women as citizens. Issues of women's rights as citizens were to surface particularly strongly in Ireland when Irish women organised a campaign to oppose the draft constitution of 1937. This was a short, intense campaign that lasted less than two months but marked a turning point in women's political campaigning in Ireland. Throughout the campaign women activists (and some men) were concerned with the implications of certain articles, particularly articles 9, 16, 40, 41 and 45, for women's citizenship rights and their status as workers (see appendix). The omission of article 3 of the 1922 constitution, which guaranteed equal citizenship, was also of grave concern. Their assault on the draft constitution was informed by their understanding of both the 1916 Proclamation and certain articles in the 1922 constitution. From the 1916 Proclamation the phrase, 'The Republic guarantees religious and civil liberty, equal rights and equal opportunities to all its citizens', was the standard against which the draft constitution was measured, and found wanting. The women fought for the reinsertion of the phrase 'without distinction of sex', found in articles 3 and 14 of the 1922 constitution, but excluded from the draft constitution. They were also incensed by the phrase 'inadequate strength of women' which was seen in article 45.4.2. With regard to women, the debate over the draft constitution was about women's rights as citizens and their right to work. While many women welcomed the constitution's attempts to reinforce the status of women as wives and mothers, they

[1] For recent work on the role of women in politics in these years see Maryann Gialanella Valiulis, 'Defining their Role in the New State: Irishwomen's Protest against the Juries Act of 1927', *Canadian Journal of Irish Studies*, 17, 1 (July 1992), 43–60; *idem*, 'Power, Gender and Identity in the Irish Free State', *Journal of Women's History*, 6/4/7/1 (Winter/Spring 1995), 117–36; Mary E. Daly, 'Women in the Irish Free State, 1922–1939: The Interaction between Economics and Ideology', *Journal of Women's History*, 6/4/7/1 (Winter/Spring 1995), 99–116; Caitriona Beaumont, 'Women, Citizenship and Catholicism in the Irish Free State, 1922–1948', *Women's History Review*, 6, 4 (1997), 563–85.

[2] Commission of Inquiry into the Civil Service, 1932–5, R. 54/2 (Dublin, 1935): Addendum C by Mrs M. Kettle, cited in Mary E. Daly, *Women and Work in Ireland* (Dundalk, 1997), 49.

were not willing to support this move when it appeared simultaneously to undermine their rights as workers. The campaign was also about the ambiguities of language and women's ability to trust governments and politicians. As a campaign it can also be seen as the last major battle of the suffrage feminists; many of the women heading the campaign had been active suffragists. And while the women could claim some success in their campaign, it marked the end of an era and witnessed the emergence and development of new political strategies for women activists.

The publication of the draft constitution

On 24 May 1934 Eamon de Valera, president of the executive council, established a committee of four civil servants to examine the Irish Free State Constitution of 1922. That committee's report was available by 3 July 1934, but detailed drafting of the new constitution did not begin until the summer of 1936.[3] De Valera had limited the circulation of a draft document before its publication and it became available to the executive council for discussion on 16 March 1937. The *Irish Times* was to record on 7 April that 'very little is known about the Constitution'. The final proof of the document became available on 29 April. On 1 May 1937 a draft of the proposed constitution was finally published.

Women's fears about their political position in Ireland had been heightened as early as 1936. On 1 July the Joint Committee of Women's Societies and Social Workers wrote to de Valera concerning 'women's constitutional and economic condition'. At this stage they were anxious about women's future representation in the new Senate being created by de Valera. It took the Joint Committee from July 1936 to 29 January 1937 to arrange a delegation to meet with de Valera on this issue of representation. A departmental memo, summing up his response to the meeting, noted:

> The president pointed out that any inadequacy in the representation of women in the legislature and public bodies was attributable to the state of public opinion. It would be difficult to do anything to give women a larger role in public life while public opinion remains as it is.[4]

Such a response revealed the unwillingness of the government to take the women's concerns seriously. Women's organisations were, however,

[3] Sean Faughnan, 'The Jesuits and the Drafting of the Irish Constitution of 1937', *Irish Historical Studies*, 26, 101 (May 1988), 79–80.

[4] Memo regarding the deputation from the Joint Committee of Women's Societies and Social Workers who met with the President on 29 January 1937. Department of the Taoiseach File, S 9880, 'Women, Position under the Constitution, 1937', National Archives of Ireland, Dublin [hereafter D/T, NAI].

to join forces, even if only briefly, when the draft constitution was published. Feminists, the Catholic Church, parliamentarians and women republicans all had something to say on the position of women in the constitution. The appearance of the draft constitution marked the beginning of sustained interest, if not always fruitful debate, on the position of women in Irish society that had not occurred since the suffrage campaign. Two early letters published in the *Irish Times* outlined what were going to be considerable problems for women activists.[5] Both letters remarked on the political apathy of women generally, and particularly noted the lack of women in formal political life. The various political parties had ignored the issue of women candidates in elections 'having not thought it worth their while to respond to women's organisations on the subject'. It was clear to these correspondents that public opinion, ill informed as it was regarding women's political needs, would be difficult to organise in any campaign to support women's political advancement.

The response: Costello

Dáil Deputy, John A. Costello, Fine Gael, and ex-attorney general, was one of the first to draw attention to the position of women under the draft constitution. In a long article in the *Irish Independent* on 6 May, which contained two paragraphs on women, he wrote, 'We read the somewhat grandiose statement that all citizens shall be held equal before the law, but we then discover that the substance of that declaration is taken away by the provision that the State may, if it likes, in its legislation declare them to be unequal.' He argued that in introducing legislation the state, because it could take 'due regard to differences of capacity, physical and moral, and of social function', was allowing itself immense powers. That provision, he argued, read in conjunction with the constitutional declaration of 'the inadequate strength of women', and the omission of the significant words, 'without distinction of sex' contained in articles 3 and 14 of the existing constitution, 'must', he noted, 'appear curious in view of the substantially equal rights of voting and otherwise at present accorded to women'. Costello claimed that, under the draft constitution, women did not have 'as a constitutional right' any claim to the exercise of the franchise on equal terms with men. As it stood, the draft offered its framer as a 'whole burnt offering to feminists and feminist associations'.

The response: Gaffney

The journalist, Gertrude Gaffney, responded to the draft constitution in her regular column in the *Irish Independent*.[6] She objected to several

[5] *Irish Times*, 28 Apr., 3 May 1937.
[6] *Irish Independent*, 7 May 1937.

assumptions made within the draft constitution and called on women to mobilise themselves into action. The 'death knell of the working woman is sounded in this new constitution' she wrote. 'Mr de Valera has always been a reactionary where women are concerned. He dislikes and distrusts us as a sex and his aim ever since he came into office has been to put us into what he considers is our place and keep us there.' Under the proposed constitution, Gaffney argued, 'we are to be no longer citizens entitled to enjoy equal rights under a democratic constitution, but laws are to be enacted which will take into consideration our "differences of capacity, physical and moral, and of social function"'. Restrictions regarding women's work were already in place since 1935.[7] Gaffney observed de Valera's skill in re-affirming the principles of 1916 but commented that the inclusion of conditional clauses would result in 'exterminating us [as workers] by degrees'. Were de Valera to descend to reality, she observed, he would see that 'ninety per cent of women who work for a living in this country do so because they must'. The argument revolved around commonly held beliefs that to remove women from the workforce would immediately lead to a reduction in male unemployment. Gaffney believed that de Valera, conscious of the 'nightmare of unemployment', was using the cue of economic depression as a means further to restrict women's rights as workers. It was, for Gaffney, and many other women activists, a complete rejection of the principles of the 1916 Proclamation.

The two feminist organisations that sought changes to the draft constitution were the National University Women Graduates' Association [WGA] and the Joint Committee of Women's Societies and Social Workers. The WGA had been established as the Women Graduates and Candidate Graduates' Association in 1902, with the original aim that all advantages of a University education would be equally available to men and women. It later became involved in a number of campaigns relating to the status of women. In 1925, for instance, they campaigned against the Civil Service Amendment Bill. The active core of the WGA was small; in 1930 it had a membership of sixty seven, less than half the number of women who graduated from University in 1929–30. However, the association had a number of distinguished female scholars who were publicly recognised and respected for their opinions. These included Professors Mary Hayden, Agnes O'Farrelly and Mary Macken. The second organisation, the Joint Committee of Women's Societies and Social Workers, had been formed in March 1935. The Joint Committee was made up of representatives from a number of women's organisations, including the Irish Women Workers' Union, which met initially to discuss

[7] The 1935 Conditions of Employment Act gave the minister for industry and commerce power to restrict the employment of women.

a response to the rejection of proposed amendments to the Criminal Law Amendment Act of 1935.[8]

The response: Women Graduates' Association

Within a few days both the Joint Committee and the Women Graduates' Association took up Costello's and Gaffney's points. At a meeting of the WGA it was noted that 'the omission of the principle of equal rights and opportunities enunciated in the Proclamation of 1916 and confirmed in Article 3 of the Constitution of Saorstát Eireann [Free State] was deplored as sinister and retrogressive'.[9] It was clear to the WGA that articles 40, 41 and 45 opened the possibility of reactionary legislation being enacted against women. It was decided to appoint an emergency committee to publicise the issues relating to women arising from the draft constitution, to work with other groups to delete the 'offending' articles and to restore article 3 of the Free State Constitution. A deputation was appointed to meet with de Valera, and other influential Dáil members, and a subscription fund inaugurated.[10] The republican, Dr Kathleen Lynn, was to note in her diary that 'women are rizz and rightly'.[11]

Mary Hayden, referring to Gaffney's article, wrote that the new constitution was not a return to the middle ages but something worse:

> Let not the empty promises of needless 'safeguards' and vague declarations of the value of 'her life within the home' blind our women to the fact that under this proposed Constitution her opportunities of earning, her civil status, her whole position as a citizen, will depend on the judgement of, perhaps, a single minister or a single state department as to her 'physical or moral capacity' and that even ministers and departments are not always infallible or unprejudiced.[12]

Mary Kettle, chairwoman of the Joint Committee, called upon women to examine carefully the so-called 'protection' clauses of the new constitution. She maintained that, if these articles became law, no working woman, whether she worked in trade, factory or profession, would have any security whatever. Since the establishment of the state, she added, women had become accustomed to regard article 3 of the 1922 constitution as the charter of their liberties. If de Valera disliked

[8] The Joint Committee was disbanded in 1993, after fifty-eight years in existence. Throughout this time, the number of organisations on the committee fluctuated, but initially comprised nine societies, and later rose to fourteen.

[9] *Irish Times*, 11 May 1937.

[10] National University Women Graduates' Association, minute book, 11 May 1937, 2/21, University College Dublin Archives [hereafter WGA, UCDA]. *Irish Times*, 17 May 1937.

[11] The diaries of Kathleen Lynn, 21 June 1937. Royal College of Physicians of Ireland, Dublin [hereafter, Lynn diaries, RCPI].

[12] *Irish Independent*, 12 May 1937. In an article in the *Cork Examiner*, 26 June 1937, Hayden noted that this new constitution, 'with all its possibilities of injustice', contained a 'mixture of flattery and insult'.

the phraseology of that article so much he could always fall back on the 'classic simplicity' of the proclamation of the republic, which stated: 'The Republic guarantees religious and civil liberty, equal rights and equal opportunities to all its citizens.' Such a statement, Kettle concluded, was unequivocal and would satisfy all women.[13]

The suffrage and republican activist Hanna Sheehy Skeffington wrote to the *Irish Independent* stating that the rights guaranteed to all citizens in the 1916 proclamation were being scrapped for a 'fascist model' in which women would be relegated to permanent inferiority, their avocations and choice of callings limited because of an 'implied invalidism as the weaker sex'. She believed that such rights had already been seriously encroached upon since the foundation of the Free State

> first by the Cosgrave government, which deprived women of the right of trial by their peers by excluding women from jury service, discriminating against them in the civil service, and lately, in even more marked fashion, under the recent employment Act, excluding them, at the whim of the minister for industry, from work in industry.[14]

While many of the letters written by the Joint Committee and the Women Graduates' Association appeared in all three national papers it was the *Irish Press* which responded most vociferously to the women's demands.[15] The *Irish Press*, of course, was the paper owned by de Valera and the organ of the Fianna Fáil party, and as one commentator has noted, it was the 'necessary coping stone to all the speeches, lectures and propaganda of the Fianna Fáil party'.[16] The paper reacted immediately to Gaffney's column. It maintained that the *Irish Independent* had found a new angle from which to attack the constitution and that it aimed 'by the methods of prejudice and distortion' to enlist the women of the country in opposition against it. It claimed that the *Irish Independent* had purposely employed Gaffney to attack the constitution as 'sounding the death knell of the working woman', though it noted that such a view was 'a distortion of the constitution' and a 'figment of Miss Gaffney's imagination'. It continued:

> On Miss Gertrude Gaffney's competence to chronicle the movements, the vagaries, and the tittle tattle of what is called Society, or to deal with the nuances of fabrics, the fashion of garments, the models of hats, or the style and ensemble which constitute the last word in chic, we are not qualified to express an opinion, but at the risk of being unpolite we must tell her that she makes a sorry exhibition of herself when she ventures on an incursion into politics, of which she has yet to learn the rudiments.[17]

[13] *Irish Times*, 11 May 1937. The letter was published in all of the national newspapers.

[14] *Irish Independent*, 11 May 1937.

[15] The *Cork Examiner*, while supportive of the women's campaign, regarded it as entirely their affair noting that if the women graduates can convince two-thirds of their non-graduate sisters the 'fate of the constitution will be decided', 26 June 1937.

[16] Tim Pat Coogan, *Ireland in the Twentieth Century* (2003), 146.

[17] *Irish Press*, 8 May 1937.

The anti-feminist tone of the *Irish Press* was symptomatic of its entire coverage of the women's campaign.

De Valera met a deputation from the Joint Committee and a separate deputation from the Women Graduates' Association on 14 May. He informed the deputations that 'Whilst he did not at all share their apprehensions, he would nevertheless give careful consideration to have a barrier set up against the possibility of the enactment of any law discriminating against women in the matter of citizenship and the franchise.'[18] He had already, on the previous evening in the Dáil, indicated to Deputy Costello that he would make such a change. It appears that the women's opinions had little real impact on him. A meeting of the WGA on 18 May heard a report by Mary Macken on the deputation's meeting with de Valera. It was noted that over two hours had been spent with him, and his assurance had been received about clauses to safeguard the political rights of women to be inserted in articles 9 and 16. He had given no hope, however, of amending or deleting the clauses in articles 40, 41 and 45, which the WGA regarded as threatening to women.[19] With this result the WGA decided to campaign for a complete rejection of the constitution by the public. But even on this there was a dilemma. The vote on the constitution was to take place on the same day as a general election. The WGA were determined that the campaign would not be fought on party political lines, what they wanted was a vote against the constitution. However, they were aware of the reality of Irish political life where party loyalty often overrode concerns about party policy. The WGA tried to get the message across that voters could vote against the constitution without voting against Fianna Fáil. The *Irish Press* however, attacked the feminists' campaign because they saw it as hostile to the government and the Fianna Fáil party.[20]

Dáil response

The women's organisations lobbied all the Teachtaí Dála [TDs] with regard to the contentious articles. However, it would be an exaggeration to say that women's rights commanded much attention on the part of deputies, who were far more concerned with other aspects of the constitution. Reporting on 26 June the *Irish Independent* noted that de Valera had shelved the 'fair sex' question, and as an amendment supportive of the feminists got pushed aside, the 'deputies took off their metaphorical coats and got down to the most controversial issue of the debate – the powers of the President'.

[18] *Irish Press*, *Irish Independent*, 15 May 1937.

[19] WGA, minute book, 18 May 1937, UCDA.

[20] Rosamond Jacob diary, 27 May 1937. MS 32,582 (81), National Library of Ireland, Dublin [hereafter Jacob diary, NLI]. WGA minute book, 11 May 1937, UCDA.

Opposition contributors to the debate included John Costello, Patrick McGilligan, John Marcus O'Sullivan and Robert J. Rowlette. Amongst the three women TDs, Margaret Pearse, Fianna Fáil, did not speak in the debate. Helena Concannon, Fianna Fáil, a member of the Women Graduates' Association and elected by the National University of Ireland constituency, mentioned the concerns of women to the president and asked de Valera to satisfy himself that future interpretations of the constitution could not lessen the status of women.[21] She informed the WGA deputation that as a disciplined member of the Fianna Fáil party she could not propose any amendments to the draft constitution.[22] Bridget Redmond, Fine Gael, put forward an amendment to article 9 (that no citizen shall be placed by law under any such disability or incapacity by reason of sex, class or religion) which failed, and on which she spoke only briefly.[23]

Deputy Rowlette noted that 'there has not been for many years such a condition of alarm among the women, as to their rights as citizens of the country, as has been aroused by certain clauses in the constitution'.[24] Deputy O'Sullivan declared that women were much more afraid of economic discrimination than political discrimination. He also noted that 'these women are not all of the class who hold advanced views. Many of them are moderate, conservative women, who hold views which are by no means advanced.'[25] These women, he said, feared 'for their political position' but they were much more afraid of what may happen in practice as to the taking away of opportunities to work.[26] Mrs Concannon observed on 12 May that 'it would be unfitting that this debate should close without a woman's voice being heard in connection with this matter'. She then noted the concerns raised by the Joint Committee and the Women Graduates' Association and asked de Valera to satisfy himself that any future interpretation of the disputed articles could not lessen the status of women. It was clear to her, at least, that 'the framers of the constitution had no intention in their minds to interfere in the slightest way with the rights of women and I am glad to have that assurance'.[27] Deputy McGilligan was later to observe that Concannon would 'walk blindly' behind her leader into the lobby and proclaim to all the world that there was no question of sexual discrimination.[28]

[21] Dáil Debates, cols. 241–7, 12 May 1937 [hereafter DD].
[22] WGA, minute book, 8 May 1937, UCDA.
[23] DD, vol. 67, col. 1307, 28 May 1937.
[24] DD, vol. 67, col. 1587, 2 June 1937.
[25] DD, vol. 67, cols. 1594–5, 2 June 1937.
[26] DD, vol. 67, col. 1594, 2 June 1937.
[27] DD, vol. 67, cols. 241–7, 12 May 1937.
[28] DD, vol. 68, col. 177, 9 June 1937.

During the Dáil debate on the draft constitution articles 9 and 16 were, amongst others, amended. The phrase 'without distinction of sex' was inserted in article 16,[29] and a clause was added to article 9 which read that 'No person may be excluded from Irish nationality and citizenship by reason of the sex of such person.'[30] De Valera had been resolute that the phrase 'without distinction of sex' was superfluous. He saw it, he said, as a badge of women's previous inferiority, an inferiority he insisted that no longer existed under the draft constitution, but his subsequent decision to include it in article 16 was an acknowledgement of the pressure brought to bear by campaigners on this issue.

The Catholic Church

On 6 May Dr Kathleen Lynn noted in her diary that the newspaper the '*Irish Catholic* says constitution is a noble document! That damns it if nothing else.'[31] The writer Rosamond Jacob also observed in her diary on 24 May 1937 that 'de Valera [was] too damn Catholic'.[32] Whatever views might have been expressed in private about the Catholic nature of the draft constitution it would have marked the death of the women's campaign to air such views in public. Much has been written about the role of the Catholic hierarchy in constructing and advising de Valera on the constitution. Ultimately, however, it was, as one commentator has noted, 'de Valera who decided what should or should not be included in the draft Constitution'.[33] The Catholic press strongly supported the draft constitution. The *Irish Catholic*, on 6 May, concluded that 'Irish Catholics will rejoice in the fact that the fundamental principles of the new Bunreacht are in close accord with Catholic social teaching.' A statement from the Catholic organisation, An Rioghacht,[34] quoted extensively from Papal Encyclicals and noted that for anyone who 'reads

[29] Also inserted in article 16 was the guarantee that 'No law shall be enacted placing any citizen under disability or incapacity for membership of Dáil Eireann on the grounds of sex or disqualifying any citizen from voting at an election for Dáil election on that ground'. DD, vol. 68, col. 153, 9 June 1937.

[30] DD, vol. 67, cols. 1305–7, 28 May 1937.

[31] Lynn diaries, 6 May 1937, RCPI. The following were also noted by Lynn in her diary, '13 May, Mrs Kettle says she works night and day with protest against new constitution's rules for women, of course they are reactionary. 18 May, evening meeting of women graduates to hear deputation's reports. Dev [de Valera] much pained we should not think his constitution perfect for women when there is so much discrimination in many sections. What could be expected from man made laws, however, he said he approved of equal pay for equal work, wonderful he doesn't apply it. Women will fight.'

[32] Jacob diary, 24 May 1937, NLI.

[33] Faughnan, 'The Jesuits and the Constitution', 102.

[34] An Rioghacht, the League of the Kingship of Christ, was established in Ireland in 1926. It was modelled on associations such as Action Populaire in France and the Catholic Social Guild in Britain.

these and other similar passages of the encyclicals and compares them with the passages of the draft constitution which touch on the same subject, it is impossible to escape the conclusion that the draft constitution, in this matter, derives its inspiration from the encyclicals'.[35] While the statement from An Rioghacht admitted that women might have some grievances,[36] it believed that a satisfactory solution could only be found in the acceptance of Catholic social teaching, basically that women should be wives and mothers.

The WGA felt the need to respond to this statement but had to be very careful not to appear anti-Catholic or anti-clerical. The response, printed in all the national papers,[37] came from Professor Mary Macken. She stated that Catholic women were in 'whole-hearted agreement' with the principles of the encyclicals. 'These women', she added, 'are practical Catholics, devoted to the Church and the Holy Father.' Macken observed that 'Encyclicals and Constitutions move in very different spheres.' An encyclical was an exhortation issued by the Holy Father to the Faithful. It was designed to meet certain definite situations in the world of morals, economics, education, etc., 'when such situations seem to him to call for exhortations or instruction'. However, a constitution was, she wrote, 'a charter of the rights and liberties of the citizen within the framework of the State'. It was amenable to interpretation in the courts of law, and 'it implies (for the implication of those clauses that have aroused the fears of women) legislation which may be exploited to the detriment of those it is supposed to protect'.[38] Women supported the encyclicals, she argued, because they 'had a vital interest in the purity of conjugal life, in the happiness of the home and the bringing up of children'. She made it absolutely clear that women's objections to certain clauses in the constitution did not imply any opposition to the teachings of the church. Women were simply 'wary of legislation and nervous of directives to such legislation' which might 'restrict unfairly under cover of "protection"'.[39]

The debate with An Rioghacht occupied the newspapers from 20 to 28 May. An Rioghacht went on to accuse Macken of 'unchristian liberalism believing that religion must be excluded from public life'.[40] It claimed that the feminist groups were 'mixed or neutral' bodies. Lacking an exclusive Catholic membership such groups of women were suspect on many levels. Similar views were expressed by the *Standard*, which deemed that many of the country's 'spokeswomen' were steeped in the spirit of

[35] *Irish Catholic*, 27 May 1937.

[36] See for instance, letter from B. B. Waters, chairman of An Rioghacht in *Irish Times*, 22 May 1937.

[37] *Irish Independent*, 26 May 1937, *Irish Times*, *Irish Press* 27 May 1937.

[38] *Ibid.*

[39] *Ibid.*

[40] *Irish Independent*, 27 May 1937, *Irish Press*, 28 May 1937.

'neo-paganism'. 'Who', the *Standard* asked, missing the main point in the women's argument, 'would question the right to private property? Who would object to the forbidding of divorce? Who, with any knowledge of Catholic tradition and Catholic teaching, would dispute that woman's place was in the home?' It was, the article concluded tellingly, the duty of the state to assist the church in all these matters.[41] Though it is difficult to assess the impact of such views, the reaction of the Catholic press may well have harmed the women's campaign.

That there was some clerical concern with the women's campaign is evident in the McQuaid papers. Father John Charles McQuaid, in an undated note to de Valera, observed:

> The feminists are getting angry and are moving into action. They seem stung by the suggestion that the normal place for a woman is the home. I shall shortly have another note to meet these persons. Their thoughts are very confused. Both *Casti Connubii* and *Quadraesimo Anno* answer them.[42]

He later noted that

> It is to misconstrue Art. 40.1 to read into it an attack on women, or any special class, or a threat of future attack. It is a graver error still to see in it any tincture of modern fascism. No article of the draft constitution even attempts to deny women's fundamental rights as a human being.

However, he also noted, it is 'an unreality to imagine that the possession of an electoral vote abolishes for either men or women or for both diversity of social function. Nothing will change in law and fact of nature that woman's natural sphere is in the home.' As Caitriona Beaumont has observed this statement suggests that under the draft constitution men and women were not considered equal citizens.[43] Ultimately, the women got no support for their campaign from the Catholic Church. Within the women's camp the most significant response to the draft constitution came from the Irish Women Workers' Union, the most notable group of women trade unionists in the country.

Irish Women Workers' Union

Louie Bennett, leader of the union, wrote to de Valera as president of the executive council stating the views of the Irish Women Workers' Union [IWWU] on the draft constitution.[44] She noted that their objection

[41] Cited in *Irish Press*, 14 May 1937.

[42] McQuaid to de Valera, undated. De Valera papers, 1091, cited in Sean A. Faughnan, 'De Valera's Constitution: The Drafting of the Irish Constitution of 1937' (MA thesis, UCD, 1988), 106.

[43] 'Rights of women', John Charles McQuaid Papers, section 5, file 48, Dublin Diocesan Archives. See also, Beaumont, 'Women, Citizenship and Catholicism', 575.

[44] The letter was published in the *Irish Press*, 12 May 1937.

to certain clauses in the constitution was 'inspired by a real anxiety to safeguard the position of women irrespective of class or party prejudices'. 'Most of us', she continued, 'would wish to subscribe without cavil to the proposed constitution, but for many of us it contains points of serious danger', not for what it actually expressed but for the ambiguity of the clauses and the danger of multiple interpretations. The IWWU believed that article 40.1 'tends to place women in a different category of citizenship from men and in a different position from men' with regard to the law. Given the evidence of fascist governments Bennett argued that this clause gave power to the government to initiate legislation that would be detrimental to women's equality. The letter went on to suggest that article 41.2 (1) should be amended to acknowledge 'women's work for the home' rather than within it. It was, she declared, invidious to have in the constitution a clause that makes it 'appear that only the women *within* the home can contribute to the common good'. She also argued that section 2.2 of article 41 would become superfluous if the 'principles of just distribution of wealth contained in article 45 are put into practice. Abolish poverty and unemployment and the need to protect mothers disappears.' The 'most indefensible' clause, however, was section 4.2 of article 45. It took from women the right to choose their own avocation in life. The letter argued that this clause would give the state power to decide what avocations were suited to a citizen's sex and strength. 'It would be hardly possible', the letter continued, 'to make a more deadly encroachment upon the liberty of the individual than to deprive him or her of this right.' The union urged the deletion of this clause because it offered 'a false solution of one of the problems of poverty' and as being offensive to a large number of citizens. The same clause, it argued, opened the door to 'fascist legislation of a very objectionable type'.[45] A deputation from the IWWU met with de Valera on 14 May, and on 24 May Bennett wrote to de Valera reminding him of his commitment to amend article 45.4 in line with the union's suggestion. She also reiterated her dissatisfaction with article 40.1 which, she stated, carried 'interpretations offensive to a large section of the community and [is] fundamentally different from your own intention'.[46] After another meeting with de Valera on 27 May what the IWWU referred to as the obnoxious phrase, 'the inadequate strength of women', was deleted from the draft constitution. The IWWU also secured the substitution of the word 'citizen' for 'women and children' in article 45.4.2. With this success the IWWU withdrew from the women's campaign. The minutes of the union for June of 1937 record that:

> We have had rather a victory in getting our amendment to clause 45 through in practically the form we suggested. Dr Rowlette piloted it, and we wrote thanking him . . . there is

[45] *Ibid.*

[46] Quoted in Rosemary Cullen Owens, *Louie Bennett* (Cork, 2001), 88–9.

> hope of an amendment to clause 40, the second paragraph of which is undesirable. The other women's societies were rather disappointed that we did not go on with the public meeting, but after our interview with the president we thought it wiser to hold our hand. The result justified our judgement. We have written to the other societies, explaining all this.[47]

While the Union was still prepared to co-operate with the women's societies they were not officially represented at the mass meeting organised by the Women Graduates' Association in the Mansion House in Dublin on 21 June. In later minutes Bennett referred to the censure of the women graduates on their action in not going on with the campaign against clauses in the new constitution which were not amended. While 'we agree', she wrote, 'that the social formation clause, for instance, to being undesirable', the fact that they had secured amendments to the constitution meant that now 'the matter is to be allowed drop'.[48] Even with their withdrawal from the campaign Bennett still wrote letters to the press on the draft constitution. On 7 June, for instance, she wrote that 'The tribute to women in the home contained in article 41.2 is superfluous.' 'A constitution', she declared, 'is hardly the place for the expression of vague and chivalrous sentiments. Mothers would prefer concrete proposals, which would release them from the pressure of economic necessity to work outside the home.' The real danger with this clause was it might be used as a pretext for undue interference with the liberty of women.[49]

The withdrawal of the IWWU certainly weakened the campaign. Bennett publicly explained the reasons why the IWWU had withdrawn. While they still supported the fight for equal rights there was a disagreement about the best means to carry that fight through. 'My committee', she noted, 'consider that amendments to articles 9, 16 and 45 have removed the really serious menace to the position of women.'[50] While there were important issues on which to campaign she believed that a woman's trade union owed its first allegiance to the trade union movement. It was now up to the women's union to make male trade unionists and the labour movements fight for the principle of equal pay and equal opportunities for men and women. What is also crucial to the position of the IWWU was that Bennett, and many women trade unionists, believed that women's place was in the home and Bennett, like

[47] Irish Women Workers' Union minute book, June 1937. Irish Labour History Museum, Dublin. My thanks to Theresa Moriarty for facilitating access to these records. Rosamond Jacob was to note the withdrawal of the IWWU from the campaign because Bennett 'had a private talk with DeV [de Valera] and he was going to alter certain wording, but not apparently, anything vital'. Jacob diary, 28 May 1937, NLI.

[48] Irish Women Workers' Union minute book, 8 July 1937.

[49] *Irish Independent*, 7 June 1937.

[50] *Labour News*, 26 June 1937.

de Valera, believed that male breadwinners should earn enough to allow wives to remain in the home.[51]

Republican women

While the actions and views of the major groups involved in the debates on the position of women in the draft constitution have been noted there is one other group that deserves mention. Where did activist republican women stand on this matter? Kathleen Clarke, Kate O'Callaghan and Maud Gonne, while not actively involved, noted their support for the women's campaign. Republican women's opposition was motivated by what they saw as a betrayal of the principles of the 1916 proclamation. Maud Gonne, for instance, wrote in *Prison Bars*, in July 1937:

> With one of our provinces cut off, and the Republican Army outlawed and 44 Republicans in jail and hundreds of good men in their keeping, it seems absurd to talk of a permanent constitution for Ireland. We have the Proclamation of the Republic – a noble, clear concise document – as our charter of liberty. It has been endorsed by the whole nation. The substitution of another document is a weakening of our national position. If, when Ireland is free, a more detailed constitution were needed the articles concerning women and the articles providing for special courts [art. 38.3] in Mr de Valera's draft constitution would damn it in my eyes.

A statement from Cumann na mBan observed that

> This constitution does not satisfy the aspirations of the Irish people. If the Proclamation of Easter Week meant anything, it meant the end of capitalism and the introduction of equal rights and opportunities for all. Our charter of freedom was laid down in the proclamation of Easter week. Only the establishment of a republic in accordance with that proclamation will satisfy our aspirations.[52]

They called on the men and women – whose rights were being threatened under the proposed new constitution 'to abstain altogether from voting at this election'. Cumann Poblachta na hEireann (the Irish Republican Party), seeing no great difference between the 1922 Free State Constitution and de Valera's draft constitution, observed that 'The present Free State constitution at least has the advantage in that it does not permit us to forget our slavery: the proposed new one would cover our chains with a faded tricolour.'[53]

Margaret Buckley, president of Sinn Féin, observed that no one took the new constitution seriously, but if she did take it seriously she would have had something to say of the way in which de Valera treated women as if they were 'half-wits'.[54] Cumann na mBan was deeply engrossed in organising a protest against the coronation of George V and, as it did

[51] Cullen Owens, *Bennett*, 89–90.
[52] *Irish Independent*, 26 June 1937.
[53] *Ibid.*
[54] *Irish Independent*, 30 June 1937.

not recognise the state, could not therefore legitimately campaign against the constitution. Old Cumann na mBan,[55] which did recognise the Free State, wrote to de Valera, objecting to articles 9,16 40(1), 42 (2) and 45 (2), for the same reasons they had been objected to by the Joint Committee and the Women Graduates' Association. Old Cumann na mBan were particularly annoyed with the 'inadequate strength of women' phrase noting that in the Anglo-Irish and Civil Wars they engaged in 'heavy muscular toil' conveying machine guns, heavy explosives and rifles'.[56] They were also incensed by their unequal treatment under the Military Service Pensions Act of 1934. Overall, the protest of Republicans did not receive wide press coverage. On the eve of polling, however, a letter on behalf of Old Cumann na mBan appeared in the *Irish Press*, addressed to de Valera, observing

> we wish you to know that your amendments to the clauses regarding women in Bunreacht na hEireann meet with our complete approval. Further, you have stated that the rights of women are not restricted, and we accept your word. Our association unanimously accepts Bunreacht na hEireann and advocates all Irish women voting for it.[57]

Kathleen Lynn was to record in her diary that the letter, signed by Bridie O'Mullane, was 'well starred, saying how much C[umann] na mB[an] think of Dev's constitution. [We are] very worried over it, for some weeks ago she was quite sound. They got her to do it. Penance, they felt our opposition so much.'[58]

The level of disappointment amongst republican women was best expressed by Dorothy Macardle. Macardle, a respected writer and intellectual, member of Fianna Fáil, a staunch supporter of de Valera, and the author of *The Irish Republic*, a major work on the fight for Irish freedom, wrote privately to de Valera arguing against those clauses which appeared to limit women in society. She concluded that 'as the constitution stands, I do not see how anyone holding advanced views on the rights of women can support it, and that is a tragic dilemma for those who have been loyal and ardent workers in the national cause'.[59]

De Valera's response

A cartoon on the cover of the June issue of *Dublin Opinion*, titled 'A Dream of Fair Women', shows de Valera dreaming that he was being threatened by Queen Maeve and Grainne O'Malley, with the caption, 'Say, big boy, what about those articles in the new constitution?'[60] De Valera certainly

[55] Cumann na mBan had split in 1933.
[56] Letter from Association of Old Cumann na mBan, 18 May 1937, S 9880, D/T, NAI.
[57] *Irish Press*, 30 June 1937.
[58] Lynn diaries, 6 May 1937, RCPI.
[59] Macardle to de Valera, 21 May 1937, S9880, D/T, NAI.
[60] *Dublin Opinion*, 16, 184 (June 1937).

found himself on the defensive when dealing with women's criticisms of the constitution and during the election and referendum campaign devoted considerable attention to refuting the arguments advanced by the women critics. De Valera remained incredulous to the women's fears and in the Dáil on 11 May stated:

> Let us consider this whole question of women's rights. I seem to have got a bad reputation. I do not think I deserve it. I myself was not conscious at any time of having deserved all those terrible things that I am told I am where the rights of women are concerned. So far as I know, wherever there was a question of working to ensure that women would have equal rights, I have worked for it, and there is nothing in this constitution which in any way detracts from the rights which women have possessed here. I took out the phrase 'without distinction of sex' and I make no apology for this.[61]

De Valera knew, perhaps by looking into his own heart, that '99 per cent of the women of this country will agree with every line of this [constitution].' He also noted that Ireland had one of the most advanced Citizenship Acts in the world, 'with which women's associations are most satisfied'. There was, he claimed, no intention of weakening or interfering with the rights of women in any way.[62]

The *Irish Press* made extensive critiques of the position of women who opposed the constitution and rejected all the feminist arguments against it. It consistently came back with the argument that the women were deliberately distorting the character and content of the constitution. It even accused the feminists of being the dupes of political parties. De Valera, in a speech in Carlow in which he dealt at length with the position of women, said that the whole issue was started as a political move by the ex-attorney general, John Costello.[63] De Valera also noted that when Costello began the campaign he had his tongue in his cheek, never expecting it to be taken seriously by the feminists.[64]

Conclusion

The referendum on the constitution was held on election day, 1 July 1937. Kathleen Lynn noted she 'voted early. We put no for constitution and Restore the Republic on voting paper.'[65] The constitution was accepted by 685,105 votes to 526,945, a majority of 158,160. In five constituencies there was a majority vote against the constitution: these were Dublin

[61] DD, vol. 67, col. 64, 11 May 1937.

[62] *Irish Press*, 3 June 1937. On the issue of citizenship see Mary E. Daly, 'Irish Nationality and Citizenship since 1922', *Irish Historical Studies*, 32, 127 (May 2001), 377–407, and *idem*, 'Wives, Mothers, and Citizens: The Treatment of Women in the 1935 Nationality and Citizenship Act', *Éire/Ireland*, 38, 2 and 3 (Autumn/Winter 2003), 244–63.

[63] *Irish Press*, 26 June 1937.

[64] *Irish Independent*, 6 May 1937.

[65] Lynn Diaries, RCPI, 1 July 1937.

township, Dublin County, Cork County West, Sligo and Wicklow.[66] It is impossible to know what impact the women's campaign had on the voting. Mary Kettle believed that in some of these constituencies 'largely owing to the fight women put up, the Constitution was defeated and certainly it reduced the number of votes cast for it'.[67] De Valera also believed that the women's campaign against the constitution had cost him votes.[68] However, in a recent television documentary on women in twentieth-century Ireland a number of women remarked that they remembered nothing about the women's campaign against the draft constitution, one adding that she was probably having a baby at the time.[69] How relevant it was to the 'ordinary' woman, may be seen in another *Dublin Opinion* cartoon, which depicts a woman surrounded by household chores and demanding children while her husband explains her position under the new constitution.[70] The number of women involved in the campaign was very small. It was a campaign organised and run by middle-class women, and very much confined to the Dublin area, reaching country districts primarily through the newspapers.

The argument over the constitution continued to the end of the year. In December 1937, at a Fianna Fáil meeting in Glynn, County Wexford, the minister for agriculture repeated the charge that women, when challenged to quote the articles in the new constitution which deprived them of privileges, failed to do so. At the same meeting the Revd P. Murphy said that the opposition to the new constitution had come mainly from a number of noisy women and from politicians.[71] Séan T. O'Kelly, minister for local government, addressing a meeting on the constitution in Dublin queried the nationalist credentials of the organisers of the women's opposition and said they would rather the country to be still 'under the Union Jack'.[72] Mary Hayden, and other women, responded to these speeches. Hayden defended the women's interpretation of the controversial clauses, and referred specifically to the Condition of Employment Act (1936), regarded when passed as of doubtful legality but now within the new constitution as perfectly legal. After the publication of these letters the *Irish Press* had a leading article headed 'Women Graduates Again'. This leader accused women of misrepresenting the implications of the constitutional articles. It invoked Pius XI and the encyclical *Quadrasgesimo Anno* in relation to article 45. The

[66] *Irish Press*, 17 July 1937.

[67] *Irish Independent*, 25 Nov. 1937.

[68] See his speech at the Fianna Fáil Ard Fheis in October 1937 in *Speeches and Statements by Eamon de Valera, 1917–73*, ed. Maurice Moynihan (1980), 334.

[69] Hoodwinked: Irish Women since the 1920s. Broadcast on RTÉ television in 1997.

[70] *Dublin Opinion*, 16, 184 (June 1937).

[71] *Irish Independent*, 6 Dec. 1937.

[72] *Irish Independent*, 14 Dec. 1937.

leader concluded by advising the women of the country to 'pray to be saved from the advocacy of the academic group who have constituted themselves their champions'.[73]

Mary E. Daly has noted that the constitutional emphasis on the importance of women's role within the home at a time when the 'overwhelming majority of Irish women – married, widowed and single, were based within the home' suggests that the constitution can be viewed as 'giving status to many members of Irish society who were otherwise ignored'.[74] However, the recognition of that status within the constitution had no practical benefits for women. Yvonne Scannell has observed that the effect of the constitution was to relegate women to a life of domesticity and powerlessness.[75] This, however, is an exaggeration. Irish women continued to engage in work outside the home; levels of emigration, fuelled by poor economic prospects in Ireland, forced many women to England and beyond.

The advent of a women's political party, founded on 24 November 1937 and named the Women's Social and Political League, was a direct consequence of the women's campaign against the draft constitution. It was to be non-party and non-sectarian and its aim was to promote and protect the political, social and economic status of women and to further their work and usefulness as citizens. Proposing the formation of the party Dorothy Macardle said she considered 'the organisation of the body a humiliating necessity and she never before thought that such a necessity would arise in Ireland. It had arisen because men had organised the sexes separately and to the detriment of women.'[76]

What did change, however, was the form of women's political activism. There was an increased emphasis on the needs and rights of wives and mothers. The formation of the Irish Housewives' Association [IHA] in 1942 saw campaigns to protect the housewife against rising prices and focused on women's rights as consumers. With a new generation of feminists the IHA was particularly influential in maintaining feminist protest in Ireland throughout the remainder of the twentieth century. The Joint Committee continued to call for equality of treatment between men and women. While the IHA managed at times to get publicity for their activities, for many of the other women's organisations this proved to be difficult. Political agitation became more hidden and evidence of that agitation can be found to a greater extent in departmental files and minute books than in the public domain.

[73] *Irish Press*, 17 Dec. 1937.
[74] Daly, 'Women in the Irish Free State, 1922–1939', 111–12.
[75] Yvonne Scannell, 'The Constitution and the Role of Women', in *De Valera's Constitution and Ours*, ed. Brian Farrell (Dublin, 1988), 123–36.
[76] *Irish Independent*, 25 Nov. 1937.

At a fundamental level the campaign against the draft constitution was about ambiguity in language, about the inadequate reflection of the reality of women's lived experience, about the mistrust that women had of male politicians. It was a protest against the discursive construction within the constitution that all women, whatever their marital status, and whether they were mothers or not, were enmeshed in traditional families. It is significant that the campaign was undertaken at all. It was the last high profile feminist campaign until the revival of feminism in Ireland in the 1970s.

Appendix

CONTENTIOUS ARTICLES

Draft constitution 1937

Article 9.1 The acquisition and loss of Irish nationality and citizenship shall be determined in accordance with law.

Article 16.1.1 Every citizen who has reached the age of twenty-one years, and who is not placed under disability or incapacity by this Constitution or by law, shall be eligible for membership of Dáil Eireann.

Article 16.1.2 Every citizen who has reached the age of twenty-one years who is not disqualified by law and complies with the provisions of the law relating to the election of members of Dáil Eireann, shall have the right to vote at an election for members of Dáil Eireann.

Article 40.1 All citizens shall, as human persons, be held equal before the law. This shall not be held to mean that the State shall not in its enactments have due regard to differences of capacity, physical and moral, and of social function.

Article 41.2.1 In particular, the State recognises that by her life within the home, woman gives to the State a support without which the common good cannot be achieved.

Article 41.2.2 The State shall, therefore, endeavour to ensure that mothers shall not be obliged by economic necessity to engage in labour to the neglect of their duties in the home.

Article 45.4.1 The State pledges itself to safeguard with especial care the economic interests of the weaker sections of the community, and, where necessary, to contribute to the support of the infirm, the widow, the orphan, and the aged.

Article 45.4.2 The State shall endeavour to ensure that the inadequate strength of women and the tender age of children shall not be abused, and that women or children shall not be forced by economic necessity to enter avocations unsuited to their sex, age or strength.

1922 Constitution

Article 3

Every person, without distinction of sex, domiciled in the area of the jurisdiction of the Irish Free State (Saorstát Eireann) at the time of the coming into operation of this Constitution, who was born in Ireland or either of whose parents were born in Ireland or who has been ordinarily resident in the area of the jurisdiction of the Irish Free State (Saorstát Eireann) enjoy the privileges and be subject to the obligations of such citizenship: provided that any such person being a citizen of another state may elect not to accept the citizenship here and termination of citizenship in the Irish Free State (Saorstát Eireann) shall be determined by law.

1916 Proclamation

'The Republic guarantees religious and civil liberty, equal rights and equal opportunities to all its citizens . . . '.

ROYAL HISTORICAL SOCIETY
REPORT OF COUNCIL
SESSION 2004–2005

Officers and Council

- At the Anniversary Meeting on 26 November 2004, Professor M.J. Daunton, MA, PhD, Litt D, FBA succeeded Professor J.L. Nelson as President. After the meeting Professor Daunton wrote in the Autumn 2004 'Newsletter':

> In November, Jinty steps down from the Presidency of the Royal Historical Society – four years of hard work for her, and four years of success for us. She has made her mark in many ways, not least in being – at last – the first woman President of the Society.
>
> Jinty's time as President has been marked most significantly, perhaps, by her commitment to outreach and inclusion. The Society is better known and more accessible across a wider geographical area than ever before. It is largely due to Jinty's enthusiasm and her strong links with continental scholars that we are now planning to visit not only the cities of the British Isles, but also mainland Europe, entirely appropriate for an historian of the age of Charlemagne. She has built up our roster of corresponding fellows, and maintained our role in the British National Committee of the International Congress of Historical Sciences. Knowledge of what we do and how we do it is now out in the public domain as a result of Jinty's determined efforts to ensure that the Society has a public face as well as being a respected academic institution both within Britain and in the global scholarly community. We are more effective than ever in defending the interests of history in education, in public debate and in preserving the archive.
>
> Those of us who have worked closely with Jinty will testify not only to her hard work and determined efforts on behalf of the Society, but also to the fact that this work has always been undertaken with good humour, common sense, and an open friendliness both to her close colleagues and to the wider circle of historians. The Society has become truly sociable.
>
> She has also educated and entertained us with her Presidential addresses, with her comments on lectures, and her interventions in discussions around the Council chamber. Alas, her time in the Presidency coincided with a bear market on the Stock Exchange so that she has faced difficult financial decisions. But we have gone through a continued bull market intellectually and organisationally which shows no sign of breaking.

- Mr David Morgan resigned as Honorary Librarian after thirteen years' service and the Society owes him a great debt for his quiet efficiency and effective service over the years; Dr Jon Lawrence, BA, PhD, succeeded Dr Aled Jones as Literary Director; the remaining Officers of the Society were re-elected.

- The Vice-Presidents retiring under By-law XVII were Professor P.J. Corfield and Professor L. J. Jordanova. Dr J.E. Burton, BA, DPhil and Dr P. Seaward, MA, DPhil were elected to replace them.
- The Members of Council retiring under By-law XX were Professor J.A. Green, Professor H.E. Meller and Professor R.J.A.R. Rathbone. In accordance with By-law XXI, amended, Professor G.W. Bernard, MA, DPhil, Dr C.A. Holmes, MA, PhD and Professor R I Frost, MA PhD were elected in their place.
- The vacant post of Honorary Librarian was re-designated as Honorary Librarian and Fellowship Officer, with the intention that the new incumbent would have special responsibility for promoting closer relations and better communications between Council and the Fellowship and membership, including the maintenance and enhancement of the Society's website.
- Two new Officers were elected during the year, in accordance with By-law XVIII. Council accepted the proposals from the Election of Officers Subcommittee that Dr Mark Smith become the new Honorary Librarian and Fellowship Officer, with effect from 23 September 2005 and that Dr Jon Parry succeed Professor Julian Hoppit as Honorary Treasurer with effect from the Anniversary Meeting on 25 November 2005.
- Professor J.S. Morrill succeeded Professor D.S. Eastwood as Convenor of the *Studies in History* Editorial Board.
- The Society's staffing arrangements have changed over the year. In February 2005 Joy McCarthy resigned after 17 years' stellar service as Executive Secretary and has been succeeded by Jane Boland. The Society's Administrative Assistant, Amy Warner, resigned in January 2005 and her post is now filled by Melanie Batt.
- haysmacintyre were appointed auditors for the year 2004–2005 under By-law XXXIX.
- Cripps Portfolio continued to manage the Society's investment funds.

Activities of the Society during the Year

The Society continues to be an active voice for the historical discipline and allied professions in the rapidly changing landscape of higher education.

Contacts with government have been maintained by meetings with Charles Clarke, the then Secretary of State for Education and Skills and his Under-Secretary of State, on history teaching from the primary to tertiary sectors, and such links are now being renewed following ministerial reshuffles.

The Society has contributed to the Research Assessment Exercise 2008, welcoming the appointment of the President as Chair of Panel N and Professor Stafford, a former Vice-President, as Chair of the History

Sub-Panel. The Society submitted nominations for membership of the History Sub-Panel, and in September 2005 provided a detailed response to the draft criteria and working methods.

The Society has maintained close relations with the Arts and Humanities Board, which became a Research Council in April 2005, commenting on the workings of the Peer Review College and the aborted idea of a Journal Reference List. A proposal on 'The History of Trust', drawn up by Professor Hosking, was submitted by the Society for consideration for the next round of AHRC Strategic Programmes.

The creation of the AHRC was marked by the Society by holding a workshop in June which reviewed key features of research funding – past, present and future – by the AHRB/C. Among those present was Professor David Robey, Programme Director of ICT for the AHRC, who outlined the ICT in Arts and Humanities Research Initiative.

The Society has responded to other consultative documents circulated by national bodies, principally the Green Paper from the Department for Culture, Media and Sport entitled 'Understanding the Future: Museums and 21st Century Life. The Value of Museums'.

The Society's on-line Bibliography goes from strength to strength, with over 13,000 new records added to the database in the year to September 2005. Thanks are due to Simon Baker who works mainly on the data of the current year, and Simon Harratt (funded entirely by the Society) who has helped in improving retrospective indexing, and filling in the gaps. Peter Salt, our longest serving team member, continues to provide the essential forward thinking and technical expertise. The project has been working hard on inter-operability, adding links to World Cat via Google, and providing full text access via EDINA's Get Copy service to electronically available articles. The value of this service will improve when J-STOR becomes a target for EDINA linkage, which should happen in the near future. Meanwhile cross-searchability with Oxford DNB and the National Register of Archives is imminent. We are most pleased, however, by the developing collaboration with Irish History On-Line, funded by the Irish Research Council for the Humanities and Social Sciences and directed by Professor Jacqueline Hill from NUI Maynooth. This is an extremely significant international collaboration, which has already yielded another 22,000 records in an under-represented area of the Society's bibliography by May 2005.

The Literary Directors have been vigorously pursuing a couple of initiatives to make the Society's publications available electronically. An agreement has been signed with J-STOR for the digitisation of all volumes of *Transactions*, and a very successful campaign has been conducted to secure formal assignment of rights for electronic dissemination from editors of previous Camden volumes. A number of digitisation projects are underway, including Carnegie Mellon's Million Books and the well publicised Google enterprise. The assignment of these rights means that the Society will be able to bring its publications to a wider audience. We remain keen, however, to be put in touch with the executors of any deceased editors and anyone knowing of such persons should contact the Literary Directors.

The 20th Quinquennial Congress of the International Congress of Historical Sciences was held in Sydney, Australia, on 3–9 July 2005. The Society, which administers the British National Committee, helped organise and fund the participation of over 40 scholars from the UK. A full report from Professor Andrew Porter, one of the delegates, will appear in the next newsletter.

The Society continues to take a close interest in the unfolding Bologna Process to create the European Higher Education Area by 2010. The outgoing President was in contact with the Quality Assurance Agency for Higher Education on the importance of these proposals, and in May 2005 Professor Wendy Davies, a 'Bologna Promoter' and Pro-Provost (European Affairs) at UCL, gave an authoritative presentation to the Research Policy Committee on recent developments. The Government is now talking a more active role in the process, and the Society is monitoring announcements and exploring ways to contribute to the unfolding debate.

As part of its initiative to foster closer relations with other Learned Societies, the Society now meets annually with the Bibliographical Society and exchanges information about meetings and other events of mutual interest. The two Societies are to sponsor a one-day conference in March 2006 on 'Historians and Bibliographers in Conversation'.

A standard feature of research application forms is a section on ethical information and many universities and individual departments have recently devised their own statements on research ethics. The Society felt it was an appropriate moment to compose its own Ethics Statement, from its distinctive perspective as a Learned Society defending and advancing the interests of history, which can be consulted on the Society's website.

The Society continues to work closely with HUDG, now re-branded as History UK (HE), with the Historical Association and with the Institute of Historical Research, and monthly meetings of the four groups have been established to co-ordinate activities and exchange information.

The Society has supported attempts to close the gap between history teaching in the secondary and tertiary sectors. It was a co-sponsor with the Institute of Historical Research of a successful conference on 'History in British Education' on 14–15 February 2005 at Senate House, and is backing a follow-up conference on 29 September, 'History in Schools and Higher Education: Issues of Common Concern', organised by the Institute of Historical Research. The Teaching Policy Committee has been monitoring the developments over the proposed reform of 'A' Level history, and over the past year members have attended meetings between the OCR 'A' Level Board and the History Faculties of Cambridge and Oxford. The Society is convening a workshop on 26 October 2005 to bring together senior examiners and subject officers of the three English 'A' Level Boards, with academics from the Society, the Historical Association and History UK (HE). Dr Clive Holmes represented the Society at the launch of the Historical Association's Curriculum Development Project, 'History 14–19'. The President has taken a leading role in promoting the Specialist Schools' Trust, and is working closely with its chair, Sir Cyril Taylor. Prof. Harry Dickinson speaks for the Society on the History Subject Association group on the Qualifications and Curriculum Authority.

The Society maintains its links with the Subject Centre for History, Classics and Archaeology. On behalf of the Society, Dr Andrew Foster attended the History Advisory Panel meeting in Oxford in April 2005. Once again the Society supported the National Awards for Teaching in Higher Education, which recognises innovation and excellence in teaching, and Dr Andrew Foster represented the Society on a panel of judges in March 2005.

Council and the Officers record their debt of thanks in a challenging transitional year to the Executive Secretary Joy McCarthy and to her successor Jane Boland, and to the Administrative Assistant Amy Warner and her successor Melanie Batt, for their expert and dedicated work on these and other activities.

Meetings of the Society

5 papers were given in London this year and 2 papers were read at locations outside London. Welcome invitations were extended to the Society to visit the History Departments at the University of the West of England and the University of Southampton. (Future visits are planned to include Dublin universities on October 21 and 22 October 2005, the University of Hull, 31 March 2006 and the University of Hertfordshire, Friday 20 October 2006).

Conferences

i) a joint conference was held with the North American Conference on British Studies and the British Association for American Studies, 'Crosstown Traffic: Anglo-American Cultural Exchange since 1865', at the University of Warwick on 4 – 6 July 2004;
ii) a further one day seminar to commemorate the Society's former President, Professor Gerald Aylmer, on 'digitisation' was held at The National Archives, Kew, on 27 November 2004;
iii) a joint conference with the Institute of Historical Research and the Historical Association on 'History in British Education' was held at the IHR on 14–15 February 2005;
iv) a conference on 'History and Music' was held at CRASSH, Cambridge, on 19–20 March 2005;

v) a joint conference with the Centre for English Local History was held at the University of Leicester to mark the 50th Anniversary of W.G. Hoskins' *Making of the English Landscape* on 7–10 July 2005;

The Colin Matthew Memorial Lecture for the Public Understanding of History – previously known as the Gresham Lecture – was given on 3 November 2004 by Dr Gareth Griffiths, Director of the British Empire and Commonwealth Museum, Bristol on 'Presenting unwanted histories: the project to establish the British and Commonwealth Museum'. These lectures continue to be given in memory of the late Professor Colin Matthew, a former Literary Director and Vice-President of the Society. The lecture in 2005 will be on Wednesday 2 November when Dr. Michael Wood, TV presenter and documentary film maker will speak on 'Travels in Time: History and Identity in Today's World'.

Future conferences are to include:

i) a one day conference with the History of Parliament Trust to mark the 400th anniversary of the Gunpowder Plot, to be held at Westminster Hall on 4 November 2005;
ii) a conference on 'New Directions in British Historiography of China' to be held at the Institute of Historical Research on 26 November 2005;
iii) a joint conference with the YMCA, 'Christian Movements', to be held in Birmingham on 17–19 February 2006;
iv) a conference, 'Cultures of Political Counsel?', to be held on 7–9 April 2006, at the University of Liverpool;
v) a joint conference with the German Historical Institute London on 'How violent were the Middle Ages?', to be held in July 2006 at Cumberland Lodge, Windsor;
vi) a joint conference with the National Maritime Museum, on the Seven Years War, on 14–15 July 2006 at Greenwich, and
vii) a conference to mark the Tercentenary of the Union with Scotland is scheduled to be held in 2007.
viii) Professor Miri Rubin would be hosting a conference on 'The Global Middle Ages' in 2007.

Prizes

The Society's annual prizes were awarded as follows:

- The Alexander Prize was not awarded in 2005.
- The David Berry Prize for 2004, for an essay on Scottish history, was awarded to Dr Clare Jackson for her essay, '"*Assize of Error" and the independence of the criminal jury in Restoration Scotland.*'

The judge's citation read:

'This essay is an acute and original analysis of a notorious episode, the intimidation of Scottish juries under Charles II. The author analyses in detail the trial and conviction of seven jurymen in 1681 for 'wilful error' in having acquitted nine suspected Presbyterian rebels. She traces also the legal background (back to the 1470s), and examines the broader implications of the trial in England as well as Scotland. She convincingly calls into question many entrenched beliefs about the character of Restoration criminal justice, demonstrating that the conviction of the jurors was a hollow victory for the Crown, which never again prosecuted jurors for wilful error. I have no hesitation in recommending that this submission be awarded the David Berry prize.'

- The Whitfield Book Prize for a first book on British history attracted 38 entries. The generally high quality of the entries was again commended by the assessors.

The Prize for 2004 was awarded to:

M. J. D. Roberts, *Making English Morals: Voluntary Association and Moral Reform in England, 1787–1886*, Cambridge: Cambridge University Press, 2004.

The judges wrote:

'This is an impressive book, the product of many years of research. It addresses a sphere of activities that has been understood historically as distinctively English – the voluntary movement – and examines the ideas and social practices which created it. The discussion is always clear, both at the empirical and at the conceptual level. Roberts argues convincingly that voluntary activity arose from the combined presence of greater leisure in the lives of many of the 'middling sort' and a desire for more effective integration of 'local cultures' into a national one' (p. 298). He traces the argument throughout the age of William Wilberforce, Elizabeth Fry, Josephine Butler and W T Stead. Yet this type of voluntary activity failed to pass on 'its vision of a non-sectarian, hierarchical yet community based active citizenship to a new generation' (pp. 288–9) into the twentieth century.

Making English Morals should be required reading for ministers and civil servants, pundits and educators. It is relevant to current debates on the voluntary sector and community building. It is probably far too subtle for some of those readers, but for that subtlety and for its ambition it earns our admiration and with it the Whitfield Prize'.

M. J. D. Roberts is Associate Professor in the Department of Modern History, Macquarie University, Sydney, Australia.

Runners Up

Jason Peacey, *Politicians and pamphleteers: Propaganda during the English Civil War and Interregnum*, Aldershot: Ashgate, 2004.

'Dr Peacey approaches a turbulent period in English politics from an angle hitherto unexplored by historians. By considering the intricacies of the world of printing and publishing it offers insight into the work of writers like Milton and Marchamont Nedham. Dr Peacey has not only created a new approach but has imposed himself on the subject through careful analysis of the language of political debate, the motivations of writers and printers and their patrons. He thus offers conclusions which will interest historians, scholars of literature, and the growing ranks of those interested in the history of the book and reading practices'.

J. L. Laynesmith, *The Last Medieval Queens: English Queenship 1445–1503*, Oxford: Oxford University Press, 2004.

'Dr Laynesmith argues vigorously for the historical importance of studying the late medieval queens as a group. The book is based on a wide range of sources – visual and textual – from account-books to chronicles, liturgies to rolls of parliament. The thematic structure creates a rounded view of the institution of queenship as it was experienced in private and in public, among kin, courtiers and even subjects. The book is written in a lively manner and displays mastery of concepts as well as sources. It will be read with equal pleasure by historians of politics, of family, of women and of courts'.

- Thanks to the continuing generous donation from The Gladstone Memorial Trust, the Gladstone History Book Prize for a first book on a subject outside British history was again awarded. The number of entries this year was 30.

  The Prize for 2004 was awarded to:

  Nikolaus Wachsmann for his book *Hitler's Prisons: Legal Terror in Nazi Germany*, published by Yale University Press, 2004.

  The judges wrote:

  'The Gladstone Prize for a first book on non-British History attracted thirty entries, of which a number proved to be ineligible. Of the eligible entries Nikolaus Wachsmann's study of the operation and function of legal terror in the Third Reich stood out for its depth of research and outstanding scholarship. As the author demonstrates, for most of the Nazi era state prisons held more inmates than the concentration camps, and yet the former have not received comprehensive study. Drawing on an impressive range of archives, from the records of the Ministry of Justice, to regional prison records and personal diaries, the author shows how the courts and the penal system were important in providing a veneer of legality for Nazi terror, and in criminalizing political dissent'.

  The judges also commended:

  Daud Ali, *Courtly Culture and Political Life in Early Medieval India*, published by Cambridge University Press, 2004, a study of the royal court as a social and cultural institution, and Daniel Power, *The Norman Frontier in the Twelfth and Thirteenth Centuries*, published by Cambridge University Press, 2004, a study of the borderlands of the duchy of Normandy and the communities of the frontier regions.

- In order to recognise the high quality of work now being produced at undergraduate level in the form of third-year dissertations, the Society continued, in association with *History Today* magazine, to award an annual prize for the best undergraduate dissertation. Departments are asked to nominate annually their best dissertation and a joint committee of the Society and *History Today* select in the autumn the national prizewinner from among these nominations. The prize also recognizes the Society's close relations with *History Today* and the important role the magazine has played in disseminating scholarly research to a wider audience. 39 submissions were made.

First prize was awarded to Andrew Arsan [University of Cambridge] for his essay 'Shukri Ghanem and the Ottoman Empire 1908–1914'; *Proxime Accessit* was awarded to Sebastian Walsh [University of Durham] for his essay 'Informal Power within the Elizabethan Polity: the case of Sir Nicholas Throckmorton'.
Highly Commended was Thomas Neuhaus [University of Essex] for his essay '"Sing me a swing song and let me dance": The Swing Youth and cultural dissent in the Third Reich'.

Articles by all three prize-winners presenting their research have appeared or will appear shortly in *History Today* editions in 2005.

At the kind invitation of the Keeper, all entrants and their institutional contacts were invited to a celebratory lunch and a behind the scenes visit to The National Archives at Kew in January 2005.

- The German History Society, in association with the Society, agreed to award a prize to the winner of an essay competition. The essay, on any aspect of German history, including the history of German-speaking people both in within and beyond Europe, was open to any postgraduate registered for a degree in a university in either the United Kingdom or the Republic of Ireland. The prize was presented at the Annual General Meeting of the German History Society, and was considered for publication in *German History*.

  The judges of the prize, now in its second year have emphasized that each of the 3 essays submitted was of good quality, covering interesting subjects in a mature and capable manner.
  The winning essay in 2004 was by Christian Goeschel [Darwin College, Cambridge] for his essay entitled 'Suicide at the end of the Third Reich'.

- Frampton and Beazley Prizes for A-level performances were awarded following nominations from the examining bodies:

  Frampton Prizes:

  AQA:
  Clare Harrisson, Greenhead College, Huddersfield
  Edexcel Foundation incorporating the London Examination Board:
  No award
  Oxford, Cambridge and RSA Board:
  Natalie Claire Whitty, Camden School for Girls, London
  Welsh Joint Education Committee:
  Thomas R.J. Davies, Penglais School, Aberystwyth

Beazley Prizes:
Northern Ireland Council for the Curriculum Examinations and Assessment:
Victoria M.R. Brownlee, The Royal School Armagh
Scottish Examination Board:
Alasdair J. Macleod, Portree High School, Isle of Skye

- The Director of the Institute of Historical Research announced the winner of the Pollard Prize, at the Annual Reception on 6 July 2005. The prize is awarded annually to the best postgraduate student paper presented in a seminar at the IHR.

  The Pollard Prize winner 2005 was Lucy Marten, 'The Shiring of East Anglia: an alternative hypothesis'.
  There were two runners up – Dianne Payne. 'Rhetoric, reality and the Marine Society' and Sam Worby, 'Kinship: the canon law and the common law in 13th century England'.

Publications

Transactions, Sixth Series, Volume 14 was published during the session, and *Transactions*, Sixth Series, Volume 15 went to press, to be published in November 2005.

In the Camden, Fifth Series, *Appeasement and All Souls: A Portrait with Documents*, ed. Sidney Aster (vol. 24) and *Foreign Intelligence and Information Gathering in Elizabethan England: Two English Treatises on the State of France, 1580–1584*, ed. David Potter (vol. 25) were published during the year. *Newsletters from the Caroline Court, 1631–1638: Catholicism and the Politics of the Personal Rule*, ed. Michael C. Questier (vol. 26) and *The Clarke Papers, Volumes V and VI*, ed. Frances Henderson went to press for publication in 2005–6.

The *Studies in History* Editorial Board continued to meet throughout the year. The second series continued to produce exciting volumes. The following volumes were published, or went to press, during the session:

- *Britain and the Papacy in the Age of Revolution, 1846–1851*, Saho Matsumoto
- *Navy and Government in Early Modern France, 1572–1661*, Alan James
- *Culture, Identity and Nationalism: Flanders in the Nineteenth and Twentieth Centuries*, Tim Baycroft
- *War, politics and finance in late medieval England: Bristol, York and the crown, 1350–1400*, Christian Liddy
- *Debating England's Aristocracy in the 1790s: pamphlets, polemics and political ideas*, Amanda Goodrich

- *The making of the Jacobean regime: James VI and I and the government of England, 1603–1605*, Diana Newton

As in previous subscription years, volumes in *Studies in History* series were offered to the membership at a favourably discounted price. Many Fellows, Associates and Members accepted the offer for volumes published during the year, and the advance orders for further copies of the volumes to be published in the year 2005–2006 were most encouraging.

The Society acknowledges its gratitude for the continuing subventions from the Economic History Society and the Past and Present Society to the *Studies in History* series.

Papers from the conference, 'Churchill in the Twenty-First Century', with a new introduction by Professor David Cannadine, were published by Cambridge University Press in Autumn 2004.

Papers Read

- At the ordinary meetings of the Society the following papers were read:
  - 'Putting the English Reformation on the map'
    Professor Diarmaid MacCulloch (7 July 2004: Prothero Lecture)
  - 'The Environmental History of the Russian Steppes'
    Dr David Moon (22 October 2004 at the University of the West of England)
  - 'The Witch and the Western Imagination'
    Dr Lyndal Roper (28 January 2005)
  - 'Africa and the "Birth of the Modern World"'
    Professor Megan Vaughan (4 March 2005)
  - 'Land and Freedom in Early Medieval Europe'
    Dr. Matthew Innes (26 April 2005 at the University of Southampton)
  - 'Trust and Distrust: a Suitable Theme for Historians'
    Professor Geoffrey Hosking (20 May 2005)
- At the Anniversary meeting on 26 November 2004, the President, Professor Janet L. Nelson, delivered her final address on 'England the Continent in the Ninth Century IV: Bodies and Minds'.

Finance

- The Society welcomed a substantial legacy bequest of £39,000 from the estate of deceased Fellow Miss Vera C. M. London of Shropshire.
- The Society's financial position improved in 2004–5, its overall worth rising by over twelve per cent compared to the previous year, largely because of rises in the value of its investments and the generous legacy from Miss London. Even so, the Society still has less funds in total than in each of the years in the period 1997–2000, a position that is more

marked when the effects of inflation are considered. Consequently, it has continued to be necessary to keep costs under close control. There are signs of light at the end of the tunnel, but the signs are still rather faint.

- Council records with gratitude the benefactions made to the Society by:
  - Mr. L.C. Alexander
  - The Reverend David Berry
  - Professor Andrew Browning
  - Professor C.D. Chandaman
  - Professor G. Donaldson
  - Professor Sir Geoffrey Elton
  - Mr. E.J. Erith
  - Mr. P.J.C. Firth
  - Mrs. W.M. Frampton
  - Mr. A.E.J. Hollaender
  - Professor C.J. Holdsworth
  - Miss V.C.M. London
  - Professor P.J. Marshall
  - Mr. E.L.C. Mullins
  - Sir George Prothero
  - Dr. L. Rausing
  - Professor T.F. Reddaway
  - Miss E.M. Robinson
  - Miss J.C. Sinar
  - Professor A.S. Whitfield

Membership

- Council was advised and recorded with regret the deaths of 16 Fellows, 13 Retired Fellows, 1 Vice-President, 2 Associates and a former President of the Society.

  These included
  Mr. T.F.T. Baker – Fellow
  Mr. B. Blackwood – Associate
  Professor N.F. Cantor – Fellow
  Dr. D.G. Chandler – Retired Fellow
  Professor P.G. Cornell – Retired Fellow
  Professor J.M. Cornwall – Fellow
  Mrs Ann K. B. Evans – Retired Fellow
  Mr. R. A. Fletcher – Fellow
  Professor Richard Fletcher – Fellow
  Professor R.L. Greaves – Fellow

Fr. Michael B. Hackett O.S.A – Retired Fellow
Dr. Francis J. Hebbert – Associate
Dr. J.S. Hurt – Retired Fellow
Mr J.D. Jarrett – Retired Fellow
Joseph Kennedy – Retired Fellow
Professor M.J. Larkin – Retired Fellow
Professor M. Lynn – Fellow
Professor H.J. Perkin – Retired Fellow
Colonel G.S. Powell – Retired Fellow
Dr. W.J. Rowe – Retired Fellow
Professor C.S.R. Russell – Fellow and Vice-President of the Society
Miss M.D. Slatter – Retired Fellow
Dr Lawrence S. Snell – Fellow
Dr. D.G. Southgate – Fellow
Professor D. Syrett – Fellow
Dr. William Taylor – Retired Fellow
Dr David O. Thomas – Retired Fellow
Professor J.A.F. Thomson – Retired Fellow
Professor A.P. Thornton – Fellow
Mr. R.C. Trebilcock – Fellow
Professor Sir Glanmor Williams – Retired Fellow
Professor A.H. Woolrych – Retired Fellow
Mr. C.P. Wormald – Fellow
and Professor Sir Rees Davies, former President.

- 94 Fellows and 38 Members were elected to the Society. 1 Corresponding Fellow was invited to accept election. The membership of the Society on 30 June 2005 numbered 2953, comprising 1990 Fellows, 573 Retired Fellows, 16 Life Fellows, 14 Honorary Vice-Presidents, 97 Corresponding Fellows, 70 Associates and 193 Members.
- The Society exchanged publications with 15 Societies, British and Foreign.

Representatives of the Society

- The representation of the Society upon other various bodies was as follows:
  - Professor David Ganz on the Anthony Panizzi Foundation;
  - Dr. Julia Crick on the Joint Committee of the Society and the British Academy established to prepare an edition of Anglo-Saxon charters;
  - Professor N.P. Brooks on a committee to promote the publication of photographic records of the more significant collections of British Coins;

- Professor G.H. Martin on the Council of the British Records Association;
- Mr. P.M.H. Bell on the Editorial Advisory Board of the *Annual Register*;
- Professor C.J. Holdsworth on the Court of the University of Exeter;
- Professor M.C. Cross on the Council of the British Association for Local History; and on the British Sub-Commission of the Commission International d'Histoire Ecclesiastique Comparée;
- Professor L.J. Jordanova on the Advisory Council of the reviewing committee on the Export of Works of Art;
- Professor W. Davies on the Court of the University of Birmingham;
- Professor R.D. McKitterick on a committee to regulate British co-operation in the preparation of a new repertory of medieval sources to replace Potthast's *Bibliotheca Historica Medii Aevi*;
- Dr. W.R. Childs member of the Court of the University of Sheffield;
- Dr. J. Winters on the History Data Service Advisory Committee;
- Dr. R.A. Burns on the user panel of the RSLP Revelation project 'Unlocking research sources for 19 and 20 century church history and Christian theology';
- Dr. M. Smith on the Court of Governors of the University of Wales, Swansea;
- Dr. R. Mackenney on the University of Stirling Conference;
- Professor N. Thompson member of the Court of the University of Wales;
- Dr. C.J. Kitching on the National Council on Archives.

- Council received reports from its representatives.

Grants

- The Royal Historical Society Centenary Fellowship for the academic year 2004–2005 was awarded to P.H.M. Porter studying for a doctorate at Magdalen College, Oxford and working on a thesis entitled "New Jerusalems: Blood Sacrifice and Redemption in the Protestant War Experience, 1914–1918".
- The Society's P.J. Marshall Fellowship is not awarded in the academic year 2004–2005. The next Fellowship will be awarded in 2005–2006.
- The Society's Research Support Committee continued to provide grants to postgraduate students for attendance at training courses or conferences, and funding towards research within and outside the United Kingdom. Funding is also available to organizers of workshops and conferences to encourage the participation of junior researchers.

- A new scheme – the Royal Historical Society Postgraduate Speakers' Series (RHSPSS) was introduced at the beginning of the financial year, July 2005, on a trial basis. The scheme is intended to enhance the impact of the Society's support by bringing postgraduate speakers already in receipt of the Society's Research Funds to speak at participating departments around the country. A review would be made at the end of the Society's financial year.
- Grants during the year were made to the following:

Travel to Conferences [Training Bursaries]

- Shin AHN, PhD, University of Edinburgh
  The 19th World Congress of the International Association for the History of Religions: 'Religion – Conflict and Peace', held in Tokyo, Japan, on 23–31 March 2005.
- Jackson Webster ARMSTRONG, PhD, Trinity Hall, University of Cambridge
  Fifteenth-Century Conference: The Peoples of the British Isles, held at the University of Wales Swansea, 8–10 September 2005.
- Manuel BARCIA PAZ, University of Essex
  World History Association Annual Meeting held at the University of Ifrane, Morocco, 27–29 June 2005.
- Jonathan Gilder BATESON, DPhil, University of Oxford
  Annual Meeting of the American Association for the History of Medicine, held in Birmingham, Alabama, USA, 7–10 April 2005.
- Kimberly BERNARD, PhD at the University of Wales, Swansea
  'Crosstown Traffic', held at the University of Warwick, 4–7 July 2004.
- Robert Gregory BODDICE, PhD at the University of York
  Northeast Conference on British Studies held at McGill University, Montreal, 1–2 October 2004.
- Thomas Edward CADOGAN, PhD at SOAS, University of London
  The 47th Annual Meeting of the African Studies Association, held in New Orleans, USA, 11–15 November 2004
- Vanessa Ann CHAMBERS, PhD, Institute of Historical Research, London
  The Social History Society 30th Annual Conference, held at Trinity College, Dublin, on 7–9 January 2005.
- Nancy COLLINS, PhD at University College London
  Seventh Annual International Conference of the Urban History Association held in Athens-Piraeus, Greece, 27–30 October 2004.
- Catherine FERRIS, PhD, University College London
  Social History Society Annual Conference, held at Trinity College, Dublin, on 7–9 January 2005.

- Lauren French FOGLE, PhD, Royal Holloway, University of London
  22nd Annual Conference of the Illinois Medieval Society, held at the University of Southern Illinois, USA, on 22–25 February 2005.
- Miguel GARCIA-SANCHO, PhD, Imperial College, London
  Conference, 'Gathering Things, Collecting Data, Producing Knowledge', held at Ischia, Italy, 28 June–5 July 2005.
- [Thomas] Michael GOEBEL, PhD, University College London
  Conference, Xo Jornadas Interescuelas/Departamentos de Historia, held at Rosario, Argentina, 20–23 September 2005.
- Kristian GUSTAFSON, PhD, Downing College, Cambridge
  Royal Military College of Canada Annual Military History Symposium, held at Kingston, Ontario, on 16–18 March 2005.
- Nicola Claire GUY, PhD, University of Durham
  Second Southeast European Studies Association Conference, held at Ohio State University, USA, on 28–30 April 2005.
- Jane HAMLETT, PhD at Royal Holloway, University of London
  North American Conference on British Studies, held in Philadelphia, USA, 29–31 October 2004.
- David Ian HARRISON, PhD, University of Liverpool
  Conference, 'We Band of Brothers', held at the University of Sheffield, 17–19 November 2004.
- Emma JONES, PhD, Royal Holloway, University of London
  Conference, 'Health and History: International Perspectives', 9th Biennial conference of the Australian Society of History of Medicine', held at Auckland, New Zealand, on 16-19 February 2005.
- Heidrun KUGELER, DPhil, Faculty of Modern History, University of Oxford
  Fourth International Interdisciplinary Conference on Germany-speaking Europe, held at Duke University, Durham, NC, USA, 7–10 April 2005.
- Simone LAQUA, DPhil at the University of Oxford
  Sixteenth-Century Studies Conference 2004, held in Toronto, Canada, 28–31 October 2004.
- Amanda MARTINSON, PhD at the University of St Andrews
  Conference on 'The World of Henry II', held at the University of East Anglia, 13–17 September 2004.
- Stamatina MASTORAKOU, DPhil, University of Oxford
  Seventh Biennial History of Astronomy Workshop, held at the University of Notre Dame, USA, 7–10 July 2005.
- Matthew MILNER, PhD at the University of Warwick
  2004 Sixteenth Century Studies Conference held in Toronto, 28–31 October 2004.
- Izabel Anna ORLOWSKA, PhD at SOAS, University of London

Conference, 'The Power of Expression: Identity, Language and Memory in Africa and the Diaspora', held in New Orleans, USA, 11–14 November 2004.

- Eyal POLEG, PhD, Queen Mary, University of London
Conference, 'Bookish Traditions: Authority and the Book in Scripturalist Religions', held at the Central European University, Budapest, 4–15 July 2005.
- Manjeet Kaur RAMGOTRA, PhD at the London School of Economics
American Political Science Association 100th Annual Meeting, 'Global Inequalities', held in Chicago on 2–5 September 2004.
- Meredith L.D. RIEDEL, DPhil at Exeter College, Oxford
19th Annual Texas Medieval Conference held at the University of Dallas, Texas, on 16–18 September 2004.
- James Thomas ROBERTS, PhD, Institute of Medieval Studies, University of Leeds
International Society of Anglo-Saxonists, Biennial Conference 2005 'England and the Continent', held at the International Society of Anglo-Saxonists, Bavarian American Centre, Munich, on 1–6 August 2005.
- Nicole ROBERTSON, PhD, University of Nottingham
Social History Society Annual Conference, held at Trinity College, Dublin, on 7–9 January 2005.
- Jason ROCHE, PhD at the University of St Andrews
'Society for the Study of the Crusades and the Latin East; Istanbul Conference', held in Istanbul, Turkey, 25–29 August 2004.
- Carlos SANTIAGO CABALLERO, PhD, London School of Economics and Political Science
European Society for Environmental History Third International Conference, 'History and Sustainability', held in Florence, Italy, on 16–19 February 2005.
- Ayako SAKURAI, PhD, Department of History and Philosophy of Science, University of Cambridge
Annual meeting of the Japanese Socio-Economic History Society, held at Hitotsubashi University, Tokyo, 30 April–1 May 2005.
- Gareth SHAW, PhD at the University of Hull
'Conference of Quaker Historians and Archivists', held at the George Fox University, Portland, Oregon, USA, 25–27 May 2004.
- Erik SPINDLER, DPhil, Faculty of Modern History, University of Oxford
40th International Congress of Medieval Studies, held at the campus of Western Michigan University, Kalamazoo, Michigan, USA, 5–8 May 2005.

- John STRACHAN, PhD, University of Manchester
  51st Annual Meeting of the Society for French Historical Studies, held at Stanford University, USA, on 17–19 March 2005.
- Anke TIMMERMANN, PhD, Robinson College, Cambridge
  Conference, 'Material Cultures and the Creation of Knowledge', held at the University of Edinburgh, 22–24 July 2005.
- Jelmer Antoon VOS, PhD at SOAS, University of London
  The 47th Annual Meeting of the African Studies Association, held in New Orleans, USA, 11–14 November 2004.
- Konstantinos ZAFEIRIS, PhD at the University of St Andrews
  Sixth Conference of the Society for the Study of the Crusades and the Latin East: '1204: A Turning Point in Relations Between Eastern and Western Christendom' held in Istanbul, Turkey, 26–29 August 2004.

[38]

Research Expenses Within the United Kingdom:

- David John CLAMPIN, PhD at the University of Wales Aberystwyth
  Visits to The National Archives, Kew
- Julie DAY, PhD, University of Leeds
  Visit to various archives in England, November 2004–July 2005.
- Daniel ENGLUND, PhD at the University of Durham
  Visits to libraries and archives in London and Gloucester, June–July 2004.
- Nicola GUY, MA at the University of Durham
  Visits to the School of Slavonic and East European Studies Library, the Maughlin Library, King's College London and The National Archives, 8–12 June 2004 and visit to Somerset Record Office, December 2004, and The National Archives, January 2005.
- Ashfuque HOSSAIN, PhD, University of Nottingham
  Visit to Glasgow University Archive Services.
- Zehra MAMDANI, MPhil, Hughes Hall, University of Cambridge
  Visit to The National Archives, Kew.
- Swapnesh MASRANI, PhD at the University of St Andrews
  Visits to archives in Dundee, Edinburgh, Forfar and Tayport, August–September 2004.
- Christine V SEAL, PhD, University of Leicester
  Visit to various archives in England from February–December 2005
- Elizabeth Kate VIGURS, PhD, University of Leeds
  Visit to archives in the London area, January–March 2005.
- Mark WALLACE, PhD at the University of St Andrews
  Visits to The National Archives and the Library and Museum of Freemasonry, 10–13 August 2004.

[10]

Research Expenses Outside the United Kingdom:

- Katharine Sarah AYLETT, PhD, University of Leeds
  Visit to the National Library of Russia, St. Petersburg.
- Noah Londer CHARNEY, PhD, St. John's College, Cambridge
  Visit to various archives in Italy, 5 February–5 March 2005.
- Delphine DOUCET, PhD at Royal Holloway, University of London
  Visits to archives in Germany, 10 August–2 September 2004.
- Michael GOEBEL, PhD at University College London
  Visits to archives and libraries in Buenos Aires, Argentina, 21 September–20 December 2004.
- Vassiliki KARALI, PhD, University of Edinburgh
  Visit to various archives in Maryland, U.S.A.
- Mohammed KARIM, PhD at De Montfort University
  Visits to the Republic of Uzbekistan State Archives, September–October 2004.
- EE Hong (Agnes) KHOO, PhD at the University of Manchester
  Visits to archives in South Korea, 1–21 September 2004.
- Mikhail KIZILOV, DPhil, Merton College, Oxford
  Various archives in Austria, April 2005.
- Philippa Constance LANE, PhD, University of Essex
  Visit to various archives in South Africa.
- Georgios LIAKOPOULOS, MPhil/PhD, The Hellenic Institute/History Department, Royal Holloway, University of London
  Visit to The Ottoman Archives, Istanbul, Turkey, 1 July–1 August 2005.
- Katherine LIM, DPhil at the University of Oxford
  Visits to Archives in Venice, August 2004–September 2005.
- Jaime MORENO TEJADA, PhD, King's College London
  Visits to various archives in Ecuador, 20 June–20 December 2005.
- James MARSHALL, MLitt at the University of Newcastle
  Visits to Museums and Fieldwork in Greece, October–November 2004.
- Jennifer McNUTT, PhD, University of St. Andrews
  Visit to archives in Geneva, August 2005
- Paolo NATALI, PhD, University of Cambridge
  Visit to various archives in the U.S.A.
- Gabriela Edreva PETKOVA-CAMPBELL, PhD at University of Newcastle upon Tyne
  Visit to the History Department, School of East European Studies of Sodertorns Hogskola, Sweden.
- Mihail Raychev RAEV, PhD at Trinity College, Cambridge
  Visit to archives in Russia, Ukraine and Belarus.
- Ignacio RIVAS, PhD, University College London
  Visit to various archives in Spain, June–September 2005.

- David Rodriguez SARIAS, PhD at Sheffield University
  Visit to various archives in the U.S.A.
- Charlotte SCHRIWER, PhD at the University of St Andrews
  Visits to Archives and Libraries in Cyprus, Jordan and Syria, 1 July–1 September 2004.
- Paul Daniel SHIRLEY, PhD, University College London
  Visit to various archives in the Bahamas and the US, May–July 2005.
- Seumas SPARK, PhD at the University of Edinburgh
  Visits to War Cemeteries in Egypt, Germany, the Netherlands and Italy, summer 2004.
- John STRACHAN, PhD, University of Manchester
  Visit to archives in France, 15–23 February 2005.

[23]

Conference Organisation [Workshop]

- Malcolm BARBER, Conference, 'The Medieval Chronicle IV', held at the University of Reading on 15–19 July 2005.
- Lawrence BLACK
  Conference, 'Taking Stock: The Co-operative Movement in British History', held at the People's History Museum, 13–14 May 2005.
- Patrick J. BONER
  British Society for the History of Science Postgraduate Conference held at the Department of History & Philosophy of Science, University of Cambridge, 5–7 January 2005.
- Caroline BOWDEN
  Conference, 'Consecrated Women: Towards a History of Women Religious of Britain and Ireland', held at the University of Cambridge, on 16–17 September 2005.
- Janet BURTON and Karen STÖBER
  Conference, 'Monasteries and Society in the Later Middle Ages', held at Gregynog Hall, Newtown, Mid Wales, 4–7 April 2005.
- Penelope J. CORFIELD
  Conference, 'The Political and Cultural Left in Britain in the 1790s', held at the Institute of Historical Research, London, 29 June 2005.
- Ildiko CSENGEI
  The British Society for Eighteenth-Century Studies, 34th Annual Conference, held at St. Hugh's College, Oxford, 6–8 January 2005.
- Flora DENNIS
  Conference, 'Domestic Encounters: 1400 to the Present', held at the Royal College of Art, London, on 14 March 2005.
- C.C. DYER
  Conference, 'W.G. Hoskins and the Making of the British Landscape', held at the University of Leicester, 7–10 July 2005.

- Dagmar ENGELKEN and Abayomi KRISTILOLU
  'Critical Perspectives on Empire and Imperialism: Past and Present, Interdisciplinary Postgraduate Conference', held at the University of Essex, 24–25 September 2004.
- David FRENCH
  Conference, 'Anglo-American Relations from the Pilgrim Fathers to the Present', held at University College London on 17–10 February 2005.
- K.S.B. KEATS-ROHAN
  Conference, 'Prosopography: Approaches and Applications', held at Jesus College, Oxford, 15–18 July 2005.
- Andy KING
  'War and Peace; New Perspectives on Anglo-Scottish Relations, c. 1286–1406', held at the University of Durham, 1–2 September 2004.
- Beat KUMIN
  Third Warwick Symposium on Parish Research, held at the University of Warwick, on 14 May 2005.
- Michael LEWIS
  Conference, 'Beyond Imperial Centre and Global Periphery: Reconnecting the Global and the Local Location', held at the Centre for Research in the Arts, Humanities and Social Sciences (CRASSH), Cambridge, on 11–12 March 2005.
- Simon MACLEAN
  Conference, 'Interpreting the Past in Medieval Germany', held at the University of St. Andrews, on 19–22 July 2005.
- Rachel MAIRS
  'Current Research in Egyptology IV', held at the University of Cambridge, 7–9 January 2004.
- Amy McKINNEY
  Conference 'Religious Thought and Practice in Ireland, 1700–1980', held at Queen's University, Belfast, on 19 March 2005.
- Nicola MILLER
  Conference 'When was Latin America modern?', held at UCL and the Institute for the Study of the Americas, London, on 16–18 February 2005.
- Luc RACAUT
  European Reformation Research Group annual conference 2005, held at the University of Newcastle upon Tyne, on 1–3 September 2005.
- Patricia SKINNER
  'Texts, Histories, Historiographies: the Medieval Worlds of Timothy Reuter', held at the University of Southampton, 24–26 July 2004.
- Naomi TADMOR
  Conference, 'Kinship in Britain and Beyond, 500–2000', held at the University of Cambridge and Downing College, 25–26 July 2005.

- Duncan TANNER
  Conference, 'New directions in modern British political history, c. 1867–2001: from the body politic to the politics of the body', held at the Centre for Contemporary British History, Institute of Historical Research, London, 7–9 April 2005.
- Craig TAYLOR
  Conference, 'France and England in the Later Middle Ages', held at the Centre for Medieval Studies, University of York 2–5 April 2005.
- Joan TUMBLETY
  'Spaces and places': the 19th annual conference of the Society for the Study of French History, held at Avenue Campus, University of Southampton, 4–5 July 2005.
- Alexandra WALSHAM
  Conference, 'Syon Abbey and its Books, c. 1400–1700', held at the University of Exeter, Crossmead Conference Centre, 7–8 October 2005.
- Katherine D. WATSON
  Conference "'Assaulting the Past": Placing Violence in Historical Context', held at St. Anne's College, Oxford, on 7–9 July 2005.
- Bjorn WEILER
  Conference, 'Thirteenth-Century England 11: Plantagenet Britain, 1180–1330', held at the University of Wales Conference Centre, Gregynog, on 9–12 September 2005.
- Charlotte WILDMAN
  Conference, 'Modern Britain: New Perspectives', held at the University of Manchester, 3 November 2004.
- Deborah YOUNGS
  The Fifteenth Century Conference, 'The peoples of the British Isles', held at the University of Wales Swansea, on 8–10 September 2005.

[30]

Bursaries for Holders of ORS Awards

- Katherine CHAMBERS, St John's College, Cambridge.
- Natalya CHERNYSHOVA, King's College London.
- Cameron Mitchell SUTT, St. Catharine's College, Cambridge.

[3]

[Total = 104]

29 September 2005

THE ROYAL HISTORICAL SOCIETY
FINANCIAL STATEMENTS
FOR THE YEAR ENDED 30 JUNE 2005

haysmacintyre
Chartered Accountants
Registered Auditors
London

LEGAL AND ADMINISTRATIVE INFORMATION

Members of Council:

Professor J L Nelson, PhD, FBA	President – Officer (to November 2004)
Professor M J Daunton, MA, PhD, FBA	President – Officer (from November 2004)
K C Fincham, MA, PhD	Honorary Secretary – Officer
I W Archer, MA, DPhil	Literary Director – Officer
Jon M Lawrence, BA, PhD	Literary Director – Officer
Professor J Hoppit, PhD	Honorary Treasurer – Officer
D A L Morgan, MA, FSA	Honorary Librarian – Officer (Position vacant from Autumn 2004)
C J Kitching, CBE, PhD, FSA	Vice-President
Professor D R Bates, PhD	Vice-President
Professor H T Dickinson, MA, PhD, D Lit	Vice President
W R Childs, MA, PhD	Vice President
Professor P J Corfield, MA, PhD	Vice President (to November 2004)
Professor L J Jordanova, MA, MA, PhD	Vice President (to November 2004)
J E Burton, BA, DPhil	Vice-President (from November 2004)
P Seaward MA, DPhil	Vice President (from November 2004)

S R Ditchfield, BA, MPhil, PhD
M Finn, MA, PhD
Professor F O'Gorman, PhD
Professor G A Hosking, MA, PhD, FBA
R S Mackenney, MA, PhD
Professor D M Palliser, MA, DPhil,
Professor J.H. Ohlmeyer, MA, PhD
Professor M E Rubin, MA, PhD
E M C van Houts, MA, LittD, PhD
Professor J A Green, DPhil (to November 2004)
Professor H E Meller, PhD (to November 2004)
Professor R J A R Rathbone, PhD (to November 2004)
Professor G W Bernard, MA, DPhil (from November 2004)
C A Holmes, MA, PhD (from November 2004)
Professor R I Frost, MA, PhD (from November 2004)

Executive Secretary:	J Boland
Registered Office:	University College London Gower Street London WC1E 6BT
Charity registration number:	206888
Auditors:	haysmacintyre Chartered Accountants Fairfax House 15 Fulwood Place London WC1V 6AY
Investment managers:	Cripps Portfolio Golden Cross House 8 Duncannon Street Trafalgar Square London WC2N 4JF
Bankers:	Barclays Bank Plc 27 Soho Square London W1A 4WA

THE ROYAL HISTORICAL SOCIETY
REPORT OF THE COUNCIL OF TRUSTEES
FOR THE YEAR ENDED 30 JUNE 2005

The members of Council present their report and audited accounts for the year ended 30 June 2005.

STRUCTURE, GOVERNANCE AND MANAGEMENT

The Society received its Royal Charter in 1868 and is governed by the document 'The By-Laws of the Royal Historical Society', which was last amended in November 2002. The elected Officers of the Society are the President, six Vice-Presidents, the Treasurer, the Secretary, the Librarian and not more than two Literary Directors. These officers, together with twelve Councillors constitute the governing body of the Society. The Society also has two executive officers: an Executive Secretary and an Administrative Assistant.

Appointment of Trustees

In accordance with By-law XVII, the Vice-Presidents shall hold office normally for a term of three years. Two of them shall retire by rotation, in order of seniority in office, at each Anniversary Meeting and shall not be eligible for re-election before the Anniversary Meeting of the next year. In accordance with By-law XIX, the Council of the Society shall consist of the President, the Vice-Presidents, the Treasurer, the Secretary, the Librarian, the Literary Directors and twelve Councillors. The President shall be *ex-officio* a member of all Committees appointed by the Council; and the Treasurer, the Secretary, the Librarian and the Literary Directors shall, unless the Council otherwise determine, also be *ex-officio* members of all such Committees. In accordance with By-law XX, the Councillors shall hold office normally for a term of four years. Three of them shall retire by rotation, in order of seniority in office, at each Anniversary Meeting and shall not be eligible for re-election before the Anniversary Meeting of the next year.

The names of the Trustees are shown on page 1. At the Anniversary Meeting on 26 November 2004, the Officers of the Society were re-elected.

The Vice-Presidents retiring under By-law XVII were Professor P J Corfield and Professor L J Jordanova. Dr J E Burton and Dr P Seaward were elected to replace them.

The Members of Council retiring under By-law XX were Professor J A Green, Professor H E Meller and Professor R J A R Rathbone. In accordance with By-law XXI, amended, Professor G W Bernard, Dr C A Holmes and Professor R I Frost were elected in their place.

Standing Committees

The Society has operated through the following Committees during the year ended 30 June 2005:

MEMBERSHIP COMMITTEE
Professor R J A R Rathbone – Chair (to November 2004)
Dr W R Childs – Chair (from November 2004)
Professor H E Meller (to November 2004)
Professor D M Palliser
Professor G A Hosking (from November 2004)

RESEARCH SUPPORT COMMITTEE
Professor P J Corfield – Chair (to November 2004)
Dr P Seaward – Chair (from November 2004)
Dr M Finn
Professor F O'Gorman

FINANCE COMMITTEE
Dr M Finn
Mr P J C Firth
Professor P Mathias
Professor F O'Gorman
Dr J Parry
The six officers (President – Chair)

PUBLICATIONS COMMITTEE
Professor D R Bates – Chair
Professor H. Meller (to November 2004)
Dr R Frost (from November 2004)
Dr R Mackenney
Professor J Ohlmeyer
The six officers

GENERAL PURPOSES COMMITTEE	Professor L J Jordanova – Chair (to November 2004)
	Dr J E Burton – Chair (from November 2004)
	Professor R J A R Rathbone (to November 2004)
	Dr S R Ditchfield (from November 2004)
	Professor D M Palliser
	Professor M E Rubin
	The six officers
TEACHING POLICY COMMITTEE	Dr W R Childs – Alternate Chair (from November 2004)
	Professor H T Dickinson – Alternate Chair
	Professor E J Evans
	Dr A W Foster
	Dr E M C Van Houts
	Dr S R Ditchfield (from November 2004)
	Dr C A Holmes (from November 2004)
	The six officers
RESEARCH POLICY COMMITTEE	Dr C J Kitching – Chair
	Professor L J Jordanova (to November 2004)
	Professor J A Green (to November 2004)
	Professor G A Hosking (from November 2004)
	Professor G W Bernard (from November 2004)
	Professor M Lynch
	Dr P Seaward (from November 2004)
	The six officers
STUDIES IN HISTORY EDITORIAL BOARD	Professor J S Morrill – Convenor
	Professor M Braddick
	Dr S Church
	Dr R Spang
	Professor M Taylor
	Dr A Walsham
	Professor M Overton
	Professor J Hunter (to November 2004)
	Professor M. Mazower (to November 2004)
	Dr N Gregor (from January 2005)
	Professor C Kidd (from January 2005)
	Dr J Lawrence – Literary Director
	Professor J Hoppit – Honorary Treasurer

OBJECTIVES AND ACTIVITIES

The Society exists for the promotion and support of historical scholarship and its dissemination to historians and a wider public through a programme of publications, papers, sponsorship of lectures, conferences and research and by representations to various official bodies where the interests of historical scholarship are involved. It is Council's intention that these activities should be sustained to the fullest extent in the future.

ACHIEVEMENTS AND PERFORMANCE

Review of activities

This year, as in previous years, it has pursued this objective by an ambitious programme of publications – a volume of Transactions, two volumes of edited texts in the Camden Series and further volumes in the Studies in History Series have appeared, by the holding of meetings in London and at universities outside London at which papers are delivered, by the sponsoring of the joint lecture for a wider public with Gresham College, by distributing nearly £22,000 in research support grants to 104 individuals, and by frequent representations to various official bodies where the interests of historical scholarship are involved.

Grant making

The Society awards funds to assist advanced historical research. It operates several separate schemes, for each of which there is an application form. The Society's Research Support Committee considers applications at meetings held 6 times a year. In turn the Research Support Committee reports to Council. A list of awards made is provided in the Society's Annual Report.

Investment performance

The Society holds an investment portfolio with a market value of about £2.25 million (2004: £1.98 million). It has adopted a "total return" approach to its investment policy. This means that the funds are invested solely on the basis of seeking to secure the best total level of economic return compatible with the duty to make safe investments, but regardless of the form the return takes.

The Society has adopted this approach to ensure even-handedness between current and future beneficiaries, as the focus of many investments moves away from producing income to maximising capital values. In the current investments climate, to maintain the level of income needed to fund the charity, would require an investment portfolio which would not achieve the optimal overall return, so effectively penalising future beneficiaries.

The total return strategy does not make distinctions between income and capital returns. It lumps together all forms of return on investment – dividends, interest, and capital gains etc, to produce a "total return". Some of the total return is then used to meet the needs of present beneficiaries, while the remainder is added to the existing investment portfolios to help meet the needs of future beneficiaries.

The Society's investments are managed by Cripps Portfolio, who report all transactions to the Honorary Treasurer and provide six monthly reports on the portfolios, which are considered by the Society's Finance Committee which meets three times a year. In turn the Finance Committee reports to Council.

The Society closely monitors its investments. The decision was taken during the year to assess the main portfolio against the FTSE APCIMS balanced benchmark along with the smaller Whitfield and Robinson portfolios.

During the year the general fund portfolio generated a total return of 15.89% compared with its benchmark return of 14.21%. The Whitfield and Robinson portfolios generated returns of 16.64% and 13.4% respectively against their benchmark of 14.88%.

FINANCIAL REVIEW

Results

The Society's finances continued to recover with total funds increasing from £1,999,895 to £2,252,861, an increase of £252,966. This was largely due to an improvement in the stock market and the receipt of a legacy of £39,069.

Membership subscriptions saw an increase of £2,415 to £73,275 and investment income amounted to £92,310 compared to £98,536 in 2004 reflecting a transfer from Government Stocks with a higher rate of return to equities with more growth potential.

Income from royalties increased from £25,148 to £28,919, income from conferences generated £13,534 and grants for awards increased from £6,601 to £8,309. Total costs increased from £228,142 to £231,807 reflecting higher conference costs and a further provision of £8,705 for slow moving publications offset by lower support costs.

Fixed assets

Information relating to changes in fixed assets is given in notes 5 and 6 to the accounts.

Risk assessment

The trustees are satisfied that they have considered the major risks to which the charity is exposed, that they have taken action to mitigate or manage those risks and that they have systems in place to monitor any change to those risks.

Reserves policy

The Council have reviewed the Society's need for reserves in line with the guidance issued by the Charity Commission. They believe that the Society requires approximately the current level of unrestricted general funds of £2.2m to generate sufficient total return, both income and capital, to cover the Society's expenditure in excess of the members' subscription income on an annual basis to ensure that the Society can run efficiently and meet the needs of beneficiaries.

The Society's restricted funds consist of a number of different funds where the donor has imposed restrictions on the use of the funds which are legally binding. The purposes of these funds are set out in note 13 to 15.

STATEMENT OF TRUSTEES' RESPONSIBILITIES

Law applicable to charities in England and Wales requires the Council to prepare accounts for each financial year which give a true and fair view of the state of affairs of the Society and of its financial activities for that year. In preparing these accounts, the Trustees are required to:

- select suitable accounting policies and apply them consistently;
- make judgements and estimates that are reasonable and prudent;
- state whether applicable accounting standards have been followed, subject to any material departures disclosed and explained in the accounts;
- prepare the accounts on the going concern basis unless it is inappropriate to presume that the Society will continue in business.

The Council is responsible for ensuring proper accounting records are kept which disclose, with reasonable accuracy at any time, the financial position of the Society and enable them to ensure that the financial statements comply with applicable law. They are also responsible for safeguarding the assets of the Society and hence for taking reasonable steps for the prevention and detection of error, fraud and other irregularities.

AUDITORS

A resolution proposing the appointment of auditors will be submitted at the Anniversary Meeting.

By Order of the Board

25 November 2005 Honorary Secretary

INDEPENDENT REPORT OF THE AUDITORS FOR THE YEAR ENDED 30 JUNE 2005

We have audited the financial statements of The Royal Historical Society for the year ended 30 June 2005 which comprise the Statement of Financial Activities, the Balance Sheet, and the related notes. These financial statements have been prepared under the historical cost convention (as modified by the revaluation of certain fixed assets) and the accounting policies set out therein.

This report is made solely to the charity's trustees, as a body, in accordance with the regulations made under the Charities Act 1993. Our audit work has been undertaken so that we might state to the charity's trustees those matters we are required to state to them in an auditor's report and for no other purpose. To the fullest extent permitted by law, we do not accept or assume responsibility to anyone other than the charity and the charity's trustees as a body, for our audit work, for this report, or for the opinions we have formed.

RESPECTIVE RESPONSIBILITIES OF TRUSTEES AND AUDITORS

The trustees' responsibilities for preparing the Annual Report and the financial statements in accordance with applicable law and United Kingdom Accounting Standards are set out in the Statement of Trustees' Responsibilities.

We have been appointed as auditors under section 43 of the Charities Act 1993 and report in accordance with regulations made under section 44 of that Act. Our responsibility is to audit the financial statements in accordance with relevant legal and regulatory requirements and United Kingdom Auditing Standards.

We report to you our opinion as to whether the financial statements give a true and fair view and are properly prepared in accordance with the Charities Act 1993. We also report to you if, in our opinion, the Trustees' Report is not consistent with the financial statements, if the charity has not kept proper accounting records or if we have not received all the information and explanations we require for our audit.

We read the other information contained in the Trustees' Report and consider whether it is consistent with the audited financial statements. We consider the implications for our report if we become aware of any apparent misstatements or apparent material inconsistencies with the financial statements.

BASIS OF AUDIT OPINION

We conducted our audit in accordance with United Kingdom Auditing Standards issued by the Auditing Practices Board. An audit includes examination, on a test basis, of evidence relevant to the amounts and disclosures in the financial statements. It also includes an assessment of the significant estimates and judgements made by the Trustees in the preparation of the financial statements, and of whether the accounting policies are appropriate to the charity's circumstances, consistently applied and adequately disclosed.

We planned and performed our audit so as to obtain all the information and explanations which we considered necessary in order to provide us with sufficient evidence to give reasonable assurance that the financial statements are free from material misstatement, whether caused by fraud or other irregularity or error. In forming our opinion we also evaluated the overall adequacy of the presentation of information in the financial statements.

OPINION

In our opinion the financial statements give a true and fair view of the state of the charity's affairs as at 30 June 2005 and of its incoming resources and application of resources in the year then ended and have been properly prepared in accordance with the Charities Act 1993.

haysmacintyre
Chartered Accountants
Registered Auditors

Fairfax House
15 Fulwood Place
London
WC1V 6AY

THE ROYAL HISTORICAL SOCIETY

STATEMENT OF FINANCIAL ACTIVITIES FOR THE YEAR ENDED 30 JUNE 2005

	Notes	Unrestricted Funds £	Endowment Funds £	Restricted Funds £	Total Funds 2005 £	Total Funds 2004 £
INCOMING RESOURCES						
Donations, legacies and similar incoming resources	2	43,587	–	–	43,587	5,167
Activities In Furtherance Of The Charity's Objects						
Grants for awards		–	–	8,390	8,390	6,601
Conferences		13,534	–	–	13,534	1,220
Subscriptions		73,275	–	–	73,275	70,860
Royalties		28,919	–	–	28,919	25,148
Activities To Generate Funds						
Investment income	6	90,796	–	1,514	92,310	98,536
Other		964	–	–	964	1,015
TOTAL INCOMING RESOURCES		251,075	–	9,904	260,979	208,547
RESOURCES EXPENDED						
Cost of Generating Funds						
Investment manager's fee		15,064	238	–	15,302	11,979
Charitable Expenditure						
Grants for awards	3	32,723	–	1,413	34,136	40,326
Conferences and Receptions		36,271	–	–	36,271	10,961
Publications		74,751	–	–	74,751	81,571
Library		3,183	–	–	3,183	4,294
Support costs		56,528	–	–	56,528	64,596
Management and administration		11,636	–	–	11,636	14,415
TOTAL RESOURCES EXPENDED	4	230,156	238	1,413	231,807	228,142
NET INCOMING/(OUTGOING) RESOURCES		20,919	(238)	8,491	29,172	(19,595)
Other recognised gains and losses						
Net gain on investments	6	217,053	6,741	–	223,794	78,124
NET MOVEMENT IN FUNDS		237,972	6,503	8,491	252,966	58,529
Balance at 1 July 2004		1,938,176	54,392	7,327	1,999,895	1,941,366
Balance at 30 June 2005		£2,176,148	£60,895	£15,818	£2,252,861	£1,999,895

THE ROYAL HISTORICAL SOCIETY

BALANCE SHEET AS AT 30 JUNE 2005

	Notes	2005 £	2005 £	2004 (restated) £	2004 (restated) £
FIXED ASSETS					
Tangible assets	5		741		308
Investments	6		2,257,250		1,982,297
			2,257,991		1,982,605
CURRENT ASSETS					
Stocks	7	4,168		12,921	
Debtors	8	12,218		13,827	
Cash at bank and in hand		3,634		38,207	
		20,020		64,955	
LESS: CREDITORS					
Amounts due within one year	9	(25,150)		(47,665)	
NET CURRENT (LIABILITIES)/ASSETS			(5,130)		17,290
NET ASSETS			£2,252,861		£1,999,895
REPRESENTED BY:					
Endowment Funds	13				
A S Whitfield Prize Fund			42,076		36,630
The David Berry Essay Trust			18,819		17,762
Restricted Funds	14				
A S Whitfield Prize Fund – Income			1,409		1,574
BHB Fund			5,679		5,534
P J Marshall Fellowship			8,390		–
The David Berry Essay Trust – Income			340		219
Unrestricted Funds					
Designated – E M Robinson Bequest	15		123,123		108,735
General Fund	16		2,053,025		1,829,441
			£2,252,861		£1,999,895

Approved by the Council on 25 November 2005

President ....

Honorary Treasurer ....

The attached notes form an integral part of these financial statements.

THE ROYAL HISTORICAL SOCIETY

NOTES TO THE ACCOUNTS FOR THE YEAR ENDED 30 JUNE 2005

1. ACCOUNTING POLICIES

a) *Basis of Preparation*
The financial statements have been prepared in accordance with the Statement of Recommended Practice 2000 "Accounting and Reporting by Charities" and with applicable accounting standards issued by UK accountancy bodies. They are prepared on the historical cost basis of accounting as modified to include the revaluation of fixed assets including investments which are carried at market value.

b) *Depreciation*
Depreciation is calculated by reference to the cost of fixed assets using a straight line basis at rates considered appropriate having regard to the expected lives of the fixed assets. The annual rates of depreciation in use are:

Furniture and equipment	10%
Computer equipment	25%

c) *Stock*
Stock is valued at the lower of cost and net realisable value.

d) *Library and archives*
The cost of additions to the library and archives is written off in the year of purchase.

e) *Subscription income*
Subscription income is recognised in the year it became receivable with a provision against any subscription not received.

f) *Investments*
Investments are stated at market value. Any surplus/deficit arising on revaluation is included in the Statement of Financial Activities. Dividend income is accounted for when the Society becomes entitled to such monies.

g) *Publication costs*
Publication costs are transferred in stock and released to the Statement of Financial Activities as stocks are depleted.

h) *Donations and other voluntary income*
Donations and other voluntary income is recognised when the Society becomes legally entitled to such monies.

i) *Grants payable*
Grants payable are recognised in the year in which they are approved and notified to recipients.

j) *Funds*
Unrestricted: these are funds which can be used in accordance with the charitable objects at the discretion of the trustees.
Designated: these are unrestricted funds which have been set aside by the trustees for specific purposes.
Restricted: these are funds that can only be used for particular restricted purposes defined by the benefactor and within the objects of the charity.
Endowment: permanent endowment funds must be held permanently by the trustees and income arising is separately included in restricted funds for specific use as defined by the donors.

The purpose and use of endowment, restricted and designated funds are disclosed in the notes to the accounts.

k) *Allocations*
Wages and salary costs are allocated on the basis of the work done by the Executive Secretary and the Administrative Secretary.

l) *Pensions*
Pension costs are charged to the SOFA when payments fall due. The Society contributed 10% of gross salary to the personal pension plan of one of the employees.

2. DONATIONS AND LEGACIES

	2005	2004
	£	£
G R Elton Bequest	1,648	2,857
Donations via membership	260	944
Gladstone Memorial Trust	600	600
Sundry income	41,079	766
	£43,587	£5,167

3. GRANTS FOR AWARDS

	Unrestricted Funds	Restricted Funds	Total 2005	Total 2004
	£	£	£	£
Alexander Prize	24	–	24	268
Sundry Grants	259	–	259	200
Research support grants (see below)	21,814	–	21,814	20,886
Centenary fellowship	500	–	500	5,425
A-Level prizes	500	–	500	500
A S Whitfield prize	–	1,065	1,065	1,099
E M Robinson Bequest				
– Grant to Dulwich Picture Library	–	–	–	2,375
Gladstone history book prize	432	–	432	1,103
P J Marshall Fellowship	–	–	–	6,700
British History Bibliography project grant	–	–	–	1,258
David Berry Prize	–	348	348	512
	£32,723	£1,413	£34,136	£40,326

During the year Society awarded grants to a value of £21,814 (2004: £20,886) to 104 (2004: 125) individuals.

GRANTS PAYABLE	2005	2004
	£	£
Commitments at 1 July 2004	2,850	5,573
Commitments made in the year	34,136	40,326
Grants paid during the year	(35,336)	(43,049)
Commitments at 30 June 2005	$1,650	$2,850

Commitments at 30 June 2005 and 2004 are included in creditors.

4. TOTAL RESOURCES EXPENDED

	Staff Costs	Depreciation	Other Costs	Total	2004
	£	£	£	£	£
Cost of Generating Funds					
Investment manager's fee	–	–	15,302	15,302	11,979
Charitable Expenditure					
Grants for awards (Note 3)	–	–	34,136	34,136	40,326
Conferences	9,645	–	26,262	36,271	10,961
Publications	17,547	–	57,204	74,751	81,571
Library	255	–	2,328	3,183	4,294
Support costs	29,910	554	26,064	56,528	64,596
Management and administration	–	–	11,636	11,636	14,415
Total resources expended	£57,957	£554	£173,296	£231,807	£228,142

STAFF COSTS	2005	2004
	£	£
Wages and salaries	51,157	49,230
Social Security costs	4,931	5,129
Other pension costs	1,869	3,738
	£57,957	£58,097

The average number of employees in the year was 2 (2004: 2). There were no employees whose emoluments exceeded £50,000 in the year.
During the year travel expenses were reimbursed to 30 Councillors attending Council meetings at a cost of £4,198 (2004: £5,028). No Councillor received any remuneration during the year (2004 nil).

Included in management and administration is the following:

	2005	2004
	£	£
Audit fee	7,373	6,698
Other services	558	540

5. TANGIBLE FIXED ASSETS

	Computer Equipment	Furniture and Equipment	Total
	£	£	£
COST			
At 1 July 2004	30,360	1,173	31,533
Additions	987	–	987
At 30 June 2005	31,347	1,173	32,520
DEPRECIATION			
At 1 July 2004	30,052	1,173	31,225
Charge for the year	554	–	554
At 30 June 2005	30,606	1,173	31,779
NET BOOK VALUE			
At 30 June 2005	£741	£–	£741
At 30 June 2004	£308	£–	£308

All tangible fixed assets are used in the furtherance of the Society's objects.

6. INVESTMENTS

	General Fund	Robinson Bequest	Whitfield Prize Fund	David Berry Essay Trust	Total
	£	£	£	£	£
Market value at 1 July 2004	1,825,937	108,735	38,204	9,421	1,982,297
Additions	420,524	2,561	662	9,200	432,947
Disposals	(381,788)	-	-	-	(381,788)
Net gain on investments	205,040	12,013	5,684	1,057	223,794
Market value at 30 June 2005	£2,069,713	£123,309	£44,550	£19,678	£2,257,250
Cost at 30 June 2005	£1,767,777	£80,408	£36,318	£10,730	£1,895,233

	2005	2004
	£	£
U K Equities	1,456,751	1,092,060
U K Government Stock and Bonds	586,362	705,188
Overseas equities	59,074	75,993
Uninvested Cash	155,063	109,056
	£2,257,250	£1,982,297

Dividends and interest on listed investments	91,953	97,980
Interest on cash deposits	357	556
	£92,310	£98,536

7. STOCK

	2005	2004
	£	£
Transactions Sixth Series	1,015	819
Camden Fifth Series	2,195	8,611
Camden Classics Reprints	958	3,491
	£4,168	£12,921

8. DEBTORS

	2005	2004
	£	£
Other debtors	9,621	8,619
Prepayments	2,597	5,208
	£12,218	£13,827

9. CREDITORS: Amounts due within one year

	2005	2004
	£	£
Sundry creditors	2,175	7,713
Subscriptions received in advance	3,376	11,238
Accruals and deferred income	19,599	28,714
	£25,150	£47,665

10. LEASE COMMITMENTS

The Society has the following annual commitments under non-cancellable operating leases which expire:

	2005	2004
	£	£
Within 1–2 year	–	–
Within 2–5 years	15,272	12,615
	£15,272	£12,615

11. LIFE MEMBERS

The Society has ongoing commitments to provide membership services to 16 Life Members at a cost of approximately £50 each per year.

12. UNCAPITALISED ASSETS

The Society owns a library the cost of which is written off to the Statement of Financial Activities at the time of purchase. This library is insured for £150,000 and is used for reference purposes by the membership of the Society.

13. ENDOWMENT FUNDS

	Balance at 1 July 04	Incoming resources	Outgoing resources	Investment gain	Balance at 30 June 05
	£	£	£	£	£
A S Whitfield Prize Fund	36,630	–	(238)	5,684	42,076
The David Berry Essay Trust	17,762	–	–	1,057	18,819
	£54,392	£–	£(238)	£6,741	£60,895

A S Whitfield Prize Fund

The A S Whitfield Prize Fund is an endowment used to provide income for an annual prize for the best first monograph for British history published in the calendar year.

The David Berry Essay Trust

The David Berry Essay Trust is an endowment to provide income for an annual prize for the best essay on a subject dealing with Scottish history.

14. RESTRICTED FUNDS

	Balance at 1 July 04	Incoming resources	Outgoing resources	Transfers	Balance at 30 June 05
	£	£	£	£	£
A S Whitfield Prize Fund Income	1,574	900	(1,065)	–	1,409
BHB Fund	5,534	145	–	–	5,679
P J Marshall Fellowship	–	8,390	–	–	8,390
The David Berry Essay Trust Income	219	469	(348)	–	340
	£7,327	£9,904	£(1,413)	£–	£15,818

A S Whitfield Prize Fund Income
Income from the A S Whitfield Prize Fund is used to provide an annual prize for the best first monograph for British history published in the calendar year.

BHB Fund
The British History Bibliographies project funding is used to provide funding for the compilation of bibliographies in British and Irish History.

P J Marshall Fellowship
The P J Marshall Fellowship is used to provide a sum sufficient to cover the stipend for a one-year doctoral research fellowship alongside the existing Royal Historical Society Centenary Fellowship at the Institute of Historical Research in the academic year 2004–2005.

The David Berry Essay Trust Income
Income from the David Berry Trust is to provide an annual prize for the best essay on a subject dealing with Scottish history.

15. DESIGNATED FUNDS	Balance at 1 July 04	Incoming resources	Outgoing resources	Investment gain	Transfers	Balance at 30 June 05
	£	£	£	£	£	£
E M Robinson Bequest	£108,735	£3,230	£(885)	£12,013	–	£123,123

E M Robinson Bequest
Income from the E M Robinson bequest is to further the study of history and to date has been used to provide grants to the Dulwich Picture Gallery.

16. GENERAL FUND	Balance at 1 July 04	Incoming resources	Outgoing resources	Investment gain	Transfers	Balance at 30 June 05
	£	£	£	£	£	£
	£1,829,441	£247,845	£(229,271)	£205,040	–	£2,053,025

17. ANALYSIS OF NET ASSETS BETWEEN FUNDS

	General Fund	Designated Fund	Restricted Funds	Endowment Funds	Total
	£	£	£	£	£
Fixed assets	741	–	–	–	741
Investments	2,069,713	123,309	1,749	62,479	2,257,250
	2,070,454	123,309	1,749	62,479	2,257,991
Current assets	6,096	–	13,924	–	28,725
Less: Creditors	(23,380)	(186)	–	(1,584)	(21,884)
Net current (liabilities)/assets	(17,284)	(186)	13,924	(1,584)	(5,130)
Net assets	£2,053,025	£123,123	£15,818	£60,895	£2,252,861